DE GAULLE'S REPUBLIC

By Philip Williams

Politics in Post-War France

De Gaulle's Republic

PHILIP M. WILLIAMS
AND
MARTIN HARRISON

GREENWOOD PRESS, PUBLISHERS
WESTPORT, CONNECTICUT

Library of Congress Cataloging in Publication Data

Williams, Philip Maynard.
   De Gaulle's Republic.

   Reprint of the ed. published by Longmans, London.
   "Constitution of the Fifth Republic": p.
   Includes index.
   1. France--Politics and government--1945-
2. Gaulle, Charles de, Pres. France, 1890-1970.
3. Algeria--History--1945-1962. I. Harrison, Martin,
1930-   joint author. II. France. Constitution,
1958. English. 1979.
DC420.W54 1979   944.082   78-23520
ISBN 0-313-21085-3

First published 1960

Reprinted with the permission of Longman Group Ltd.

Reprinted in 1979 by Greenwood Press, Inc.
51 Riverside Avenue, Westport, CT 06880

Printed in the United States of America

10 9 8 7 6 5 4 3 2 1

CONTENTS

ACKNOWLEDGMENTS

We are indebted to our colleagues, the Warden and Fellows of Nuffield College, Oxford, who made it possible for this book to be written. We are grateful to Messrs. P. Campbell, D. Lachance, J. Plamenatz and P. Renshaw, who read the entire manuscript, and to Professors Duverger, Goguel, Gonidec and Robinson, Mr. B. Donoughue and Monsieur P. Emanuelli, who read parts of it. They saved us from many inaccuracies and infelicities; for those that remain, they bear no responsibility.

The text was completed early in December 1959, and the Epilogue early in February 1960.

PHILIP M. WILLIAMS
MARTIN HARRISON

Oxford
February 1960

ABBREVIATIONS

A.G.E.A.	Association générale des étudiants algériens (Lagaillarde).
A.G.E.L.C.A.	Association générale des élèves des lycées et collèges d'Algérie (Roseau).
C.C.C.	Comité Consultatif Constitutionnel.
C.G.T.	Confédération Générale du Travail; largest trade union federation, mainly Communist.
C.N.I.	Centre National des Indépendants; conservative (Duchet, Pinay, Reynaud).
C.R.S.	Compagnies Républicaines de Sécurité; riot police.
C.S.P.	Comité de Salut Public.
D.C.F.	Démocratie Chrétienne de France; right-wing M.R.P. (Bidault).
E.D.C.	European Defence Community.
F.L.N.	Front de Libération Nationale; Algerian nationalists.
G.G.	Gouvernement-Général; the headquarters of government in Algiers.
G.P.R.A.	Gouvernement Provisoire de la République Algérienne; the F.L.N. 'provisional government'.
J.O.	*Journal Officiel de la République Française: Débats Parlementaires (Assemblée Nationale).*
M.N.A.	Mouvement National Algérien (Messali Hadj).
M.R.P.	Mouvement Républicain Populaire; Christian Democrat (Pflimlin, Schuman).
M.T.L.D.	Mouvement pour le Triomphe des Libertés Démocratiques (Messali Hadj's former party).
P.R.	Proportional Representation.
P.R.A.	Parti du Regroupement Africain (Senghor).
P.S.A.	Parti Socialiste Autonome; left-wing Socialist (Depreux).
R.D.A.	Rassemblement Démocratique Africain (Houphouet-Boigny).
R.F.S.P.	*Revue française de science politique.*
R.P.F.	Rassemblement du Peuple Français; de Gaulle's party 1947–53.
R.T.F.	Radiodiffusion-Télévision Française.
S.A.S.	Sections administratives spécialisées (administering Algerian villages; military, under civilian control).
U.F.D.	Union des Forces Democratiques; left-wing anti-Gaullist alliance of U.G.S., P.S.A., Mendès-France, Mitterrand, etc.
U.F.N.A.	Union française nord-africaine; Algiers ultras (Martel).
U.G.S.	Union de la Gauche Socialiste; neutralist and left-wing Socialist (Bourdet).
U.N.R.	Union pour la Nouvelle République; Gaullist party 1958 (Soustelle, Debré, Michelet, Chaban-Delmas, Chalandon).
U.S.R.A.F.	Union pour la Salut et le Renouveau de l'Algérie française (Soustelle).
U.T.B.	Unité territorial blindée.

PART I

The Ancien Régime

1. The Balance-Sheet of 'The System'

Amid the sharp words, assemblies are dominated by the fear of action.

2. The Loss of Empire

No régime, in the long run, can stand against the will of a nation.

3. The Cost of Algeria

Armies exist to serve the policies of States.

Quotations from Charles de Gaulle, *Le Salut,* pp. 40, 47 and 148.

B

1

The Balance-Sheet of 'The System'

The Fourth Republic was conceived on 21 October 1945, when Frenchmen (and Frenchwomen, voting for the first time) were called to the polls by General de Gaulle. They had first to elect a new Assembly, and secondly to decide whether a new constitution should be drafted or the old one restored. Out of an electorate of twenty-five million, nineteen million voted; fewer than 700,000 favoured a return to the pre-war Third Republic.

Thirteen years later its successor was no less unanimously condemned. In the referendum of 28 September 1958, four voters out of five accepted the constitution of the Fifth Republic; but the spokesmen of the minority had all insisted that their opposition to the new system implied no approval of the old one, which most of them had indeed criticized throughout its brief existence.

Few good words are said today for the Fourth Republic, least of all in France. Yet the nation's prospects in 1958 were far better than in 1939. Then the country was ending a century of decline. Her birth-rate had touched bottom; her industry, coddled by protection and riddled by class war, lagged far behind her rivals; her standard of living was low, her social legislation backward, her armed forces far inferior to those of the Reich; her foreign policy was bitterly disputed between those who were content for her to remain a British satellite and those who preferred German (or Russian) leadership.

In 1958 France presented a very different picture. Her birth-rate since the war had been the highest for a century; the new generation, coming to maturity in the 1960s, was bound to prove a force for change—if not necessarily for progress. Industry was booming; the heavy investments of the immediate post-war years were at last bringing results.

The modernized sector of French industry could compare, and compete, with any in Europe; and, although the gap between the new and the backward firms and regions grew ever wider, French industrial production after 1953 expanded about as fast as German and far faster than American or British.

The benefits accrued in social stability. The standard of living rose rapidly. Already the liberation governments had given France an advanced social security system. Though the Communists still polled a quarter of the vote, the Party's revolutionary potential had been sapped by the unimaginative rigidity of its ultra-Stalinist leadership and the growing prosperity of its rank and file. There was far more direct danger to French democracy in the nationalist bitterness aroused by the country's loss of power in the world. Yet French foreign policy had not failed; in contrast to the 1930s, French statesmen had taken the lead in a successful recon-ciliation with the ancestral enemy through an imaginative programme of European union which—despite vicissitudes —was steadily progressing against the resistance of protect-ionists, nationalists and Communists. It was in the French possessions overseas, above all in Algeria, that weak govern-ment and weak leadership proved fatal to the regime.

.   .   .   .

The conflicts of the war and liberation are crucial to an understanding of the Fourth and even the Fifth Republics. Outside France, the struggle against Vichy and the occupying Germans was led by General de Gaulle, whose view of the future was dominated by his determination to restore France to great power status, and to strengthen her system of government as a means to that end. Within the country a small section of the Resistance, mainly in the army and administration—Michel Debré was among its most influential members—shared in these preoccupations. But for most Resisters—not only Communists but Socialists and left-wing Catholics too—the movement was a social revolution as well as a struggle for national freedom. Naturally Free French-men and Resisters shared many common objectives, but their priorities often differed widely.

4

Thus there was always tension between the Gaullists and most internal Resisters, even the non-Communists. But the two groups were forced into alliance by a common fear: that the Allies would impose on France a provisional government of their own choice under one of those discredited and reactionary senior officers for whom the Roosevelt Administration had so strange a weakness. For the internal Resistance, de Gaulle was far preferable to Darlan or Giraud; for de Gaulle, its confidence was a major asset in his campaign for Allied recognition. But this alone was not enough. The Allies were deeply suspicious of this prickly general, of whose aims they knew so little, and obscure and potentially dangerous Resistance leaders were no reassurance to them. They wanted the comfort of familiar names; and so, to assert his legitimacy, the General was driven to revive the old discredited political parties, and to give places and status in his Consultative Assembly to Radical, Conservative and Centre leaders from the remote days of that Third Republic which both he and the internal Resistance meant to reconstruct from top to bottom.

So the game became four-handed. For the Communists, the Resistance was to be a springboard to power. For their allies it offered a chance to build a truly democratic, socially transformed, *République pure et dure*. For de Gaulle and his group, constitutional reform was the key to French revival; the General himself hoped to achieve this with the co-operation of Socialists and M. R. P., whose social programme he was quite willing to accept. Finally, the traditional parties which had controlled the Third Republic hoped to stem the reforming ardour of these new groups which they had formerly kept from power, and to retain all they could of the old order.

From the Allied invasion of 1944 until the eruption of the cold war in 1947, French politics centred on the Communist bid for power. As the Allied armies invaded the north, the Germans withdrew from the south. In much of the Midi power was seized by local Liberation Committees, often Communist controlled, and there was bitter settling of accounts. Similar situations in other countries—Greece and Belgium—were resolved by the intervention of Allied forces. But in France the Communists, after furious internal dissensions, decided to seek power by legal means. No violent clash took place, and the de Gaulle government peacefully imposed its authority on the Liberation Committees and disarmed the partisan forces. For a year after the liberation, de Gaulle held power as head of an all-party provisional government working with a nominated Consultative Assembly.

There was a general election in October 1945 for a Constituent Assembly; the constitution it drafted was rejected at the referendum of May 1946. A new Constituent Assembly was chosen in June. Its constitutional proposals were approved by referendum in October, and in November the first National Assembly of the Fourth Republic was elected. All these three assemblies were dominated by three great parties, the Communists, the Socialists, and the Catholic M. R. P., each having roughly a quarter of the seats; the other quarter was shared between the Third Republican parties (anti-clerical Radicals and pro-clerical Conservatives), and a handful of independents and Gaullists.

The General's provisional government failed to impose stringent austerity measures; their chief advocate, Mendès-France, resigned in April 1945. It did put through some sweeping measures of nationalization, social reform and political change—among them P. R. and woman suffrage. But the harmony between de Gaulle and the Resistance survived for barely three weeks after parliamentary government was restored. There were too many conflicts between the General and the Resistance, with whom—especially with the Socialists—he was genuinely anxious to work. They disliked his insistence on building up a powerful army, and they retained all the French democrat's traditional fears of the strong executive, free from detailed parliamentary control, which de Gaulle thought essential. He soon became frustrated at his impotence; though head of the government, he could not take a step without the consent of three huge, solid and mutually suspicious parties. He could still, had he chosen, have rid himself of them by a *coup d'état*. But he was too much of a democrat to take this course, and in January 1946 he suddenly resigned office. He thought himself indispensable; for twelve years it seemed he had proved utterly mistaken.

6

At the centre of his miscalculation lay the third great party, M.R.P. Newly founded in 1944, by a group of young Catholic democrats of socially progressive views, its sudden electoral success had astounded everyone, not least its leaders. A conservative, Catholic, bourgeois and peasant electorate, unwilling to vote for the weak and discredited parties of the Third Republic, alarmed at the growth of Communism and Socialism, turned with surprising discipline to this one available bulwark against the danger from the Left. But while its voters were largely conservative and Vichyite, its leaders had set themselves the aim of reconciling Catholicism with social progress and democracy. De Gaulle, disappointed with the Socialists, could surely turn for help to the party of Catholic Resistance.

Perhaps he could; but not by withdrawing from politics. For M. R. P. to follow him into the wilderness would have left Socialists and Communists alone in the cabinet, and with a small majority in the all-powerful legislature. Rightly fearing this *tête-à-tête*, the M.R.P. leaders continued for another year and more to shore up the rickety structure of three-party rule—*tripartisme*—while the pretence of common ground between the three parties grew ever more shallow. But when Socialists and Communists combined to support a draft constitution giving complete power to the National Assembly, M.R.P. took the lead against it; to the general surprise the draft was defeated in the May referendum. In this campaign they had no active help from General de Gaulle (who did not even vote). A constitutional solution had now become urgent. All three parties recognized the need for compromise, and from their mutual concessions the constitution of the Fourth Republic was born.

The strongest reason for haste was the discredit into which all the parties in power were falling. *Tripartisme*—control of the government by three solid, disciplined, mutually antagonistic organizations—was utterly contrary to French political traditions. During 1946 it came to seem intolerable. None of the three parties could impose a coherent policy of its own; each was quite strong enough to obstruct the wishes of its rivals; all three suffered from the unpopularity of the government. So each sought to divert public discontent from itself by attacking its partners in office, and to compensate for unpopularity by treating its own ministries as the private property of the party; in both these activities the Communists set the pace. The consequent ministerial chaos further intensified the discredit of *tripartisme*, though indeed unpopularity was the inevitable reward of governing in a time of food shortage and industrial penury. But with both Communists and non-Communist Resisters under fire, there seemed to be an opportunity opening for the other players in the 'four-handed game'—the Third Republic parties (Radicals and Conservatives) now in opposition, and the Gaullists.

It was in these circumstances that the constitution of October 1946 was produced. A complex, elaborate compromise, it kept real power in the hands of the Assembly, tempering it slightly with a restored but feeble upper house, the Council of the Republic, and a President elected by Parliament. Both houses were to be elected by P.R. (which was, however, largely abandoned for the Council in 1948 and greatly modified for the Assembly in 1951). Each major party could thus rest assured that its two big partners would not obtain exclusive control, and the three arranged the details of the system so as to handicap their smaller rivals.

On 18 June 1946, at Bayeux, General de Gaulle had sketched out his own constitutional ideas, which were in essence to be realized twelve years later. The compromise constitution of the *tripartiste* allies fulfilled none of his requirements. His denunciation of their work found an echo in the country, and—despite the obvious drawbacks and dangers of a further spell of provisional government—the second draft constitution was almost rejected. Only nine million people voted for it; eight million were hostile and eight and a half million stayed at home. De Gaulle still would not listen to those followers who wanted him to return to politics; but the onset of the cold war changed his mind, and in April 1947 he launched his new party, the R.P.F. It was meant to attract followers from all parties except the Communists. But Socialists and M.R.P. would not let their followers join, while Radicals and Conservatives rushed for the bandwagon. So, contrary to the General's intentions, the R.P.F.

8

developed into a new party, which soon shed most of the little left-wing following it acquired.

The Communists too had been growing increasingly discontented. Their rejection of armed revolt in 1944 had gained them little. They had been denied control of the crucial posts, Defence, Interior and Foreign Affairs, by both General de Gaulle in 1945 and his successors in 1946. They had failed in their hopes of absorbing the Socialists into a Communist-dominated government—let alone a Communist-controlled party. By 1947 there were even signs that their hold on the trade unions was weakening. The domestic, foreign and colonial disputes came to a head simultaneously; in May the Communists voted against the government, and their ministers were dismissed. Politicians and administrators now faced the question that had haunted them for three years: could a destitute and desperate nation be governed against its organized trade unions? And this challenge was to be met, not by a united anti-Communist front, but by a weak combination of two discredited parties backed by only a quarter of the country. For when the October municipal elections gave the voters their first chance to express themselves since the end of *tripartisme*, all its enemies enrolled under the R.P.F.'s banner. In the big cities the new movement won startling victories, with 40 per cent of the votes, to 30 per cent for the Communists and only 25 per cent for Socialists and M.R.P. together. It was the crest of the Gaullist wave.

A month after this setback for the Communists, their trade union followers of the C.G.T. launched a violent nation-wide strike, which in some places (notably Marseilles) was revolutionary in temper. It was ruthlessly broken by the Socialist Minister of the Interior, Jules Moch. A non-Communist minority broke away from the C.G.T. to form a small new federation, *Force Ouvrière;* millions of members deserted the trade union movement altogether. Another violent strike in the coalfields was broken a year later. The C.G.T. had been ruined as a Communist political weapon; it had been put out of action almost as effectively as an organization to defend working-class claims.

Those claims needed defending. For the departure from office of the Communists had revolutionized the parliamentary situation. The R.P.F. voted regularly with them to upset centre governments. Thus, Socialists and M.R.P. together were in a minority of 100 in the 600-member Assembly. To survive, any centre government needed the backing of fifty of the 150 Radicals and Conservatives, whose decisive marginal votes came therefore to weigh more and more heavily on policy. But these deputies feared to lose their discontented electoral following to the R.P.F., which exploited demagogically many of their own themes—nationalism abroad, opposition to government spending at home, violent denunciation of supposed scandals, attacks on the politicians in power and their sordid 'System', demands for constitutional reform. The Socialists were on the defensive against these right-wing assaults from 1947 onwards, and for a few months in 1950, in the Bidault government, they were driven into opposition.

Under the disguise of Gaullism, the men and parties of the Third Republic were on the way back. Although the R.P.F.'s leaders were genuine Gaullists, the label was to prove a sham, thinly concealing the reality of Radical and Conservative revival. Most Radicals had found by 1949, and many Conservatives discovered within the next two years, that they could win seats without accepting the General's patronage—and instructions. In 1951 the electoral law was changed to help parties which could form electoral alliances—in practice the centre groups—at the expense of R.P.F. and Communists. These two between them won nearly half the votes, but barely a third of the seats. The R.P.F., unable to paralyse government by voting with the Communists, had no blackmailing power while it stayed in opposition; but its votes were coveted by the Right and Centre parties who hoped to drive the Socialists out of the Government. In these conditions few Gaullists (Jacques Soustelle and Michel Debré among the few) proved immune from the lure of office. The party split in 1952 when its conservative wing went over to M. Pinay (who has never been forgiven for it by loyal Gaullists). Next year the rump moved into the majority camp, and General de Gaulle abandoned politics.

These were years of repression in Morocco and Tunisia, scandal and disaster in Indo-China. M.R.P., the party mainly responsible, tolerated do-nothing policies (*immobilisme*) at home and abroad in order to retain Conservative support for their cherished European Defence Community. But what they gained on the Right they lost on the Left; and the mounting Socialist and Radical opposition was reinforced by many Gaullists, who regarded the European Army—and often also the Indo-China war—as ruinous to French influence in Europe. The Dien Bien Phu disaster in May 1954 crystallized this strange coalition, which (with the Communists) carried to power in June an unorthodox Radical, the chief critic of the Indo-China war, Pierre Mendès-France.

In his seven months of office Mendès-France liquidated many legacies of his predecessors. He settled the Indo-China war on terms approved at the time by 462 deputies (some of whom later accused him of treason for it). He offered Tunisia internal autonomy (and so, his enemies later claimed, began the slide downhill in North Africa). He brought the E.D.C. treaty up for decision; on a free vote it was lost by fifty-five. He earned the lasting hatred of M.R.P. for not staking his cabinet's life on it, and of the Communists for accepting an alternative plan for German rearmament. When he was beaten in February it was on his Tunisian policy, which the Assembly approved both before and afterwards. But he retained his popularity. As leader of the victorious Left in the 1956 election, he seemed at last to have emerged from the wilderness where he had so long remained after he resigned, in 1945, in solitary protest against de Gaulle's economic caution.

.   .   .   .

France faced a grave economic problem at the end of the war. She had long ago chosen social stability at the cost of progress, and her economy had gradually been frozen by high protection and legislation in favour of the small man. In the early years of the slump she suffered less than other industrial countries, but they made a far better recovery; in 1938 her industrial production was still a quarter below that of 1929 (where Germany's was up by a quarter and Britain's by a sixth). Thus the terrible destruction and demoralization of the war struck at an economic system which

11

had long been relatively stagnant, and had recently been in sharp decline.

The Monnet plan was intended to remedy this situation by an organized but voluntary effort. It sought to win the consent of all categories—workers, employers, peasants—for a concentration in the coming years on the basic industries which were the key to future expansion. The plan was not completely fulfilled, but great strides were made in such crucial sectors as railways and electricity (where 1957 production was nearly treble that of 1938). Most of this investment had to be made through government agencies. Total public expenditure increased little (5 per cent) between 1938 and 1950 (while the national income rose 10 per cent); but the proportion directed to productive purposes soared from 5 per cent to 38 per cent. France regained her pre-war level of industrial production within three years of victory. After 1918 it had taken her twice as long.

The Monnet plan would have fallen much further behind but for Marshall Aid. This aid was used for the constructive purposes for which it was given, although the ministers who insisted on this priority often lost popularity by doing so. By 1954–5 France was producing 36 per cent more capital goods than in 1929, and 28 per cent more fuel and power, while consumption was 1 per cent lower. The rewards of this abnegation would soon be reaped, but only because post-war governments had resisted the anti-austerity demagogy of the Right and the Communists with a determination and political courage for which they have had little credit.

In the last years of the Fourth Republic, industrial production was expanding fast. Production *per head* increased by 4 per cent per annum between 1949 and 1958. The standard of living thereafter improved markedly, though in some sectors—notably housing—there was still much lost time to retrieve. Even the backward agricultural sector was making progress; by 1955, 10 per cent fewer workers were producing 25 per cent more than in 1938. The many justified criticisms of post-war French economic policy need to be seen in this generally creditable perspective.

The first error was made by General de Gaulle early in 1945. His Minister of National Economy, Mendès-France, supported by many Socialists, wanted rigorous measures on the Belgian model against war-profiteering and inflation: to call in the currency and block all bank accounts. The Minister of Finance, Pleven, resisted these proposals with the backing of business, the peasantry—and the Communist party. De Gaulle pointed out that Mendès-France had all the experts against him. 'I know a Colonel de Gaulle who had all the experts against him,' was the retort. But the General chose caution, Mendès-France resigned, the war-profiteers kept their gains, and the wage–price spiral began its disastrous course.

It took four years to bring inflation under control. Then, almost at once, it was started off again by the Korean war boom. Not until 1952 were prices stabilized at a level twelve times that of 1944. For almost forty years the currency had been losing its value; the effects on the national outlook were profound—and catastrophic. Thus 'Pinay's miracle', by which that leader succeeded in keeping prices from rising in France when they were falling throughout the world, was of the greatest psychological importance—even if it was achieved only at the cost of sacrificing productive investment for a time. From 1952 to 1955 inflation was kept in check. Another success was achieved over the balance of payments. Before the war France had paid by exports for only two-thirds of her imports. After it, she eventually managed—though with many vicissitudes—to achieve a favourable balance and to build up by the end of 1955 a comfortable reserve of foreign exchange. This was then dissipated in record time by rapid industrial expansion and the Algerian war.

The worst effects of currency instability were social. Fixed-income groups naturally suffered; productive groups fought furiously among themselves to maintain or improve their share of the cake. The conflict was made the more bitter by the notorious inequity of the fiscal system. Small businesses and farms, which are exceptionally numerous in France, are especially hard to control; consequently, the burden of direct taxation falls almost wholly on the wage and salary earners, who are a much smaller segment of the population than in most advanced industrial countries. The efforts of the different groups to shift the burden of taxation or inflation on to others make up much of the domestic history of post-war France.

Because of these difficulties, taxation cannot be used as a weapon for the redistribution of income. The social security system set up just after the war, comprehensive as it was, had a redistributive effect only *within* the working class, between the sick and the well, the employed and the jobless, the childless and the fathers of families. Trade union action was also ineffective. French workers have always been hard to organize and politically divided. Just after the war the Communist-led unions were extremely powerful, but their strength was broken in the violent strikes of 1947–8. Not until 1953 was there another important strike movement in the public sector, not until 1955 in the private. The unions play a part in administering the social security system, the (ineffective) works committees, and even the nationalized industries: but devices have been found to minimize their influence in order to prevent the Communists exploiting it.

The protests of the peasantry are loudly expressed at every price review. Ministers of the Right, suspected of favouring business, find little more approval than those of the Left, assumed to be prejudiced in favour of the workers. For, though the peasants enjoy many advantages (paying grotesquely little in direct taxes and benefiting from notorious abuses such as the alcohol subsidy), there are far too many of them, and in the poor and economically declining parts of France their conditions are often wretched. After 1953, the end of inflation and the rapid progress of industry brought prosperity to the towns and to the expanding regions of the north and east, and attracted many of the younger generation to them. But these changes only accentuated the difficulties of the poorer rural departments of the south and west.

The peasantry were not the only sufferers; the discontented small shopkeepers had even greater grievances. Distribution has felt the impact of modernization less than any other sector; the whole country has far too many shops, and in the regions where population is declining, they have no hope of retaining a sufficient clientele. When tax controls were tightened somewhat in 1953, it was the last straw. Poujade was to acquire a large (if temporary) political following by exploiting their feelings of revolt, and he attracted a good deal of peasant support also in the less prosperous areas. Yet this movement, destructive and backward-looking as it was, was not wholly an unhealthy sign. For Poujadism registered the impact of modernization on out-of-date farms and businesses. For the first time the competitive shoe was beginning to pinch. Previous movements of this type had been reactions to a general economic decline. This one, while equally ugly in itself, was a sign of growing pains.

Small business and the peasantry are the most formidable opponents of economic modernization; large industry has often adapted itself to it and even welcomed it. But the 'Poujadist' sections wielded great obstructive power in a political system where quite a small group of deputies had an effective veto on change. Some reformers, discovering the difficulty of carrying through necessary but painful economic readjustments, came to despair of circumventing the opposition within France. But they hoped it could be out-manœuvred by changing the national framework, and that protectionist resistance could be overcome by a political move to force France to open her frontiers. This was one of the main motives for embarking on a policy of West European economic union. It is not accidental that M. Monnet of the modernization plan was also the real begetter of the Schuman plan for the Coal and Steel Community, and was to become President of its High Authority.

. . . .

The domestic motive was not, of course, the only reason for Frenchmen to welcome the idea of European unity. All the nations of Western Europe had suffered defeat and occupation between 1940 and 1945; to all of them the nation-state seemed less satisfactory and viable than it did to Englishmen whose country had survived the war intact. A united Europe presented itself as a bulwark between the two giant powers, a means of giving extra weight to French views, and a cure for the acute inferiority complex brought on by her defeat in 1940 and her exclusion from many of the crucial post-war decisions.

But the most important motive of all was the attempt to

settle the perennial German problem. The First World War
had left France victorious but exhausted, neither strong
enough to hold Germany down by herself, nor able to count
on her wartime allies to support her in peace. The past and
future cost of opposing German domination of Europe seemed
so high that between the wars many Frenchmen resigned
themselves to accepting a subordinate place in a Europe
controlled by Germany. Even among those who refused,
many in the Resistance movement itself were convinced that
the traditional nation-states could not be restored, and anxious
for reconciliation with Germany through a united Europe.

At the end of the war, however, French policy was determined by two nationalists, de Gaulle and Bidault. They
were aggrieved at America's anti-Gaullism, resentful at
their country's second-rank status, and suspicious that
Churchill and Roosevelt wished to displace France from
Syria, Indo-China and Morocco. So they attempted to balance
between the United States and Russia without committing
themselves to either. Bidault had to abandon this policy in
1947, when the western powers broke with Russia and the
French Communists turned against their partners in office.
Henceforth economic and military weakness bound France
closely to the United States, which gave firstly Marshall Aid
which saved the Monnet plan; then protection and weapons
under the Atlantic pact; finally assistance (earmarked for
Indo-China) on which hard-pressed governments came to
depend. This dependence was found humiliating by neutralists, Communists, and nationalists of all kinds—from de
Gaulle to Daladier and from Mendès-France to the far Right.
Resentment at France's junior status was fed both by suspicion of Anglo-Saxon designs on the empire, and by fear of
France again becoming a battlefield—this time as a result of
decisions taken in Washington and London. Frenchmen were
often both exasperated by the form of these decisions and
dismayed by their substance—especially when they concerned
Germany.

The evolution of French policy towards Germany, under
this pressure, has meant almost a reversal of alliances. De
Gaulle and Bidault, however equivocal their attitude to the
United States and Russia, had a clear-cut policy towards

Germany. They sought specific guarantees against her revival: political, in the refusal to authorize a central German
government; economic, in the low limit placed on her steel
production; territorial, in the special regime for the Ruhr
and the attachment of the Saar to the French economy. But
the United States, worried about Communism, and Britain,
concerned for trade recovery, were not prepared to maintain a non-self-governing slum in the centre of Europe. One
by one the safeguards were whittled away. French attempts
to cling to them only discredited her with the Anglo-Saxon
powers. It became increasingly clear that a new start was
necessary.

The change became possible when Robert Schuman replaced Bidault at the Quai d'Orsay in the summer of 1948.
He was a Catholic and a borderlander, like his opposite numbers in Germany and Italy, Adenauer and de Gasperi. Through
the Council of Europe at Strasbourg, the European federalists
tried to press their governments along their chosen path;
they came up against the indifference of public opinion and
the stubborn scepticism and reluctance of the British. By
1950 the promoters of European unity had decided that these
obstacles had to be turned, not assaulted; and they embarked
on the 'functional' programme of transferring specific
sectors of economic life to *ad hoc* supranational authorities.
Thus Britain would be confronted by institutions which
worked, and the unenlightened public would face a *fait
accompli*. When important decisions were in the hands of
international bodies, a political superstructure would plainly
be needed to ensure democratic control.

Jean Monnet and his friends were hoping to unite Europe
by stealth. For a time their strategy seemed brilliantly successful. The Coal and Steel Plan was launched by Schuman in
May 1950. It was greeted with widespread approval, not only
for its own sake but as the first major and imaginative
initiative in foreign policy taken by any French government
for sixteen years. There was naturally opposition: from
Communists, from nationalists on the Gaullist and right-
wing benches, from small business and from some protectionist big industries. But the current of support was strong,
and at the end of 1951 the plan was ratified in the National

c

Assembly by the surprising majority of 144 votes. It was to be the last victory of the 'Europeans' for five years.

For already the situation had been completely altered by the consequences of the Korean war. American policy-makers decided that it was imperative to rearm West Germany against a possible 'Korean' attack by her Eastern neighbour, and to complete the process within three years. Inevitably they met strong French opposition. Even those Frenchmen most anxious for friendship with Germany feared that rearmament would cripple the democratic forces across the Rhine with which they hoped to work. But though French opinion was virtually unanimous against rearming Germany, French ministers, dependent on American economic aid, could not resist the pressure of their allies. They therefore tried to escape from their dilemma by attaching the unpopular idea of German rearmament to the popular programme of European union. The result was nearly a catastrophe: instead of accrediting the former policy in the eyes of the public, they almost ruined the latter.

There had been warnings enough. In 1949, when France ratified the Atlantic Pact, the Assembly had insisted on keeping a veto on the entry of any new power (meaning Germany) into N.A.T.O. In 1952 a resolution in favour of a European army, garnished with a number of vital conditions which were not to be fulfilled, scraped through the Assembly by only forty votes. Though the E.D.C. treaty was promptly signed, no one was anxious to bring it up for ratification. At the end of 1952 the nationalist pressure to eliminate Schuman became irresistible; he was replaced by the much less 'European' Bidault. With the R.P.F. within the majority and soon within the ministry itself, cabinets were paralysed. They could not demand a ratification vote; and the 'Europeans' themselves did not press for it, fearing it would go against them.

Meanwhile the political alignment was changing. As the Christian Democrats consolidated their position in both Germany and Italy, the French Right became more attracted to a European union which might offer guarantees against dangerous economic experiments at home. Conversely, Socialists (and some Radicals) grew increasingly suspicious,

18

and their doubts were increased by dissatisfaction with the cautious *immobilisme* of conservative-led governments at home, and with the dissipation of French strength in Indo-China. Some of these feelings were shared by the nationalist opposition, so strong among the Gaullists, which itself found an echo among many kinds of Radical (Herriot, Daladier, even Mendès-France) and in a few Socialists like Lacoste and Lejeune. Military leaders had a great effect on Gaullist and right-wing opinion; to most of them, submerging the identity of an independent French army seemed an excessive price to pay for avoiding the resurgence of a German one. All the non-Communist opponents of E.D.C. agreed in distrusting the complexity of the treaty's machinery, the absence of any democratic political superstructure, and above all the absence of Britain from a group of countries which seemed certain to be dominated by Germany. Monnet's chickens were coming home to roost. A functional organization had been agreed upon, without British participation or democratic control. But instead of accepting the *fait accompli*, Parliament rebelled.

E.D.C., like Indo-China and Tunisia, was a poisoned chalice handed on to Mendès-France by his predecessors in office. Though the sponsors of the treaty themselves had never dared submit it to the Assembly, they nevertheless insisted that he should do so. Knowing it could not pass as it stood, he tried to have it modified; they gave him no support. He therefore declined to jeopardize his chance of achieving a new start in the colonies and at home. With the government neutral (and divided), and half the Socialist deputies defying the party whip to vote against the treaty, E.D.C. went down to the defeat which France's allies, with absurd short-sightedness, had 'refused to contemplate'. Mr. Dulles threatened an 'agonizing reappraisal'. Sir Winston Churchill (who, though himself the first leader to propose a European army, was unwilling for Britain to participate in it) spoke warningly of France's empty chair. Mendès-France and Eden hastily prepared an alternative scheme for rearming Germany and bringing her into N.A.T.O.; the former rammed it through the Assembly, and his successor (Faure) through the upper house. European union had suffered a heavy blow.

Co-operation between national units, including Britain, seemed to have become the favoured formula.

The general election of 2 January 1956 seemed unlikely to revive the cause of European internationalism. It was fought mainly on Algeria. The parties of the Left which had criticized recent policies—Communists, Socialists and especially Mendesist Radicals—gained between them two million votes. The Gaullists, now absorbed in the System they had denounced, lost three million, while Conservatives and M.R.P. held their own; all national leaders of these parties (except Bidault) stressed their liberal records and intentions. The defunct R.P.F. had two principal legatees: Mendesism, the revolt against *immobilisme* of dynamic, modern, economically progressive France, and Poujadism, the corresponding reaction of the stagnant and declining firms, farms and regions. This new, vulgar and vigorous opposition of the far Right won fifty seats and two and a half million votes (taken from every party) by violent abuse of the System, the corrupt politicians, the taxation of small shopkeepers, and the treasonable selling-out of the empire. For all their immense differences Mendesism and Poujadism both sought—like Gaullism before them—to influence the decisions made in Parliament by pressure from without. They failed too; their deputies also were quickly absorbed—or re-absorbed—by the System, and both movements declined as suddenly as they had arisen.

For the impact of the 1956 election was remarkably short-lived—even for France. Mendès-France was the undoubted leader of the victorious coalition; yet he was excluded in turn from the premiership (which went instead to the Socialist Guy Mollet), from the Quai d'Orsay (where M.R.P. vetoed him) and from any real voice over Algeria (where Mollet, after the Algiers riots of 6 February 1956, abandoned any attempt at changing policy). The Socialists, who had welcomed Mendès-France as an electoral ally, thus threw him over within a month of the vote, repudiating his foreign policy in favour of M.R.P. and his Algerian plans in favour of all-out prosecution of the war. And public opinion approved their new course. With Socialist leaders justifying the Algerian campaign, nationalist feeling revived. Poujade's sting was drawn; Mendès-France's appeal faded, and in rapid succession he lost office, control of his parliamentary group, and the leadership of his party in the country.

This time, nationalism did not impede the plans of the Europeans as it had in 1954. Socialists who had opposed E.D.C. welcomed economic integration. Many Gaullists and Radicals, who had then distrusted Germany and sympathized with Britain, now changed their views. Supporters of the Suez expedition blamed American opposition and British hesitation for the fiasco; ardent defenders of *Algérie française* were exasperated by the reticence of the N.A.T.O. allies over Algeria and their sympathy for Tunisia. Moreover, rapid economic expansion had given a new confidence to French industry, while the eagerness of her partners gave France a strong position within the Six. For Adenauer and the Italians were anxious to retrieve the E.D.C. disaster by a new economic advance, and willing for substantial sacrifices to ensure French participation.

In March 1957 the Common Market and Euratom treaties were signed at Rome, and in July they came before the Assembly. Though all the enemies of the System opposed them—Communists and Gaullists, Poujadists and Mendesists —they were ratified by a majority of 103. France had accepted Little Europe, choosing partnership with the ex-enemy across the Rhine instead of with the ex-ally across the Channel. It was a sharp change from 1954. Then all Gaullists and many Socialists and Radicals had refused a close association with Germany which excluded Britain. But no one now was willing to delay or make concessions for the sake of British participation—except Mendès-France, as generally discredited in 1957 as he had been popular in 1954.

The re-launching of Little Europe was the last success of the System. Elsewhere it was approaching collapse. With full public approval, internationalism in Europe was accompanied by nationalism over North Africa. But the Algerian war had revived inflation, had halted the rise in the standard of living, was fast dissipating the reserves of foreign exchange, and was spreading authoritarian views and practices at home. The Fourth Republic had come a long way in the two years since February 1956, when Paris gave way to the 'men on the spot' in Algeria.

2

The Loss of Empire

Listening to men on the spot was the bane of the Fourth Republic's colonial policy. Ministers in Paris were generally well-intentioned, often liberal, rarely blind or reactionary. But time and again they were too weak to impose their will upon a local administration, often supported by settlers in the colony and by powerful politicians and business interests in the capital. The government's own military and civilian representatives were occasionally enemies of any nationalist claim. But quite frequently they were sent out as liberals, chosen to enforce a new line of policy—and were either obstructed into resignation, or else gradually won over by the services which nominally were dependent on them.[1]

But, even with the best intentions, France would have had more difficulty with her colonies than Britain. For her traditions were very different; the 'Republic one and indivisible' was as centralizing, as anti-federalist, as the monarchy or empire. Frenchmen with liberal colonial views sought to hasten the promotion of native elites to French citizenship and equality of status. The old colonies and Algeria enjoyed parliamentary representation in the Third

[1] As Robert Schuman wrote after four years as the minister responsible for Morocco and Tunisia: 'they [the two Residents-General] are on the spot, they receive and provide all the information; the scope of their initiative is vast and varied and besides they have a tendency to widen it, especially if their views coincide with those of the French population; they interpret the instructions arriving from Paris and decide how these are put into effect. The *fait accompli* is the great and constant temptation which the Residents-General are to be commended for resisting in so far as they do not succumb to it. Moreover, they themselves are in a similar situation with respect to certain services (police, information, etc.). . . . Above the Residents-General the Minister for Foreign Affairs is responsible for their administration which is supposed to be in conformity with his own views. This is one of the fictions upon which the democratic régime rests. . . .' (*La Nef*, March 1953, pp. 7–9).

Republic, and assimilation was the theory of progressive minds, however imperfectly it might be applied in practice. Englishmen, tempted to discount it from the start, should remember that the United States has taken a somewhat similar course not without success. And nationalist leaders in the French colonies have almost always been French-educated, steeped in French culture, often married to French wives, and generally anxious to co-operate with France. But French policy has rarely been sufficiently flexible to exploit these assets.

The fate of the empire was one of the main issues in the constitutional debate, in which federalists and assimilationists clashed. The first draft, prepared by the Communists and Socialists, leaned heavily to federalism. The colonies were offered a fresh association based on free consent (implying a right of secession), and on the equality of Frenchmen and natives. This generous scheme perished when the draft constitution was defeated at the referendum. Although it was rejected overwhelmingly overseas wherever white settlers held the ascendancy, it was approved throughout the old colonies, where natives could vote.

During the long wrangle over the second draft, colonial reform became expendable. The original concessions were whittled away under pressure from Bidault, then Premier, from the Radical elder statesman Herriot and the settlers' spokesmen in Parliament, and from de Gaulle in the country. 'Free consent' became no more than a pious affirmation. The new text was strongly assimilationist—so long as the equality implied in assimilation need not be granted. Natives were granted an ill-defined citizenship, but few of them also won the vote. The colonies were represented in Parliament, but with far fewer seats than their population justified—and the white settlers generally retained separate representation. The most a colony could hope for under the 1946 constitution was that Paris would make it a department. Four West Indian and Indian Ocean territories were given this status (already possessed by Algeria) and administered with other departments by the Ministry of the Interior. Most other colonies became Overseas Territories, equally part of the Republic and represented in its Parliament, but under the

Ministry of Overseas France. They were granted local representative assemblies—inevitably modelled on the general councils of the metropolitan departments.

Already two of the nominally independent protectorates, Syria and the Lebanon, were lost. Those remaining, Morocco, Tunisia, and the Indo-China states (but not Cochin-China which France claimed as a colony) were encouraged to become Associated States, combining with the Republic to form the French Union. But the protectorates showed no enthusiasm for a Union which proved mostly a sham. Power remained firmly with the government of the Republic. The generous sentiments of the Preamble to the constitution turned out less significant than the restrictive terms of its text, which notably (in Article 62) required all resources to be pooled under the exclusive control of Paris. Not surprisingly the Union's institutions never acquired authority.

The first tragedy was played out in the swamps and rice-fields of Indo-China. There, as elsewhere, nationalist agitation had been vigorously repressed before the war. The defeat of France in 1940 gave the nationalists their stimulus; the encouragement of Japan gave them their opportunity. In 1945 the Vietminh nationalist movement took control locally when the Japanese left. But, menaced by the traditional enemy from the north, China, they proved willing to make an uneasy truce with the returning French. During 1946 the truce frayed rapidly. Vietminh was a popular front led by Communists. Some Frenchmen nevertheless believed that an understanding could be reached with its leader Ho Chi Minh: chief among them were M. Sainteny, then Commissioner for North Indo-China and today serving under de Gaulle, and General Leclerc, the most faithful of all de Gaulle's military followers. But the High Commissioner, Admiral Thierry d'Argenlieu, believed that Vietminh should be fought. As soon as Ho had left to seek a negotiated agreement in France (where he was to find less backing than he had hoped from the Left), d'Argenlieu in Saigon launched separatist movements to withdraw the south (first Cochin-China, then Southern Annam) from Vietminh control. In November a French colonel, encouraged from Saigon, deliberately ruined the conciliatory policy of his general by

bombarding Haiphong. By the end of 1946 an arme
was imminent. Ho appealed to Léon Blum, just
Premier; the French censor at Saigon delayed the te
until after the war had begun.

For seven years it raged on, punctuated by fre
military assurances of imminent victory. At first des
efforts were made to patch up a peace. But in 1949,
M.R.P. had taken over responsibility from the Sociali
new policy was begun; the former emperor Bao Dai
had abdicated in 1945 and accepted the Republic) was bro
from his retirement in Cannes to head a pro-French gov
ment. But Bao Dai was wary of becoming a mere puppet
insisted on concessions to nationalist feelings (notably
Cochin-China) and the French were grudgingly obliged
recede from their original intransigent position.

In 1949 also the Communists won in China, and at the e
of 1950 the French lost the key frontier post of Caoba
Henceforth the war was to become a terrible drain on Fren
morale and resources; but with the Communists consolidati
their control of Vietminh, it became part of the wider col
war. In France itself *la sale guerre*, as the Communists calle
it, was as unpopular as wars in remote Indo-China hav
always been (back in 1885, Jules Ferry was overthrown afte
a minor defeat there). No minister, save Mendès-France at the
moment of opening peace talks, ever dared suggest sending
conscripts. The war was fought by professionals (especially
paratroops), the Foreign Legion, and Vietnamese; the officers
were of course French, and every year the war killed as many
as the officer schools in France turned out. Not only was it
crippling the country's military strength in Europe; it was
also bleeding her economically, absorbing in the early years
much more than Marshall Aid brought in.

In Indo-China itself the people were hostile, except for
pockets of pro-French feeling, notably among the Catholics
of Tonkin for whom M.R.P. felt an understandable tenderness.
Around the whole war floated an odour of profiteering and
scandal, caused mainly by the notoriously lucrative traffic in
over-valued Indo-Chinese piastres; when this trade was
belatedly stopped in 1953, many vested interests on the
French side were undermined. The anti-Vietminh nationalists

promptly called for independence and refused to enter the French Union—causing many Frenchmen to question the point of a war in which victory merely meant conceding to others what had been refused to Ho.

By 1953 a prominent Gaullist (M. Christian Fouchet, now Ambassador to Denmark) was calling the Indo-Chinese conflict 'the Fourth Republic's Mexican expedition'. France seemed unable either to negotiate a settlement (since the Right would make no serious concessions at all, while no party in power would negotiate with Ho) or to win a military victory (since the country would certainly not support great sacrifices, whether of money or of lives, for Indo-China). The soldiers had been set an impossible task. It was not surprising that they resented it—and blamed the politicians at home, who were indeed guilty of indecision, but were also useful scapegoats for military blunders, above all the crowning idiocy of Dien Bien Phu. That crushing disaster was the end. Britain and America could not agree on nuclear intervention; Russia urged prudence on China and Vietminh; and the Geneva agreements partitioned the country, like Korea. Mendès-France, who bore no responsibility for the war and was called on to negotiate *after* the disaster, has since been denounced for losing half Indo-China. Had the war gone on, nothing would have been saved; as it was, the one nationalist who could hold the south was Diem, who had never compromised himself with the French.

The story of the North African protectorates is less bloodstained and disastrous, but it is sorry enough. The Tunisian Neo-Destour party was the most modernized and moderate nationalist movement in any Arab land. From 1949 French centre governments undertook cautious and prolonged negotiations with it. But in December 1951 these were abruptly broken off under pressure from the powerful parliamentary lobby of the settlers. Three months later the Socialists had been driven into opposition in Paris; the Tunisian ministers (among whom Neo-Destour was represented) could now be arrested and exiled to the south. The Conservative-led Pinay cabinet began two years of repression, with the normal, dismal sequence of terrorism, counter-terrorism and guerilla warfare. This was ended in 1954 by Mendès-France, whose

negotiations were successfully concluded next year by his successor Edgar Faure. The Neo-Destour leader Bourguiba soon returned from exile to become Premier and then (in 1957 when the Bey was deposed) President. His reactionary rival Salah ben Youssef, who denounced him as too pro-French, retired to Cairo. 'Internal autonomy' (which successive governments had promised but not granted) was all that was conceded by Mendès-France, but it proved a brief halting-place on the way to full independence.

The conduct of the new state towards French settlers and pro-French Tunisians left much to be desired, and the Algerian war was soon to place Franco-Tunisian relations under almost intolerable strain. Both governments had difficulty in restraining their fire-eating extremists. But disaster was averted by the determined moderation of Bourguiba and the patient comprehension of the Frenchmen dealing with him. For all her delays and errors, France had here acted just in time to keep power in the hands of the most moderate and friendly faction which had any hope of survival.

Morocco came under French control thirty years after Tunisia. Potentially much richer, it was developing very fast, in frontier boom conditions. But it remained a more primitive country with a much smaller educated elite. The nationalist party, the Istiqlal, was less westernized than the Neo-Destour; both they and their enemies the *colons* were more disposed to violence than their Tunisian counterparts. The Sultan, Mohammed V, himself sponsored and encouraged the Istiqlal; in 1951 he was threatened with the fate of the late Bey of Tunis (deposed in 1943 by the French for collaboration), and two years later the threat was carried out (on the pretext that he was obstructing reforms, of which little was heard after his removal). The Minister responsible, Bidault, had not countenanced the act; but subsequently he covered and justified it. Two leading ministers protested (François Mitterrand, who soon resigned, and Edgar Faure). As the critics predicted, the exiled Sultan became the unchallenged spokesman of a united country, without whom no negotiation could be undertaken.

When Mendès-France came to power a year later, his hands were full with Indo-China, Tunisia and Germany; his 'majority' was suspicious and restive; and he ventured on no major change in Morocco. In June 1955 the crisis came to a head when Lemaigre-Dubreuil, millionaire champion of conciliating the nationalists, was murdered by French counter-terrorists (probably in the police). This was too much. Edgar Faure, now Premier, sent out a strong Resident, Gilbert Grandval (today one of de Gaulle's ministers) to clean up the government of Morocco.

On the spot Grandval quickly won Moslem confidence, but he met open defiance and sabotage from administration and army alike. Nor was he backed by the government which appointed him, which was deeply divided and led by a man who preferred manœuvre to decision. Grandval's mission was to devise and impose a compromise solution which would avoid a triumphant return of the exiled Sultan. But any chance of success was ruined by the stubborn resistance of the Right to any concessions at all. The Resident warned that disaster loomed if nothing had been decided by 20 August, the anniversary of the deposition; the recalcitrant ministers held firm; Grandval's resignation was offered and refused; and on 20 August the expected and horrible massacres of Europeans duly occurred (in Algeria as well as Morocco). Still the blind men of the Right held out—not against bringing the Sultan back or the Istiqlal into office, but against permitting anyone except a puppet to share in power at all. But the puppets were more alive than their masters to what was happening; and when in October el Glaoui, France's chief supporter in Morocco, made his submission to his old enemy the Sultan, no solution was left but the unconditional return of the deposed monarch.

Few episodes in recent history have shown a French government in so unfavourable a light. The Right and the Gaullists, who never tired of denouncing the weakness and incoherence of government, were foremost in sabotaging policies they had accepted and men they had appointed—with the perfectly foreseeable result of bringing about the very outcome they most dreaded. Yet, with rather remarkable magnanimity, Mohammed V has remained a bulwark of reason and moderation against the anti-French extremists—though he has not always been able to stop their excesses.

.   .   .   .

The same story of 'too little and too late' was all but repeated in Black Africa. When Madagascar broke into revolt in 1947 yet another 'strong' man made a wilderness and called it peace. Many thousands of Malagasies died in the revolt and Chevigné's repression, and the leaders of the nationalist movement were imprisoned or exiled. But order was restored. The lesson was not lost on the other territories; for the most part Black Africa remained outwardly calm. Although the 1946 'settlement' was resented, for tactical reasons criticism centred on the second-class citizenship of the Africans rather than on nationalistic demands. Embittered by the indifference of metropolitan France, many native leaders drifted for a time into fellow-travelling. But in 1950 Houphouet-Boigny, the leader of the chief West African party, the R.D.A., was won from the *progressiste* embrace by the generosity with which the Minister for Overseas France treated the Ivory Coast riot leaders. (The Minister, Mitterrand, is with Mendès-France the main target for right-wing hatred and charges of treason.) Houphouet has since proved France's staunchest friend in Africa. His chief opponent, Gabriel d'Arboussier, remained a fellow-traveller for several years, but also became eventually an advocate of co-operation with France and (in 1957) President of the Grand Council of French West Africa.

Although preoccupied with subduing Indo-China, Paris granted considerable social reform and substantial economic aid. But political reform lagged sadly, even though the colonial electorate had quadrupled by 1951 and the territories' representation in Parliament was increased. Yet assimilation was collapsing as colonial administration was steadily decentralized. Even the territorial assemblies exercised an unexpected influence over the economy and administration of their territory, and fostered a vigorous local political life. Before the débâcle at Dien Bien Phu exposed the bankruptcy of a colonial policy based on force, it was clear that changes must be made if the tranquillity of Africa was to be maintained. As early as 1953 the Ministry of Overseas

France was preparing schemes which abandoned assimilation in favour of even greater decentralization and local autonomy. In April 1954 Louis Jacquinot, Laniel's Minister for Overseas France, told the Assembly 'The hour has come to envisage decisive reforms for the future of the French Union.'

Harassed governments gave priority to more pressing problems, and the Assembly was either indifferent or paralysed. A relatively uncontroversial municipal reform, proposed in 1952, was finally voted only in 1955. Meanwhile nationalism was awakening. Reforms along Jacquinot's lines were extended to the trusteeship territory of Togo in 1955; this merely stimulated the demand for similar measures throughout Black Africa. The 1956 elections brought to the Assembly a group of moderate nationalists, determined to press for a real transfer of power.

France reacted speedily and intelligently. Reminding the Assembly of the promises made to the colonies in the constitution, Guy Mollet declared that France must now keep her word. Shaking the dust of three years from the plans for reform, Gaston Defferre, the progressive Minister for Overseas France, and Houphouet-Boigny, now Minister Delegate, expanded these into the far-reaching *loi-cadre* of June 1956. If the outline law's proposals bore the stamp of Houphouet-Boigny's federalism, its success was a triumph for Defferre, who skirted the growing disagreements between the Africans, and, by exploiting every procedural manœuvre, repeatedly thwarted the unholy alliance of the diehard Right and the Communists.

The *loi-cadre* and its attendant decrees offered the Africans as much as could legally be granted within the existing constitution—and probably more. Universal suffrage on a common roll was extended to all territories. The territorial assemblies were given wide autonomy over local affairs. Councils of government were created, elected by the assemblies; the French governors presided, but there were African vice-presidents and ministers with technical responsibilities. The way was clear for the councils of government to develop into responsible cabinets—a concession that Defferre could not make openly since the recognition of a second sovereignty was impossible within the indivisible Republic.

For the moment the Africans were satisfied. Defferre administered the reforms as liberally as they were conceived. Elections with universal suffrage were freely held throughout Black Africa in 1957. The councils of government were allowed even more control over local affairs than had been expected. Yet this could not be the final solution. The *loi-cadre* foreshadowed a revision of the constitution, essential to further progress. Unfortunately the Africans could not agree on a new shape for the French Union. Their differences, which mounted steadily after the publication of the *loi-cadre*, were to be carried unresolved into the Fifth Republic.

Houphouet-Boigny argued for the creation of a 'democratic and Franco-African community based on equality'. This would be a federation with a central government and parliament in Paris, in which the territories would be directly associated with France. The regional executives of West and Equatorial Africa, costly structures screening the territories from Paris and complicating the administration, should be pruned or abolished. The *loi-cadre* reflected his beliefs in its emphasis on increasing the autonomy of the territories and its indifference to Dakar and Brazzaville. Until 1957 he was backed by the R.D.A. Thereafter his persistent hostility to regional executives proved unpopular with many of his followers, while a militant minority led by Sekou Touré refused to accept as he did that the right to independence, once admitted, should remain symbolic.

For the moment Houphouet-Boigny remained a formidable force, an indispensable member of every cabinet. But to Léopold Sédar Senghor, the P.R.A. leader from Senegal, the *loi-cadre* imposed a disastrous 'balkanization'. The territories were individually so small and weak that they could never claim genuine independence. An advocate of pan-Africanism, he wanted the French Union to become a loose confederation, with the territories forming primary federations (corresponding to the existing regional groupings) which would associate with France on more equal terms.

The clash of doctrine over the primary federations was reinforced by personal rivalries, tribal antagonisms, and economic calculations (Ivory Coast suspected that it was to serve as milch cow to the poorer territories). The cries for immediate change became increasingly insistent; in February 1958 Madagascar demanded immediate independence within a 'French Commonwealth'. But in Black Africa it was less and less clear where the majority lay. Attempts at compromise bore little fruit. In April the R.D.A. agreed on a formula which came very close to the compromise agreed between the rival camps during the constitutional debates in the summer: recognition of the separate personality of each territory with the right to choose its form of association with metropolitan France. But the conflict developed, and in September the party split.

Meanwhile constitutional revision waited. In principle there was a majority in the Assembly for granting the right to independence and pushing decentralization even further. But the Right feared creating a precedent for Algeria, the Communist-Poujadist coalition did its wrecking work again, and the well-intentioned majority failed to break out of its lethargy. Only weeks before the Republic collapsed, the Sudanese R.D.A. leader Modibo Keita declared rather inaccurately that 'Africa has chosen, France hesitates', and warned that 'the chances of constructing the Franco-African community diminish daily. . . . If France allows the chance of creating the Franco-African community to escape, Africa will inevitably set out on the only path compatible with her dignity: independence.'

Yet although the Fourth Republic faltered at this final step, its policies in Black Africa were the most hopeful achievement of its dying years. It granted reforms before being overtaken by events. It produced, in the territorial assemblies, in the Parliament of the Republic, and even in the obscure Assembly of the French Union, the vital cadre of experienced Africans who could assume greater responsibilities. It pointed the solution of the colonial problem to its successor. It proved that France still had the will to produce liberal and far-sighted policies.

Why, then, did the very ministry which set the new course in Black Africa follow the old one in Algeria?

3

The Cost of Algeria

At first sight the Algerian problem seemed little different from the others. Algeria had been French since 1830; juridically part of France, it had sent members to Parliament in the Second and Third Republics. There were two main Moslem parties, a moderate one led by Ferhat Abbas, who until the war had aimed only at equality of status, and a more intransigent one under Messali Hadj (the P.P.A., later renamed M.L.T.D. and now called M.N.A.).[1] As elsewhere, nationalist organizations were frequently banned and their leaders interned or exiled. On VE-day, 8 May 1945, there were disorders in the Sétif area which were savagely repressed.

To give Algeria its due representation in Parliament would have strengthened fears of France becoming (in Herriot's phrase) 'the colony of her colonies'. Instead of a hundred deputies, Algeria was therefore to return only thirty (and fifteen of these would represent the settlers); but she could also elect an Assembly of her own. The Algerian statute was voted in 1947; Radicals and Conservatives had become the marginal parliamentary groups, and exploited their new-found power to whittle down its concessions and to get rid of the Governor-General, Chataigneau, who had won Moslem confidence. His successor, the Socialist Naegelen, presided over elections which became a byword for fraud on a heroic scale—those to the Algerian Assembly in 1948, and to local authorities and Parliament in the following three years.[2]

[1] Algerian People's Party; Movement for the Triumph of Democratic Liberties; Algerian National Movement. Earlier still it was called North African Star. Abbas founded the U.D.M.A. (Democratic Union for the Algerian Manifesto) in 1946.
[2] 'The pseudo-elected members, currently known by the name of "prefabs", installed in their seats thanks to electoral fraud, most often illiterate and frequently dishonest, represent nothing and no one, have no influence whatever in their constituencies, and do not even perform

D

All the administration's efforts were devoted to electing yes-men ('*beni-oui-oui*'). During the campaign for the Algerian Assembly, over half the M.T.D.L. candidates were arrested; from the victims' ranks came much of the F.L.N. leadership six years later. Messali, like Bourguiba and the Sultan, was interned.

From such developments critics rightly concluded that the Indo-Chinese, Tunisian and Moroccan errors were being repeated—and wrongly inferred that the Algerian problem was identical. They were mistaken, for French opinion, indifferent to the protectorates and unwilling to make sacrifices for them, was deeply concerned about Algeria. For this difference there were a number of reasons.

First, the French were far more solidly implanted. They had been there twice as long as in Tunisia or Indo-China, three times as long as in Morocco—and before Texas or California were part of the United States. The European population was much larger (a million, against 200,000 in Tunisia and 300,000 in Morocco), and more deeply rooted (five-sixths born there, against one-half and one-third respectively).[1] Many families had lived there for several generations; through contact with them, many Frenchmen were aware of the considerable French effort in road-building, agricultural development, and above all health. Thus there was more knowledge at home of what France had done in Algeria, more pride in it, and more sympathy for the European population—not the handful of *gros colons*, the enormously rich landowners, but the mass of postmen and clerks, small farmers and railwaymen.

Yet, secondly, the drastic fall in infantile mortality (partly due to the success of French medicine) had created an appalling population problem. Algeria has one of the highest birth-rates in the world; half the Moslem population is under

any service for the administration which created them. Few mistakes have been as tragic as that by which we have evaded our own laws in order to raise into prominence discredited characters of no intellectual or moral worth whatever.' From a report to the French government in 1955 by the Governor-General of Algeria, M. Jacques Soustelle.

[1] About half the Europeans in Algeria are of French origin, including many Corsicans. The rest are mainly of Spanish descent in the west, Italian and Maltese in the east.

twenty.) Hundreds of thousands—in some villages half the adult males—have emigrated to France when they failed to find work at home, and sent back their earnings to their families and neighbours. This invasion benefited the French economy, but was resented by many French workers, whose dislike of the *bicots* helps to explain the Communist Party's many equivocations on the Algerian problem.

Thirdly, the Army felt differently about Algeria. Since 1956, young conscripts have been engaged against the F.L.N. in a guerilla campaign of a kind which rarely stimulates either sympathy or respect for the enemy. But far more important was the attitude of the officers (and N.C.O.s). In Hitler's war the army had been divided about where its political duty lay. It emerged determined not to split again. Indo-China both re-forged its unity and developed its political consciousness. For, first, the abler young officers developed a new dimension to their conception of warfare; in a revolutionary struggle the allegiance of the civil population had proved decisive, and the Vietminh had acquired it by methods of psychological warfare which conventional tactics could not meet. Secondly, justly or not, the whole army felt betrayed by the politicians, and by the civilians at home, who would neither win the war nor settle it in time. They had seen the pro-French Vietnamese who trusted their assurances abandoned to the vengeance of their enemies. The army entered the Algerian war in a 'never again' mood, which was sharpened by their fear that Algeria was the last military province where they could feel useful and respected, and that its loss would drive them back to an indifferent, uncomprehending, anti-militarist homeland.

Nor was it only professional soldiers who saw Algeria as a last chance. Many civilians too were bitter at their country's loss of power. Since 1933 France seemed to have been perpetually retreating—and before less civilized, less democratic, less tolerant rivals. Many Englishmen felt a similar resentment at Suez; in France (far more humiliated, above all in 1940) it was much more widespread. This revolt against 'being pushed around' was rationalized into the strange belief (actively inculcated by official propaganda) that France's economic, political and strategic future depended on holding Algeria. The discovery of oil in the Sahara came opportunely to reinforce this notion.

In the 1930s most French leaders had abdicated responsibility and accepted the policies of one or other great power. Gaullism and the Resistance had been revolts against this passive acceptance of foreign domination. But the defeat of Hitler did not settle the problem of France's position in the world, and after the war the same political and temperamental clash between defeatists and resisters recurred. The cautious centre governments of the Fourth Republic were often accused, not only of *immobilisme* and lack of imagination at home, but also of subservience to foreign pressures and indifference to national interests abroad. The claim that France needed above all a psychological resurgence, a reawakening of her national self-confidence, was preached by the Gaullists but not by them alone; it found echoes in all parties, and no one made the appeal more often or more eloquently than Mendès-France. In 1956 a surge of national feeling did develop; and it was stimulated by two of the very few front-rank leaders who had consistently and staunchly supported Mendès-France: the Gaullist Soustelle and the Socialist Lacoste. Ironically, the reawakening for which he had called was to destroy him as a political leader.

By the end of 1955 the urgent need for drastic action in Algeria was common ground between the parties in the election campaign, though they might differ about what the action should be. The revolt had by then been in progress for a year. Its leaders were political unknowns, who seized their opportunity in 1954. Messali, dictatorial, intransigent, and still interned in France, quarrelled with his principal followers, who had been elected to the Algiers municipal council and who wished to co-operate with the reforming mayor, Jacques Chevallier (a minister under Mendès-France). The quarrel was bitter, the disillusionment of the rank and file deep; the way was open for the third group, the revolutionaries. They struck on 1 November 1954. Mendès-France was Prime Minister; he declared that Algeria was forever French and that the rising would be put down. Mitterrand was Minister of the Interior; he echoed his leader's determination, and suppressed both factions of the M.T.L.D. Soustelle, who was

reputed to share Grandval's strength of character and liberality
of outlook but was far more prominent in the Gaullist ranks,
was made Governor-General; as an appointee of Mendès-
France, he was received with suspicion by the very settlers
whose leading spokesman in Paris politics he was soon to
become. By the end of the year the war was spreading. Graver
still, French reprisals and F.L.N. terror were affecting moderate
Moslems, even the *beni-oui-oui* sponsored by the administration to sit in Parliament and the Algerian Assembly. In September sixty-one of them denounced indiscriminate repression,
condemned integration, and affirmed the existence of an Algerian nation. An election was due in France by June 1956; and
the government, arguing that the dying Assembly could take no
serious decisions, dissolved it six months early. (But, because of
the war, the Algerian seats were left vacant in the new house.)

The election was a victory for the Left. But the allied
Socialists and Radicals held less than a third of the seats.
They could govern only by the consent either of the Communists or of the Conservative—M.R.P. combination they had
so bitterly denounced. The latter would not hear of Mendès-
France as Prime Minister; besides, his followers were fewer
than the Socialists, and it was therefore Guy Mollet who in
January formed the new government. His Minister for Algeria was a distinguished octogenarian, General Catroux,
who had played a major part in the recent negotiations with
the Sultan of Morocco. On 6 February 1956 the new Premier
flew to Algiers. The delay had given his enemies time to
prepare, and he was met by a riotous mob organized by
'ultras'—Poujadists and Fascists—and composed, not of
rich *colons*, but of those unskilled workers and *petit-bourgeois*
who in all mixed societies show most fear and hatred for
their coloured neighbours—and who, in France, vote for the
Socialist party. General Catroux resigned; he was replaced
by Robert Lacoste. It was the anniversary of the right-wing
riots in Paris which had shaken the Third Republic exactly
twenty-two years before.

. . . .

The settlers had won an important victory. The new
departure in Algeria was not political but military; for the

37

first time a French government—and only a ministry of the Left could have done it—ventured to send conscripts to fight a colonial war. Before long there were 400,000 troops in Algeria, virtually the whole fighting strength of the army. So far Mendès-France approved. He even welcomed the growing concentration in military hands of civil powers formerly wielded by an administration which he wholly mistrusted. But he also wanted compensating measures to win Moslem confidence, and above all a purge of the Algiers administrative machine. Lacoste would not hear of it. It was not that he had any love for the European extremists, against whose more virulent leaders and organizations he was quite prepared to strike. But he was unwilling to engage in a two-front war or cripple the services with which he had to work.

In April 1956 Ferhat Abbas arrived at F.L.N. headquarters in Cairo. Educated in France, married to a Frenchwoman, he had favoured assimilation and (in 1936) denied the existence of an Algerian nation. 'I have questioned history, I have questioned the living and the dead, I have visited the graveyards, no one spoke of it to me.' But by 1943 his Algerian People's Manifesto was calling for an autonomous republic; by 1955 he was one of the sixty-one; and by January 1956 he was saying sadly, 'The methods I have defended during the last fifteen years—co-operation, discussion, persuasion—have proved ineffective.' The defection of so consistent a francophile showed the dangers of Lacoste's course.[1] In May Mendès-France resigned, amid the indifference of the public and the hostility of nearly all the deputies elected under his patronage four short months before.

Although the government's reluctance to provoke the settlers set the Fourth Republic on the road to ultimate disaster, its policy was not intentionally reactionary. Officially it was contained in Mollet's celebrated *triptyque:* first a cease-fire, three months later elections (with international observers), finally negotiations with the duly chosen representatives of the Algerian people. During the summer there were private talks in Egypt, Yugoslavia and Italy between spokesmen of

---

[1] Yet in 1959, as F.L.N. 'premier', Abbas still sent his son to a French school in Tunis.

the Socialist party and representatives of the F.L.N. The gap remained too wide to be bridged. For the F.L.N. demanded the prior recognition, not merely of Algerian independence, but of themselves as a provisional government. They asserted their claim to representative status by the assassination of all who denied it: not only pro-French Moslems but also moderate nationalists and Messali's followers, now reconstituted as the M.N.A. The struggle was waged with the utmost ferocity. The M.N.A.'s strength lay among Algerians in France; and there, during 1956, the murders of Moslems by Moslems averaged about three a day. In Algeria itself the most appalling incident occurred in the spring of 1957, when an F.L.N. band surrounded a pro-M.N.A. village near Melouza and slaughtered every male over fifteen, 300 of them in all.[1]

Whatever the F.L.N.'s misdeeds, no North African leader could conceivably oppose Algerian nationalism. But none knew better than Bourguiba and the Sultan (now King) of Morocco how precarious the war made their position. Each knew that his people sympathized with the Algerians, but had himself to take account of the French, and so could easily be outbid for popular favour by his enemies—on the Left but above all on the Right, Cairo-oriented reactionaries like Allal el Fassi in Morocco and Salah ben Youssef in Tunisia. No one had more interest in escaping from an impossible position by settling the war. So, in October 1956, the two rulers arranged a conference at Tunis. Beforehand, Ahmed Ben Bella and four other F.L.N. leaders visited Morocco to consult the King, and then set off for Tunis in his plane. But its French crew disobeyed their orders from Rabat and landed at Algiers, where the five were seized and imprisoned.

Lacoste was told of this impending *coup* after the aircraft took off, the Minister of the Army (Lejeune, Socialist) apparently earlier, Mollet only after the arrests. The Moroccans and Tunisians were understandably furious, and the minister responsible for dealing with them (yet another Socialist,

---

[1] The French account (most circumstantial, though not without discrepancies) accused the F.L.N. The F.L.N. (with no evidence) accused the French. The M.N.A. blamed the F.L.N. for the massacre and the French for making it an excuse for refusing independence.

Savary) resigned. But the capture was popular, and the Prime Minister—like M. Bidault three years before—covered and applauded an act he would not have authorized. Once more the army had imposed its will on Paris. Nor had it merely scotched whatever chance of a negotiated peace existed in October 1956; the seizure had more lasting repercussions. The French have often complained since that the F.L.N. leaders lacked political capacity and authority to make decisions. Those who had that capacity and authority lay in the Santé prison.

At the end of 1956 French policy seemed to have reached an *impasse*. Negotiation was out of the question for a time. Military victory was remote; Lacoste's *dernier quart d'heure* was a sorry joke. It was hoped that the Suez expedition would put an end to Egyptian aid to the F.L.N. by toppling Nasser, but Massu's paratroops were stopped a few hours from Cairo. (The Paris politicians naturally blamed England for the fiasco; the soldiers blamed the Paris politicians and became even more bitter against the System than before.) In Algiers, the F.L.N. were sowing panic by indiscriminate terrorism: bombs at the bus-stops, in the dance-halls and in the shopping centres. In this mood of exasperation and frustration, several disturbing and revealing events took place.

In December General Jacques Faure (a former ardent Vichyite and future Poujadist candidate) was discovered plotting to seize power in Algiers. In March 1957 another general with a heroic war record with the Free French, Paris de la Bollardière, resigned his command in protest against dishonourable methods of repression. Both officers were given minor punishments.

In January 1957 a bazooka shell was fired into the office of the commander-in-chief in Algeria, General Salan, whose A.D.C. was killed; the crime was traced to a European counter-terrorist, the former swimming champion Dr. Kovacs. Through his friend General Faure, Kovacs knew that Soustelle, Debré and others were trying to have Salan replaced by General Cogny; when he was arrested he tried to save himself by claiming to have acted on orders from a Committee of Six including Cogny, Soustelle and Debré. He succeeded. Not till 1958 did a government (de Gaulle's) dare bring him to trial;

and then he mysteriously escaped from the country, just as politically inconvenient criminals did under the Fourth Republic.[1]

The war's effects were not confined to Algeria. It poisoned the political climate in France itself. Right-wing thugs broke up meetings protesting against the repression or advocating peace—or, by merely threatening to do so, gave the authorities a pretext to ban the meetings and silence the critics. Even within the Socialist party, respected minority leaders were treated vindictively: André Philip expelled, Daniel Mayer forced to resign from the Assembly, Madame Brossolette manœuvred out of her Senate seat. But—whether from blindness, indecision or simple fear—governments took no vigorous action against the ultras who were conspiring against the security of the state, and demoralizing the army by trying to murder its commander. Instead, these offences were charged against left-wing students who distributed F.L.N. leaflets (Jean Rousset, who has been imprisoned *without trial* ever since 1956), or priests engaged on social work among Moslems in France, or journalists whose articles gave offence to the army (sometimes for saying no more than Socialist leaders had done in the election campaign). Underhand attempts were made to ruin obnoxious papers financially. A government led by a Socialist used price-control powers to force *Le Monde* to sell copies at an uneconomic figure. The same ministry started seizing opposition journals from time to time. This was illegal (unless a prosecution followed, which it hardly ever did). But it was an effective form of financial persecution, and became so normal that a colonel in the Defence Ministry could seize a paper without even thinking it necessary to inform any minister.

Officialdom especially detested journals which published charges of torture or maltreatment of prisoners. Unable to stop the abuses themselves, all too many ministers reacted by vilifying those who exposed them. Some of the charges were false or exaggerated; others were certainly true, for later governments freely admitted that these practices had

[1] Notably Peyré, central figure of the 'scandal of the generals' in 1950, which the Gaullists exploited gleefully. But Peyré was charged with corruption, not murder.

prevailed—under their predecessors.[1] When General Massu's parachutists (to whom the most ungrateful tasks were normally assigned) were ordered to break F.L.N. terrorism in Algiers, they did so by the only effective means. But they suspected that politicians who had willed the end had not only turned a blind eye to the methods used, but were also preparing dossiers against scapegoats whom it might be expedient to sacrifice.

Efforts were made to stamp out these practices. Disciplinary action was sometimes taken, though never publicized (it is traditional in France to keep secret punishments inflicted for misdeeds done in the service of the state). Mollet set up a Commission to Safeguard Individual Rights and Liberties—and also to expose false accusations; but three members soon resigned in protest against their impotence. Suspects could, under emergency powers, be interned without trial; for the families of the many who disappeared without trace, bureaucratic inefficiency was as harrowing as deliberate maltreatment.

In this as in other matters the last governments of the Fourth Republic had lost control over their services. Mollet's successor renewed unofficial contacts with the F.L.N. through Ben Bella's Tunisian lawyer, who came to Paris—only to be arrested and expelled by the Ministry of the Interior. (Such incidents, sadly typical of the decrepit Fourth Republic, have unhappily recurred under the renovated Fifth.[2] In March 1958 the Paris police demonstrated before the Assembly they were supposed to protect, nominally demanding danger-money because of F.L.N. attacks, but also shouting anti-parliamentary and anti-semitic slogans. Bourgès-Maunoury remained Minister of the Interior, though the Prefect of Police lost his post. No more was done to restore discipline. The consequences were soon to be seen.

[1] A Communist, alleged by the party to have been tortured in prison by paratroops, was soon afterwards killed while fighting with the F.L.N. Some non-Communist critics were also guilty of distortion and misrepresentation. But all too abundant evidence has come from sources as little suspect as the leaders of the Catholic and Protestant churches, the priests serving as officers in Algeria, Gaullist generals and ex-ministers: Malraux, Michelet, Billotte, Capitant, Bollardière.

[2] See below, pp. 161-2.

The rot which began under Mollet (or earlier) became worse after his fall. No subsequent ministry had either internal coherence, solid support in the Assembly, or any likelihood of lasting more than a few months. Though the Right had disliked Mollet's foreign, financial and social policies, they had welcomed his acceptance of responsibility for the Algerian war. But rather than vote taxes to pay for it, they turned him out.[1] Bourgès-Maunoury, who succeeded him, had been his Minister of Defence and the chief harrier of the 'liberal' critics, whose ministerial sympathizers now went out of office. But often in politics it takes a man of the Right to make a move to the Left (and vice versa). Bourgès-Maunoury's government reopened unofficial negotiations with the F.L.N., abolished the Algerian municipal councils (strongholds of settler influence), and introduced a reform bill, the so-called *loi-cadre*. The bill divided Algeria into provinces, some dominated by Europeans and others by Moslems—so opening the way to possible partition—and it put Moslems on the same voting roll as Europeans, so giving the former effective power. The furious settlers planned to demonstrate in Algiers; General Massu stopped them by warning that he would not hesitate to fire on them. They then called on their 'quartet' of parliamentary friends—the Gaullist Soustelle, the Conservative Duchet, Bidault of M.R.P. and the right-wing Radical Morice (Minister of Defence)—and the government was overthrown.

After five weeks of ministerial crisis (a record) another Radical, Gaillard, formed another weak and divided cabinet which passed a watered-down version of the *loi-cadre*. But reform in Algeria was soon thrust aside by successive crises over Tunisia. Here the F.L.N. now controlled the whole border area, and seemed as powerful in the country as Bourguiba himself. He appealed for arms; France made conditions; and to the fury of the French Right Britain and America supplied the weapons. Like Macarthur in Korea, the army leaders were indignant at their enemy's 'privileged sanctuary' over the border, and demanded the right of pursuit across it.

[1] Père Ubu: 'Non, de par ma chandelle verte, faisons la guerre, puisque vous en êtes enragés, mais ne déboursons pas un sou' (Alfred Jarry, *Ubu*, Scène 14).

43

The F.L.N. apparently saw a chance to lay a trap, into which the French fell headlong. Early in 1958 French planes were repeatedly fired on from the Tunisian frontier village of Sakiet. The air force commander warned that next time he would retaliate; the next attack came just before a Red Cross convoy was due—so there were impeccable witnesses to the French bombardment which followed. Once again men on the spot had faced ministers with a disagreeable *fait accompli.*

The Socialists demanded the punishment of those responsible; but the cabinet, fearing the army's reaction, left them at their posts to nurse their resentment. The raid's defenders had little satisfaction either, and Lacoste publicly denounced the apologetic attitude of the Foreign Office. In Tunisia a clash, which might have provoked the French fire-eaters to attempt a reconquest, was averted by the restraint of the French General Gambiez (and of Bourguiba). Britain and America offered their 'good offices'; Gaillard accepted. The enraged French nationalists, already bitter over the arms deliveries, now feared that Mr. Murphy and Mr. Beeley would trap France into a conference with five opponents—Britain, America, Tunisia, Morocco and the F.L.N.; and that craven but crafty politicians were plotting capitulation and using international pressure as an excuse. The army's resentment was shared by the Right, who (with the customary aid of the Communists) upset the Gaillard cabinet. The Fourth Republic had entered its last crisis.

The Right had miscalculated. Not more than 150 of the 600 deputies were willing to follow the 'quartet' in an all-out war policy. Soustelle had no chance at all of election to the premiership; Bidault was invited but stopped by his own party; the offer of a post to Morice was fatal to the next candidate (Pleven); in order to get rid of Lacoste, the Socialist Party refused office altogether. The dismayed settlers saw the crisis their friends had provoked used to eliminate every leader in whom they had confidence.

President Coty did not intend to defy them—and the army —by sending for Mendès-France or Mitterrand. He had indeed been sufficiently alarmed to make a secret approach to de Gaulle, but the General was unwilling to follow the customary procedure, and demanded powers which the Assembly clearly would not accept. So the choice fell on M. Pierre Pflimlin of M.R.P., a financial specialist with a reputation for liberal opinions on Algeria. His bid for the premiership, which was thought unlikely to succeed, was to be made on the thirteenth of May.

· · · · · · · ·

This cautious and responsible politician hardly seemed the man to provoke revolutionary opposition. But he had just stopped Bidault, and Algiers suspected he meant to negotiate with the F.L.N. Four distinct groups there were determined to prevent him. They had little in common, and it was somewhat to their own surprise that they soon found themselves committed, as the standard-bearer of their resistance, to General de Gaulle.

The first group was the handful of wealthy *colons*. Well connected in Parliament, expert lobbyists, plentifully supplied with funds by a levy on businesses and farms, they were experienced, resourceful, and determined in defence of their privileges. They had no love at all for de Gaulle; in the war they had preferred Pétain, or failing him Giraud. Until Gaillard's fall their spokesman, Alain de Sérigny, had been working for a 'Government of Public Safety' under the 'quartet'. Not until 11 May did he come out for the General.

Next came the European poor. They were terrified of being abandoned by France. The rich could move home (and many had, since the war began). But their home was in Algeria, and often had been there for generations; they were fighting for its security. Among them were many different groups (usually led, of course, by men of the middle-class). The most active and ruthless were fascist in type. The largest, the U.F.N.A., claimed 17,000 members. Its leader, Robert Martel, had been briefly interned by Lacoste; he was in touch with Paris counter-revolutionaries. Also important were the Poujadists, led by Dr. Bernard Lefèvre. Both organisations were active on 6 February 1956; from both came recruits for counter-terrorists like Kovacs. Likewise prominent in previous demonstrations had been the students' union (A.G.E.A.)

led by Pierre Lagaillarde (whose predecessor had been called up by Lacoste for rioting against the *loi-cadre*), and the secondary schoolboys' union, A.G.E.L.C.A. The ex-servicemen, whose leaders were not as determined as the others to overthrow democracy in France, were less noisy but more substantial. They alone might genuinely be attracted to de Gaulle's banner.

The third group was tiny: the knot of Gaullist conspirators. Handful though they were, they were not without assets. Many army officers had served with the Free French forces, and naturally preferred the Gaullists to their fascist rivals. Moreover, in France itself very many Gaullists had been in the state machine—administration, police, armed services—ever since liberation. Old Resistance and R.P.F. contacts were readily renewed, and enabled the Gaullists to enjoy complicity and support at home, and especially in the government's own services, which the others could not match. Furthermore, the General himself still enjoyed immense prestige among Moslems. Thus once an explosion occurred, the Gaullists were well placed to take advantage of it. But they had few reliable followers in Algeria, and no certainty whatever that de Gaulle would give them his blessing.

The fourth force was decisive: the army. It contained several factions; some had Gaullist sympathies, others were in touch with the ultras. Few had any love for the rich *colons*, whose past neglect and exploitation of the Moslems they blamed for the war; Massu had bitterly criticized Soustelle for defeating the first *loi-cadre*, saying 'These blind irresponsible fools will lose us Algeria'. But deeper still was their mistrust of the politicians, whom they blamed for all the defeats and humiliations from 1940 to Suez; who allowed the despised Parisian intellectuals and journalists to traduce and vilify the army; who permitted Tunisia to aid the rebels, then let the Anglo-Saxons interfere with her just chastisement. The soldiers found political weakness in Paris a crippling handicap in their own military task. How could they convince the Moslems that France really meant to remain, when ministries and policies changed—for incomprehensible but doubtless sordid reasons—every six months? Sooner or later some politician, accidentally tossed up by a stray parliamentary wave, would propose to abandon the struggle, capitulate to the F.L.N., and force the army again to betray men who had trusted and worked with them. But the army would not stand being humiliated again. Algeria should not go the way of Tunisia and Morocco. And if the regime could not save it, then in Bidault's words, 'Better mourn the Fourth Republic than *Algérie française'.*

The soldiers believed that French defeats and retreats were due solely to a bad political system and poor leadership. They were wrong. No French ruler could defy the rest of the world, and when de Gaulle took power he did not try; like Gaillard and Pflimlin, he conciliated instead of bullying Tunisia, and he went further than any predecessor to meet Algerian Moslem aspirations. But he, too, was both unable and unwilling to offend the army by direct negotiation with nationalists who based their claim on bullets rather than ballots. Lacoste was right to point out that his policy was being continued by de Gaulle. No one attempting a completely different course— whether more or less liberal—could have survived for long. Many criticisms of the Fourth Republic's leaders, both from the army and from the Left, were quite unrealistic.

But some were not. Too many ministers were willing to register pressures instead of resisting them, to exploit prejudices instead of trying to eradicate them, to condemn those who exposed abuses instead of those who perpetrated them, to be led by their subordinates instead of leading them. An M.R.P. leader took responsibility for deposing the Sultan, a Socialist for arresting Ben Bella, a Radical, for bombarding Sakiet. Ministers allowed policy to be made by parliamentary blackmail (over Tunisia in 1951), by military and civil service obstruction (over Morocco in 1955), by street riots (in Algiers in 1956). The murderers of Lemaigre-Dubreuil, of Salan's A.D.C., of the Communist Professor Audin went unpunished. It was much easier to repress critics of torture than torture.

Over a year before the Algerian war began, a leading journalist (Jacques Fauvet) warned prophetically that democracy was again under attack, that liberty was already in danger in North Africa, and that 'unless we take heed, before long France will go the same way'. But the consuls who should have preserved the Republic instead connived at its degradation. Ministers let disobedience become a habit, justified its deplorable consequences, and then in May 1958 were surprised to find it universal. The thirteenth of May did not kill the Fourth Republic. It drew attention to the fact that it was dead.

PART II

Cincinnatus Returns

4. *Death and 'Resurrection'*

In this conflict of duties, that of direct service to France
—in other words of obedience to me—far outweighed the
other.

5. *A Roman Dictatorship*

It was simply absurd to feign to believe that I was
smothering the Republic which I had snatched from
the tomb.

6. *De Gaulle against the Gaullists*

The nation saw by instinct that, plunged as it was into
disorder, it would be at the mercy first of anarchy, then
of dictatorship, were I not there to serve it as guide and
rallying point.

Quotations from Charles de Gaulle, *Le Salut,* pp. 146,
264 and 21.

E

4

Death and 'Resurrection'[1]

The civilian extremists in Algiers would willingly have overthrown the Republic on or after 6 February 1956. The army
opposed them; Massu, for instance, stopped their demonstration against the *loi-cadre* in September 1957. The thirteenth
of May was made possible by the changed attitude of the
military chiefs, and precipitated at that particular moment
by the conduct of Lacoste.

The army's outlook changed essentially because of resentment at internationalization, fear of capitulation, and a
growing conviction that the Fourth Republic was so incapable of consistency or determination that under it French
Algeria was ultimately doomed. The man who exploited the
soldiers' mood was Léon Delbecque. A self-made businessman,
secretary of the R.P.F. in Nord, he had served in Algeria as
a reserve officer in 1956. When the Gaullist Chaban-Delmas
became Minister of Defence under Gaillard at the end of
1957, Soustelle suggested that he should appoint Delbecque
to his staff. Back in Algiers, Delbecque set himself to turn the
explosion which he foresaw to the advantage of the General.
Without revealing this aim, he preached the impotence of
the regime to army officers, promoted contacts between them
and the civilian malcontents, and after Gaillard's fall organized a Committee of Vigilance—to which twenty-two
parties, student and ex-service groups adhered—to channel
the popular discontent in the direction he desired. Its first
demonstration—or rehearsal—was on 26 April. Its real blow
was to be struck in the late summer.

Chaban-Delmas was aware of some of these activities (later
he claimed credit for them all). Lacoste knew something too,
but not much until April, when the friend of Delbecque's
who headed the telephone-tapping branch was moved. The

[1] See Appendix to this Chapter, page 74.

51

Minister for Algeria then promptly demanded Delbecque's removal, threatening to appeal to President Coty if necessary. He was not averse to protests from Algiers against the abandonment of his policy, and at first he had even encouraged the 26 April march; but now, fearing riots, he banned it. In contrast to September, however, the army leaders refused to enforce the ban. They were gratified by the complete orderliness of the marchers, who called for a Government of Public Safety (de Gaulle's name was still not mentioned). Delbecque (who had flown back to a military airfield which Lacoste did not control) seemed to have his following well in hand.

The demonstrators were to be bitterly disappointed. Gaillard had been overthrown to make way for a tougher policy with Tunisia; instead they were now told that a 'sellout government' was likely to come in. Bidault failed, Morice was blackballed, Pflimlin was proposed, Lacoste was to be evicted. Their indignation was fed by Lacoste himself, disgusted at his spineless party which was going to abandon him and his policy, and doubtless Algeria too. Publicly and privately he warned that a 'diplomatic Dien Bien Phu' was being prepared. And on 8 May he bitterly attacked the generals for 'civic cowardice' in refusing to make their real opinions known in Paris.

In this state of mind, Lacoste seemed a promising recruit for the men who were working to stop Pflimlin. Delbecque and Sérigny saw him on 9 May and urged him to lead the protest movement by announcing that he would remain at his post in Algiers until a Government of Public Safety took office. Delegations from the Vigilance Committee and Soustelle's organization U.S.R.A.F. were mobilized by Delbecque to reinforce his plea. The Minister hesitated, then refused. Next day he left for Paris, damned as a traitor by settler opinion. But he had not given up all hope that the *colons*' discontent might be a useful weapon against capitulation, for he is alleged to have told a Senator from Algiers 'I hope you have a fine demonstration, and sack the town hall' (Mayor Jacques Chevallier—a Conservative, a Catholic and a Mendesist— was Lacoste's *bête noire*).

Delbecque, however, had no intention of using his demonstration to serve Lacoste's ends. His plan was to keep it

going until the Assembly had voted. If Pflimlin won despite
the protest, the crowd would invade the Ministry of Algeria
(universally known as the *Gouvernement-Général* or G.G.) and
the Vigilance Committee would take over as a Committee of
Public Safety. Soustelle was to fly in to lead the movement and
issue an appeal to de Gaulle. And—it is said—paratroops were
to take off at once for Paris to support a simultaneous demonstration there.[1]

Just as Delbecque did not mean to be used by Lacoste,
so others were wary of being used by Delbecque. On the night
of 12 May a Committee of Seven—Lefèvre the Poujadist,
Martel of U.F.N.A., Lagaillarde of A.G.E.A., and four other
'ultra' leaders—met and determined to steal the Gaullists'
revolution. On the next afternoon the crowd would assemble
with full official approval, for at 6 p.m. a short ceremony at
the War Memorial was to commemorate three French prisoners
whose execution (on Tunisian soil) had just been announced
by the F.L.N. As soon as the ceremony ended the ultras
would attack the G.G.; the army would have either to fire on
them or to join them. They would call on its chiefs to take over
power, and they felt confident that it would not fire.

Their confidence was not misplaced. Senior officers were
involved in one or other (or in Colonel Thomazo's case in all)
of the plots. Those who were not, Salan and Massu among
them, were equally unwilling to shoot down patriots demonstrating against a 'sell-out' which they too hated and
feared. Already, after Lacoste's bitter words on 8 May, Salan
had warned President Coty that the election of a 'sell-out
government' would have incalculable results among his
forces; General Ely, the chief of staff in Paris, had approved,
and his aide, General Petit, had encouraged the military
conspirators in Algiers by a rash promise of Soustelle's
support and an unauthorized assurance of de Gaulle's. Now,
when Lacoste at the last moment decided to ban the demonstration of 13 May, Salan again—as on 26 April—declared
himself unable to enforce the ban.

The Vigilance Committee had ordered a general strike for

---

[1] This is based on an uncorroborated statement by the Brombergers.
The Paris demonstration, which flopped, was organized by Biaggi, a
Gaullist adventurer who had been a leader on 6 February 1956.

1 p.m. on the 13th. It was complete. Among the youths who soon filled the streets, leaflets circulated charging that Pflimlin would betray Algeria by negotiations in the summer, when the town was empty; Algiers must stop him now by insisting on a Government of Public Safety with Soustelle, Bidault, Morice and Duchet. The American Cultural Center was sacked by the crowd, but the offices of the *Journal d'Alger* (which supported Chevallier) were saved by para-troops. At 5 p.m. a Vigilance Committee loudspeaker began whipping up feeling, denouncing the treacherous Paris politicians who were really responsible for the assassination of the murdered prisoners, repudiating any sell-out govern-ment, any government of the System, any authority except a Government of Public Safety. When the brief ceremony ended, at five past six, the generals went back to their head-quarters and the crowd slowly started to disperse—both unaware that a revolution was taking place a few hundred yards away.

It was not Delbecque's revolution, of course; that was not due for hours. But neither was it Lagaillarde's and Martel's; their insurrection, too, was being stolen from under their noses. For the *lycéens* of A.G.E.L.C.A. had no intention of letting their seniors of A.G.E.A. monopolize the glory of the day. Well before the ceremony ended they were climbing the wide stairway which leads up from the War Memorial to the Forum, the big car-park in front of the G.G. The C.R.S. (riot police), who held the top, enraged them by using tear-gas. A.G.E.L.C.A. loudspeakers below denounced this pro-vocation, and the under-twenties swarmed to the attack on the hated police. Schoolboy messengers sped round the city on motor-scooters to spread the word. At 6.5 p.m., as the generals left, Lagaillarde rather belatedly shouted, 'Every-one to the G.G. to smash the rotten regime.' The crowd on the steps grew. Suddenly someone—allegedly a paratroop colonel —ordered the C.R.S. back into the building, leaving the Forum open. In the G.G., Lacoste's *chef de cabinet* Maisonneuve was in charge. He phoned indignantly to the prefect (an ally of Delbecque's) and was told that parachutists were coming to take over. As none had come, Maisonneuve ordered the C.R.S. to charge and clear the Forum; they did so, and he telephoned to Lacoste in Paris that it was all over. It had not yet begun.

The parachutists now arrived and occupied the top of the stairway, but did not stop the crowd invading the square (as one demonstrator put it, 'they pushed us on while pretending to hold us back'). The *lycéens* started to wreck the parked cars of the G.G. officials who had not come out on strike. Senior officers appealed vainly (and quite inaudibly) for calm; Lacoste's military assistant Colonel Ducournau stood gesticulating impotently as his own car was turned over. At 6.15 p.m. about five hundred demonstrators began to attack the building. At one corner a few *lycéens* broke into the library and set it on fire. In front, the assailants stoned the C.R.S., who withdrew behind the gates. The paratroops let the attackers use one of their trucks as a battering-ram, and about 6.45 p.m. the gates gave way.

The C.R.S. threw more tear-gas grenades from the first floor, half a dozen shots were fired, and the crowd fell back. But Lagaillarde, aided by his parachutist lieutenant's uniform (and ignoring one officer who cried 'Stop, you're making a mistake, it's not till tomorrow') broke through into the building and from an upper floor vigorously (but again inaudibly) harangued his followers to the attack. The C.R.S. disappeared, apparently by the subway to army H.Q. The crowd stormed in and began sacking the offices and flinging papers from the windows. Parachutists prevented them getting at most police and security files, but it is said that some conveniently disappeared in the confusion, including all those on business frauds and also the dossier on the bazooka plot against Salan (there were suspects among the members of the C.S.P.). One of Lacoste's senior officials sat with his head in his hands, groaning 'Two years' work—for nothing'. A demonstrator hoisted a Poujadist flag. Another carried off in triumph the bust of Marianne, symbol of the Republic. 'No casualties, fortunately,' commented an officer later, 'except the Republic, and that's not serious.'

The chief figures of the next few days were still absent. Massu arrived at 7.30 p.m. in a state of fury, shouting '*Quel bordel*', raging at the official who had ordered tear-gas and at Lagaillarde for 'disguising himself' in uniform. (There is a widely-circulated but apparently quite unfounded story that he telephoned Paris to ask whether to fire on the crowd, but found that neither the outgoing nor the prospective premier would take the responsibility.) As for Salan, he had received a telephone appeal from the G.G. at 6.45 p.m., but hesitated some time before taking the subway from his H.Q. He reached the G.G. soon after Massu, tried to address the crowd, and was howled down. Lagaillarde and the riot leaders urged Massu to head their Committee of Public Safety; at about 8.45 p.m., with no guidance from Salan, he agreed in order (as he told a press conference next day) to keep them under control. At 9.10 p.m. he announced the C.S.P.'s membership to the crowd: three paratroop colonels and four Moslems, suggested by the army, and seven rioters. None of these except Lagaillarde was known; one, asked whom he represented, replied proudly 'The crowd.' All proved to be ultras, not Gaullists. When Lacoste phoned from Paris to warn Massu of the dangers of his course, he was already committed. And when Delbecque at last arrived soon after nine o'clock, it seemed he had duly been robbed of his revolution. 'I must admit we've got a bit ahead of your script,' Lagaillarde remarked to him cheerfully.

The Vigilance Committee were disconcerted, not only by their rivals' premature attack, but also by the absence of Soustelle. He had told Biaggi the day before that he would not himself initiate a breach of the law, but would wait for the generals to decide; 'That sentence,' replied Biaggi, 'can be spoken only in Spanish.' On the 13th itself Soustelle remained in the Assembly instead of flying to Algiers. While the C.S.P. was being formed, Delbecque was trying desperately to reach him by telephone. By the time Soustelle finally decided that Pflimlin would win after all, the government had closed the airfields. His friends had found a sympathetic commander who was willing to let him leave, but they had forgotten to specify the name under which he would be travelling. 'M. Noël Martin' had to stay in France.

Delbecque at last reached the G.G. soon after 9 p.m., declared himself Soustelle's representative, optimistically announced his patron's imminent arrival, and was made vice-president of the C.S.P. After violent arguments several other

Vigilance Committee members were also added. Meanwhile, outside the door, a determined youth named Jacques Roseau was protesting that it was 'inadmissible' to form a C.S.P. without him, the President of A.G.E.L.C.A., whose members had been the first to break into the G.G. He eventually became a member, and indeed President of the Youth Committee, in which capacity he proposed to postpone the summer examinations and abolish the oral.

In Paris, readers of that morning's *Figaro* could have pondered an astonishingly accurate forecast of events by Serge Bromberger. Yet the politicians were taken completely by surprise. Deputies coming in one by one from dinner learned that the C.S.P. had been formed, and were at once plunged into feverish excitement. But their reaction was not at all that hoped for by the demonstrators. Hesitant members, instead of voting against Pflimlin out of fear, rallied to him out of defiance. Without the demonstration against him, he would probably have lost; because of it he won comfortably, by 274 to 129. For the Communists decided to abstain. If they and their fellow-travellers had opposed him, he would have had a majority of one.

His cabinet met in a mood of indignation, resolved to 'smash the revolt' (Pierre de Chevigné, Minister of Defence), if necessary by 'starving Algeria out' (Maurice Faure, Minister of the Interior). They brought gendarmerie reinforcements into Paris, put a police guard on Soustelle, and arrested some extreme-Right leaders and dissolved their parties. But with Algiers they were circumspect. Unanimously they decided to gamble that Salan and Massu were honest in claiming to have joined the revolt only to control it. Gaillard, as outgoing premier, had already delegated civil authority in Algiers[1] to Salan, and Pflimlin confirmed this. But at the same time he displayed firmness by stopping supplies. At 6.30 a.m. President Coty as Commander-in-Chief broadcast orders to the army to obey the legal government. (One officer wrote to him expressing his desire to do so. He was court-martialled.) And at dawn, when the Forum had emptied and one foreign

[1] Whether the town or the department of Algiers became a matter of controversy between the government and the general; but certainly not the whole of Algeria as Salan successfully claimed.

journalist thought Algiers might have been brought back under control, the new Prime Minister went wearily to bed.

．　　．　　．　　．　　．　　．　　．　　．

The decision to gamble on Salan's and Massu's loyalty was understandable, for there was little other hope of regaining control of Algiers. The cabinet were unanimous in taking it, were right in believing that neither general had been involved in the plot, and were further reassured by their attitude on the 14th. For on that morning after the night before many senior officers were alarmed at what they had done. Pflimlin was in power; no political leader had come to their aid. What would become of their careers? Salan made a long phone call to Pflimlin in the morning, and Massu gave an astonishing press conference in the afternoon, in which he said the C.S.P. would sit only until a new Minister for Algeria arrived.

But the ministers were wary, and they allowed their suspicions to show, Right-wingers were arrested in Paris, suspect generals were removed. The cabinet started to whittle away the authority it had granted to Salan, and tried to keep direct contact with loyal prefects. For over a week Algeria remained partially blockaded. The army concluded that the government's fair words were meant to lull them into passivity until ministers felt ready to pounce—and then, as one said, 'it will rain close arrests'. So the wily commander-in-chief, whose nickname was 'the Chinese General', began cautiously to prepare an alternative line of action.

He was in an extraordinary position. For if the government seemed to have little confidence in him, the insurgents certainly had none. Delbecque and the Gaullists had been openly working for his replacement for months; and it was little more than a year since some of the ultras had tried to assassinate him. Most Europeans considered him 'soft' and a time-server, and they had howled him down on the night of the 13th. And yet no one wanted to offend him. The government needed his goodwill desperately. The ultras had cried '*L'armée au pouvoir!*' to frustrate Delbecque and de Gaulle, and the very existence of the C.S.P. depended on the continued favour of the military. Delbecque himself also had to look to Salan, since Soustelle had failed him; if anyone was now

to launch the appeal to de Gaulle, it must be the commander-
in-chief. Thus everyone courted Salan, assuring him earnestly
of their own friendship, and warning him amiably against
the dark designs of their rivals.

So, when he spoke from the G.G. balcony for the second time,
on the morning of Thursday the 15th, he was no longer
friendless. It was an adroit speech, and the crowd cheered.
In traditional style he ended, '*Vive l'Algérie française, vive
la France!*' As he stepped back, Delbecque confronted him.
Salan hesitated, then took a pace forward. '*Et vive de
Gaulle!*'

For the handful of devoted Gaullists it was the decisive
moment. In his concern for his own precarious position their
enemy Salan had reopened the way to the solution which, on
Tuesday night, had seemed blocked. But could they count
on de Gaulle himself to play his part?

This had always been their greatest worry. Many who were
not Gaullists had thought of the General in recent months:
Presidents Coty and Bourguiba, moderate nationalists from
Algeria and Black Africa, liberal journalists and parliamentarians. For some Gaullists had been working hard and successfully to win support on the Left, and early in 1958 the
General's keenest advocates were the left-wing critics of
Mollet and Gaillard. But de Gaulle kept his silence. He had
neither wanted nor expected the power which he would not
take illegally, and saw no prospect of obtaining legally. In
recent months, however, the many and varied public appeals
to him, and the alarming news that the army was in 'moral
rebellion', had begun to influence his attitude. He neither
approved nor even knew what Delbecque was planning. But
he did tell the conspirator late in April, and confirm early in
May, that if a crisis arose between Algeria and the homeland,
he would at last speak out. So Delbecque had had his green
light; and now the moment had come.

De Gaulle replied to Salan's appeal that same evening, with
the concise statement, 'I am ready to assume the powers of
the Republic'. There was jubilation in Algiers, and dismay on
the Left. For the General's intervention changed everything.
It staved off a possible collapse of the movement in Algeria.
It also prevented a much more likely outcome: the seizure of

power from the half-hearted Salan and the still uncommitted Massu by their impetuous and determined juniors, abetted by the ultras and eager to launch a military invasion of the mainland. But de Gaulle's statement had positive effects too. In the army in France, in the administration, and among the Algerian Moslems themselves it won for the movement a sympathy which no one else could have commanded.

To the army and the Right, de Gaulle's name stood for inflexible patriotism: he was a guarantee against a sell-out. But for many on the Left he was also the man who had restored democracy fourteen years before: a safeguard against fascism. Reassuring both sides, he was the solution which divided Frenchmen least, and the best hope of averting civil war. Next day in Parliament, to the general surprise, de Gaulle's old opponent Mollet (influenced privately by Chaban-Delmas) expressed his admiration for the General as well as his fears about the latter's present course. Did he recognize the legal government, would he disavow the C.S.P., and—if invited—would he stand for the premiership in the usual way and go back home if he lost? The Socialist leader denied indignantly that he was 'opening a dialogue' between the General who would not take power by force, and the Party without which—in this Assembly—he could not be elected. His questions, he claimed, were not an approach but a challenge. Events hardly bore him out.

All the cards had been dealt, and it remained only to play them—when suddenly a joker was slipped into the pack. Soustelle evaded his police guard, escaped into Switzerland, chartered a plane and arrived at Algiers at 1.30 p.m. on Saturday 17 May. It was a total surprise; Sérigny indeed went to the airfield expecting to meet the Moslem politician Sid Cara. For some people, especially Salan, it was also a most disagreeable shock. The commander-in-chief, still reluctant to commit himself too far, believed Pflimlin was on the point of resigning and handing over to a Government of Public Safety. Soustelle's arrival might well shatter that hope. Moreover, the former Governor-General, so popular and powerful in Algeria, was a dangerous threat to his own leadership. The meeting of the two men was so stormy that the U.T.B. (territorial tank unit) moved out to the airport to provide armed support for Soustelle. But at length a compromise was found. Salan would phone Pflimlin, and if the Prime Minister did mean to resign, Soustelle agreed to return to Switzerland forthwith. But Salan soon discovered that Pflimlin had no such intention. He and Soustelle then staged a dramatic and emotional public encounter for the benefit of the crowd in the Forum, who had no idea they had been contemplating arresting one another a couple of hours before.

Despite the reconciliation, there was no love lost between them. The army distrusted all politicians. Right-wing deputies would have flocked to Algiers at the slightest encouragement; they got none. Besides Soustelle, only two were allowed to stay: a Gaullist war-hero, Dronne, and a Corsican for whom the army had a special use, Arrighi. Half a dozen extreme Right politicians who made the journey suffered the internment or expulsion which Soustelle had so narrowly escaped —to the fury, sometimes, of their civilian sympathizers in Algiers. Soustelle himself shrewdly sought no official post, and contented himself with speechmaking. But when his Gaullist friends suggested Salan should seek advice from a political 'directory' (of Soustelle, Massu and Sid Cara) they were promptly denounced by Massu himself for undermining the authority of the army. And when the C.S.P. for Algeria and the Sahara was set up, the junior officers insisted that Massu must be co-president, to represent the military, alongside the civilian Sid Cara.

The army claimed—and believed—that it was leading, not a political movement, but a national revolt against humiliation and defeat. Radio Algiers broadcast a letter from an officer to his colonel:

> The army was simply compelled to rise and roar: 'no more "strategic withdrawals"; no more "peace with honour"; no more "internal autonomy"; no more "independence in interdependence"; no more "representative negotiators"; no more "good offices" . . .'

Obsessed with their own patriotism, its spokesmen were often virulent. Colonel Lacheroy called Pflimlin the prospective 'Kerensky of France', and Delbecque too accused the government of plotting to bring the Communists to power.

Some civilians introduced a still more sinister note. One editorialist on Radio Algiers threatened:

> There are accounts to settle. We shall judge dispassionately those we sent to Parliament. . . . Do not tolerate France being governed by Frenchmen of recent date. . . . Smash the outdated and narrow framework of the parties which have never thought of the happiness of the true people, but only of the mafia they control.

After 1 June it became clear that these fascist-minded settlers were well represented on the Committees of Public Safety, which from 13 May spread rapidly throughout Algeria (though the Constantine and Oran areas lagged somewhat behind). But for the time being the C.S.P.s were kept under control by the army.

The 13 May movement was, however, more complex than a mere conjunction of angry soldiers, fascist settlers, and Gaullist conspirators. It was also a social revolution in the relationship between the races. The change began even before Soustelle arrived. Previous wartime demonstrations by Europeans had often degenerated into anti-Moslem lynch mobs; some such incidents occurred on 13 May outside the capital. But in Algiers itself, under the army's leadership, the Europeans fraternized. And when on the 16th the military organized a Moslem demonstration in the Forum, they were rewarded by a wholly unexpected response. Freed from the fear of hostile mobs, impressed by the officers promising equality, reassured by the name of de Gaulle, the Moslems who came out voluntarily to demonstrate for the new era far outnumbered those pressed into service by the army. Algiers hailed this 'miracle of 16 May' as the first fruits of the national resurrection, a new 'night of the Fourth of August' in which, as in 1789, the privileged had voluntarily renounced their privileges.

The truth, of course, was not quite so simple. Finding themselves obliged to pay lip-service to the integration with France they had so long opposed, the *colons* naturally hoped to use it to 'tame the law of numbers' (as Martel put it) by swamping the Moslem majority in Algeria with European votes from the mainland. But they had little sympathy in the army or at home, and once they had accepted equality in principle they could no longer resist measures (in voting, local government, the administration, and education) to introduce it at their expense. Nor were Europeans the only losers. For the soldiers genuinely sympathized with the Moslem poor against their traditional exploiters of both races. (They followed up the 'Fourth of August' by a campaign to emancipate Moslem women, encouraging them to tear off their veils before the crowds.) Modernizing and almost socialistic, the whole movement has been called a 'Kemalist revolution'.

Soustelle, the first man since 13 May to cry ' *Vive la République!* ' to an Algerian audience, gave the new note. His speeches changed the whole public image of the movement. With the crypto-fascism of the extremists, and the prickly chauvinism of the army, there now mingled an authentic idealistic nationalism appealing consciously to the principles of 1789. As one broadcaster proclaimed:

> The French Revolution and her daughter, this new peaceful and fraternal Revolution we are achieving here, have powerful resources against which nothing can hold. . . . For the first time since last century France wins . . . miraculously through the power of the words which forged her grandeur, 'Liberty, Equality, Fraternity' . . . Nothing can prevent our humane revolution winning the deepest heart of Paris.

Algiers thus claimed to be guarding the true republican tradition against Frenchmen who were tarnishing it by demonstrating alongside the Communists, censoring the press, and arresting 'patriots'. The unique appeal of a revolution *for* closer union with the mother country was used to the full. Professional and 'specialized' C.S.P.s launched fraternal appeals for help and understanding to their various opposite numbers at home: fellow taxi-drivers, Auvergnats, ex-Resisters or 'rugbymen'. Again it was Soustelle who best expressed the plea:

> Ten million human beings from the Mediterranean to the Sahara have finally taken the historic resolution to remain French for ever, full members of a free community, by sweeping away in a single blow all the manœuvres and hatreds of former times.

63

They stretch their hands towards you. Will you allow these outstretched hands to fall back into the void?

．　　．　　．　　．　　．　　．　　．　　．　　．

The Pflimlin cabinet, put together before the insurrection in Algiers but voted into office just after it, had not been designed for a revolutionary situation. Efforts to strengthen the sickly infant were in progress even before its birth. First the Conservatives proposed a government of national union under Mollet (so recently turned out by themselves); some leaders favoured it, but to most members it seemed like accepting the army's veto of Pflimlin. The Prime Minister then tried to bring in the two chief party leaders, Mollet and the Conservative Pinay. But the latter was kept out by his party because the Socialists would not also accept Bidault, an open sympathizer with Algiers. Finally the Socialists came in alone, Mollet on the 14th as vice-premier, Jules Moch on the 16th returning to the Interior (where he had broken the revolutionary strikes in 1947), and Albert Gazier going to Information, where he was soon to impose a strict press and radio censorship. The newcomers stiffened the government's resistance to Algiers. At Sunday's cabinet some ministers urged strong action against both the generals and Soustelle, and even the banning of the press conference which de Gaulle had announced for next afternoon. But Pflimlin refused.

The General entered the Palais d'Orsay punctually at 3 p.m. His performance was most skilful. He wooed the Socialists, referring by name to 'my friend' Lacoste and Mollet 'whom I esteem'[1] (and to no one else), reminding them of the socialistic achievements of his previous ministry, and repudiating as absurd the idea that he would ever overturn the liberties he had himself restored. But he also praised the intervention of the army, refused to condemn the Algiers leaders, and urged the Assembly to adopt a special procedure for his legal accession to power. So carefully did he hold the balance that both sides were dissatisfied, and opinion in Algiers was ready to condemn the 'compromiser'—until the moment when the Socialists denounced his factious and

[1] He referred to their unforgettable encounter at the Arras Town Hall at the Liberation. It never happened!

unconstitutional conduct, whereupon he again found grace across the Mediterranean

Now for a moment there seemed to be a lull in the storm. The Communist general strike, called for the moment when de Gaulle was to speak, was an utter failure—like the abortive demonstrations which Biaggi and the friends of Algiers had planned for the evening of 13 May. The cabinet made no reply to de Gaulle's press conference. Behind the scenes, however, there was frantic activity: Gaullists and right-wingers preparing an insurrectionary movement in France; soldiers in Algiers perfecting plans for an invasion of the mainland; politicians exploring ways to avert honourably a disastrous civil war. Colombey-les-deux-Eglises began to receive distinguished visitors. Pinay (no Gaullist) went on Thursday the 22nd, after seeing Pflimlin the day before; he returned enthusiastic for the General. Piette, a Socialist deputy and friend of Mollet, followed on Friday; '*Personne y était*' said the critics when Mollet denied meeting de Gaulle, for in the Resistance Piette had been called 'Colonel Personne'. But at the weekend the slow-motion reel was suddenly speeded up. Algiers precipitated matters by the seizure of Corsica.

This step was decisive. The army leaders knew they had gone too far to retreat; if Pflimlin survived, they were ruined. Massu had already drawn up a 32-page plan for the airborne invasion of the mainland. But the wily Salan would not commit himself so far; a peaceful demonstration in Corsica seemed a far safer alternative. So Massu and Delbecque persuaded him to authorize an action which—whether he intended it or not—was to snap his frail link to Paris. For the expedition became an open challenge to the government.

For such a challenge the island offered several advantages. The population sympathized with the Algerian settlers, many of whom were of local origin (more Corsicans live in North Africa than at home). The garrison consisted largely of para-troops from Algeria. Gaullism was strong, and its local leader (Henri Maillot, a distant cousin of the General) was in touch with Massu. Pascal Arrighi too arrived in Algiers just in time to be useful. Being the only deputy from the island who had never held office, and having just lost a local election, he

65

jumped at the chance to distinguish himself. Salan signed his travel order; 'the Rubicon was in the inkwell'.

At 5.15 a.m. on Saturday the 24th, Arrighi landed at Calvi from a military plane. Again he was just in time; the local Gaullists were about to act—perhaps sooner than Algiers expected. The police and army were won over easily. At Ajaccio the demonstrators met at 6 p.m., and half an hour later the prefecture was in their hands. In other towns matters went equally smoothly, except at Bastia where there was token resistance from Casalta, the Socialist acting mayor, and much confusion because three distinct groups claimed the glory of forming the Committee of Public Safety.[1] But all was put in order by a delegation flown in from Algiers, including Delbecque, Sérigny, and Colonel Thomazo who joined the party at the last moment for the ride, led the troops in singing bawdy songs during the flight, and before landing found himself appointed by Salan as military governor of Corsica.

No blood was shed (when someone congratulated Arrighi, he replied 'But this is a revolution, not an election'). For the government was deserted everywhere. Even at Bastia barely a hundred people demonstrated for the Republic. The prefect stayed loyal, but five out of six sub-prefects went over at once, and the sixth later. Police and gendarmerie joined the insurgents. At Bastia the sub-prefect moaned to Casalta, 'I don't know which side will sack me,' and the Colonel, 'I don't know which side will shoot me.' The military commander, however, gave Arrighi a little trouble; it was not revolution that disturbed him, but the idea of taking part in an operation ordered by the Tenth Military Region (Algiers) when he was subordinate to the Ninth (Marseilles). Arrighi won him over, Casalta won him back, and he soon retired sadly to the mainland. But Marseilles itself tacitly connived at the action of the Calvi parachutists, who led the movement. The only threat of opposition came from C.R.S., riot police flown in from Nice on Moch's orders (in Air France planes for

[1] Casalta demanded either that (token) force be used to eject him from the Town Hall, or that the whole party should descend the steps behind him, singing the 'Marseillaise'. Eventually a compromise was reached, and he descended with his group of friends, singing a 'Marseillaise' of his own, and draped in the folds of the national flag.

fear that military ones would take them to Algiers instead).
The paratroops reached the aerodrome five minutes before the
aircraft landed, and the C.R.S., prudently observing that they
were the stronger, promptly changed sides.

The most resolute ministers still did not give up hope. Moch
and Chevigné planned to retake Bastia before dawn on Mon-
day. At 9.30 p.m. on Saturday the cabinet gave its approval.
C.R.S. were sent south and orders given to the fleet. But at
5.30 next afternoon Admiral Nomy saw Pflimlin and President
Coty, and half an hour later the plan was cancelled. It is
denied that the Navy mutinied, but certainly they were reluctant, imposed delays and obstacles, and even produced
false reports of storms in the Mediterranean. The army would
not undertake to hold the town if airborne reinforcements
arrived from Algeria. Ministers feared to deplete their few
reliable forces in France. Even economic sanctions against
Corsica broke down; the Marseilles prefect feared the reactions
of the city's many Corsicans. The impotence of the ministers
was displayed to the world—and to themselves. In Algiers
Salan's spokesman was asked what would happen if the
government used force in Corsica. 'What force?' he replied.

The French state had been withering away for years. Now
the process reached its climax. 'You are not abandoning
power,' a left-wing Gaullist told ministers in the Assembly.
'It has abandoned you.' The civil service, on Moch's evidence,
offered 'inert opposition' to cabinet decisions. In his own
Ministry, once the Republic's holy of holies, officials concealed
information from him—or gleefully supplied it, when it
seemed likely to intimidate ministers by revealing the extent
of the conspiracy. The police in the capital had shown their
sympathies sufficiently by their ugly demonstration in March;
the gendarmerie (who came under the Ministry of Defence)
shared the outlook of the army; even the firemen, so useful in
riots, were disaffected—as their colonel put it, they would
stick to their job of putting out fires—'but if the Palais
Bourbon caught alight, I doubt if they'd bother'. Moch's
own creation, the C.R.S., neither could nor would fight the
army. He thought half of them loyal, and entrusted the
defence of Paris to them—but the conspirators were convinced that these same C.R.S. were panting with eagerness to

join the revolt, and they planned to take over the capital with the very forces which the government had collected to defend it.

The navy was more or less 'neutralist'. But the air force was brazen. Openly, its planes traversed the skies in Cross of Lorraine formation; covertly, its commanders flew across to Algeria the troop-carrying planes necessary for an invasion of the mainland. The army was seething. Marshal Juin warned the President and the Premier not to count on dividing those in France from those in Algeria. The chief of staff, General Ely, resigned on the 16th. His resignation message was censored, and Pflimlin told his chief assistant, General Beaufort, 'You are mutineers, all of you'. After much trouble the government found a 'loyalist', Lorillot, to replace Ely. He promptly assured Salan that his sole aim was to keep the army united, distributed Ely's banned message to the troops, and later personally deciphered messages between de Gaulle and Salan without informing the cabinet. Four of the nine regional commanders were openly (and others more discreetly) in favour of Algiers; at Toulouse the mayor and prefect refused to speak to General Miquel.[1] The prefect himself warned the government that he was 'on a volcano'; his colleague at Bordeaux called it a powder-barrel. Similar reports were coming in from all over the country.

At the last meeting of the Pflimlin cabinet, Pleven summed matters up. 'We are the legal government. But what do we govern? The Minister for Algeria cannot enter Algeria. The Minister for the Sahara cannot go to the Sahara. The Minister of Information can do nothing but censor the press. The Minister of the Interior has no control over the police. The Minister of Defence is disobeyed by the army.'

Some ministers were still prepared for a final throw: to move the seat of government to the 'red bastion' of the northern coalfield, on the Belgian border, and arm the miners. Mollet spoke romantically of dying among them on the barricades. But would they have marched? On 19 May only 800 of the 300,000 Nord miners had struck; in the Renault

---

[1] But no doubt Miquel did not actually say, as was alleged, '*M. le Préfet, je ne suis pas ici pour défendre votre préfecture mais pour la prendre*'.

works near Paris, 3 per cent had come out. The Nord responded well to another strike call on the 27th; but in Paris it was a pathetic failure. Not even Communists would strike (or indeed always vote, as the referendum later showed) against de Gaulle. Certainly they were unwilling as well as unable to fight against him. The demonstrators who marched from the Place de la Nation to the Place de la République on 28 May were indeed impressively numerous (200–250,000 by the highest Gaullist and lowest anti-Gaullist estimates). But they were hardly the vanguard of a civil war army: and a few ribald slogans like '*De Gaulle au musée!*' and '*Le girafe au zoo!*' mingled with '*Vive la République!*', '*Front populaire!*' and '*Le fascisme ne passera pas!*'. Yet the very suggestion of a Popular Front was self-defeating, for it would have alienated the rest of the nation, and shattered in pieces the cabinet itself. 'It would have been the war in Spain,' remarked Mollet—'but without the Republican army.' And Moch advised wryly, 'Always avoid civil war—especially when you are sure to lose'.

.   .   .   .

These ministers now hoped, therefore, not to keep de Gaulle out but to wring from him guarantees offering an honourable alternative to what they most feared: an army coup, then military rule, and in the distant background probably a Communist reaction. On Sunday afternoon, 25 May, Mollet wrote the General a long letter giving the official Socialist arguments against his conduct and candidature. When he showed it to Pflimlin next morning, the Premier realized for the first time that the Socialist leaders, too, desired contact with de Gaulle. So far he had refused to approach the General for fear they should think he was betraying them. Now he could act. But de Gaulle moved first, asking both men to meet him that same night; if they refused, he would publish the fact. They agreed at once. (Moch, however, later dissuaded Mollet, urging him to bargain acceptance against a repudiation by de Gaulle of the Corsican adventure.)

Elaborate precautions were taken to preserve secrecy. The Prime Minister's secretary left in the official car, while

Pflimlin sneaked out of a back entrance followed by an assistant, who then stalled his car in the middle of the street to prevent pursuit. De Gaulle was met outside Paris by motorcycle police, who threw off the attendant journalists by defying red lights and one-way signs. The two leaders met at midnight at St. Cloud. The Prime Minister, with his eye on a Parliament still deeply suspicious of de Gaulle, asked the General to disavow the Corsican insurgents. De Gaulle, with his eye on the mutinous army, replied that to do so, except as a prospective prime minister, would destroy his usefulness as an arbiter: 'I can only disavow once'. As president of M.R.P., Pflimlin agreed to arrange for de Gaulle to meet other party leaders—but he would not abandon the post entrusted to him or the colleagues who were serving with him. He suggested they should announce their failure to agree; de Gaulle demurred. When they parted at 2 a.m., Pflimlin was convinced that he was no conspirator and would never accept power illegally; at mid-day he was therefore thunderstruck to read de Gaulle's statement, 'I have begun the regular process of forming a republican government', and his appeal to the armed forces and all citizens to maintain order. For the Prime Minister, who had told his colleagues the truth, now seemed to have lied to them—yet he dared not face the consequences of denying the announcement.

But they did not reproach him. Moch's emotion on hearing the news was not indignation but profound relief; de Gaulle, then, was not in the conspiracy but was trying to stop it. For at 10 a.m. Moch had learned from a diplomatic source (apparently the American Consul at Algiers) that the invasion of the mainland was to be launched that night. 'Operation Resurrection' would be commanded by General Miquel under orders from Algiers. Tanks from the Paris garrison were to seize Le Bourget and Villacoublay airfields; Miquel's parachutists from the south-west would begin to land at 2.30 a.m., those from Algiers at 5.30 a.m. But most of the 'paratroops' who were to take over Paris would be recalled reservists, Indo-China veterans—and the police and C.R.S. whom the government expected to oppose them. All would wear parachutist uniforms. Prefectures throughout the south would be occupied by the C.S.P.s which were waiting in the wings, while the army stood by benevolently to 'preserve order'. If the government fled northwards, it would be cut off by the troops in Germany under General Jacques Faure, hero of an earlier and abortive conspiracy.

All the generals fervently hoped to win by threats alone. Beaufort, who was to command in Paris, personally told the Elysée just what was planned, and when.[1] But this does not mean they (still less their subordinates) were merely bluffing. Moch, the strong man of the government, never believed so. He was convinced that an irretrievable calamity was imminent, and that de Gaulle had shown his good faith by intervening to stop it—thus keeping open the legal road to power which alone he was ready to take.

Moch was right in his assumption, and Algiers did postpone the attack. But in Parliament, among less informed or more incredulous deputies, resistance to de Gaulle stiffened when his extraordinary communiqué became known. The Socialists voted overwhelmingly (117 to 3) never to accept him, M.R.P. urged Pflimlin to stay in office. The Conservatives indeed ordered their ministers to resign (one refused). But a large majority of the Assembly was striving—for once—not to throw out a reluctant cabinet but to keep one in. A constitutional reform bill (proposed in the vain hope of taking the wind out of de Gaulle's sails) passed by 408 to 165: no pretext there for resignation. The Socialist Ministers urged Pflimlin to stay—not to block de Gaulle, but to give time to work on their party, for they feared a vote that day meant a Popular Front under Mitterrand. But the Premier was determined, and at 4 a.m. on Wednesday the 28th he resigned (after receiving more frequent and comfortable votes of confidence than any of his predecessors could boast).

To choose a successor was the task of the President of the

[1] Besides this top-level private 'intoxication', public operations of the same kind were carried on over Algiers radio by Roger Frey (later Minister of Information), who broadcast mysterious messages like 'We shall eat the little prune tomorrow night' (Pflimlin means little prune in Alsatian) or 'The hen will lay an egg within 24 hours' (the pro-Gaullist commander at Bordeaux was General Lecoq). Frey had hoped to sail to Algiers in Errol Flynn's yacht, but it broke down, and he had to turn to a friend of the actor's, a former British naval officer turned smuggler, to get him across the Mediterranean.

Republic, René Coty, a respectable conservative surrounded by ardent (though sometimes recent) Gaullists. In the afternoon, as the republican demonstrators were gathering in eastern Paris, he told the party leaders that the choice was de Gaulle or a Popular Front, and he would do his utmost for the former. At midnight the General came once again to St. Cloud to meet Coty's representatives, the Presidents of the two houses: for the deputies André Le Troquer, a one-armed Socialist, and for the senators Gaston Monnerville, a coloured Radical; ex-President Vincent Auriol had declined. The meeting was not a success. Twelve years before, de Gaulle had sworn he would never set foot in the Assembly again; Le Troquer insisted he must come to make the customary speech before his election. The General wanted exceptional powers for two years. 'Three months' offered Le Troquer. 'Six' was Monnerville's pacific (and only) contribution. De Gaulle demanded the right to draft a new constitution; Le Troquer would not hear of it. At 1 a.m. they parted angrily. The crisis was at its peak.

Algiers resumed its invasion plans—for the coming night, Thursday 29 May. Le Troquer spread gloom among his Socialist colleagues at their morning meeting; Moch instructed prefects to take to the *maquis* if necessary. At 3 p.m. the deputies met to hear their own President read the first and last special message from a President of the Fourth Republic. Only de Gaulle could avert civil war, declared Coty; if the Assembly rejected him, he would himself resign. Constitutionally, his powers would then pass to the President of the Assembly.

The members were standing as Le Troquer began his disapproving gallop through the presidential statement. But at Coty's threat to resign, the Communists and many Socialists sat down. When Le Troquer finished, they rose and sang the 'Marseillaise'; the Right then sang a 'Marseillaise' of their own. Opinion was at fever heat, and President Coty was bitterly reproached with behaving unconstitutionally. Certainly he had used all his authority, and perhaps more, to induce members to vote for de Gaulle—for he knew, as they did not, that civil war was only ten hours away. His motives were proper, but his tactics were imprudent. For the Socialist votes were crucial, and all he had done by threatening to resign was to harden their opposition.

The game seemed lost. Le Troquer had convinced his party that the General was haughty, intransigent and dictatorial. They were determined to vote him down—which meant putting Coty out and Le Troquer into the Elysée. Suddenly doubts began to spread. For Monnerville, it was learned, had formed quite a different impression of de Gaulle's attitude. Then Auriol released the General's reply to his letter of three days before. At last the deputies could assess de Gaulle's mind for themselves. The result was dramatic; by more than two to one the Socialists voted to negotiate. That evening de Gaulle received and accepted the invitation to form a government. But all Friday was still needed to bring Parliament round. Auriol, Mollet and Deixonne (chairman of the Socialist deputies and an opponent) flew to Colombey; all reported back favourably to the party next morning. The deputies, senators and executive members voted: 151 in all. The decision was Yes. The majority was three.

Next afternoon de Gaulle met the party leaders, twenty-six of them, at the Hôtel Laperouse (the Communists were invited, but refused). He agreed after all to appear before the Assembly, but he would not answer questions (he cited a sound precedent, set by Joseph Laniel, perhaps the least distinguished and successful of the Fourth Republic's fifteen premiers). He revealed the outline of his constitutional plans. There were a few questions, mostly about his attitude to the Committees of Public Safety. That night Gaullists and Communists clashed on the Champs Elysées, the police openly taking sides; and at Toulouse General Miquel, the prospective commander of Operation Resurrection, withstood pressure to launch the invasion after all, for some extremists were bent on averting any compromise with the hated System. At 3 p.m. on Sunday de Gaulle entered the Assembly to read the shortest investiture speech of the Fourth Republic, then withdrew for the brief debate. The house voted at twenty-five minutes to eight. Among the General's 329 supporters were forty-two Socialists; among his 224 opponents, forty-nine. Three weeks earlier he would not have had fifty votes. Georges Bidault remarked that his speech might well have been

shorter still: 'Gentlemen, between you and the Seine is
—me'.

APPENDIX TO CHAPTER 4

Sources are many, slipshod, and biased; but it is not impossible to sort
out the errors and contradictions. Nearly all the books favour the
insurgents.

M. and S. Bromberger, *Les 13 Complots du 13 Mai*, had loquacious
confidences from every conspirator in France and Algiers. Their book
is by far the best, but needs checking and supplementing.

D. Pado, *13 Mai: Histoire secrète d'une révolution* (Ed. de Paris), has
useful documents but is otherwise scrappy. P. Gerin, *L'Algérie du 13
Mai* (Gallimard), also has texts, and is good on the Algerian background
and on the army. For it, see also A. P. Lentin, *L'Algérie des Colonels*
(Petite bibliographie républicaine, hostile), and especially J. Planchais,
La Malaise de l'Armée (Plon, February 1958), a remarkable anticip-
ation. H. Pajaud, *La Révolution d'Alger* (Les 4 Fils Aymon), discusses
Algiers plots. Like Gerin he was an eye-witness of the 13 May. Lagail-
larde's story is in A. de Sérigny, *La Révolution du 13 Mai* (Plon), which
is highly disingenuous but reveals some of its author's activities; R.
Dronne, *La Révolution d'Alger* (Ed. France-Empire), also gives a good
deal away. A report by an assistant of Lacoste is published in J. P.
Tournoux, *Carnets secrets de la politique* (Plon). Paris politics are
treated (better than by the Brombergers) in J. Ferniot, *Les Ides de Mai*
(Plon; hostile). The reasons for de Gaulle's success are best analysed
in L. Hamon, *De Gaulle dans la République* (Plon). For Corsica, see P.
Arrighi, *La Corse—Atout décisif* (Plon), and on the mood of Gaullists
in France, J. Dauer and M. Rodet, *Le 13 Mai sans Complots* (La Pensée
moderne), and especially A. Dominique's novel *Le Gorille en Révolution*
(Gallimard). There are well-informed articles in several left-wing journals, notably *L'Express*, 15, 22 and 29 May, 12 June and 31 July; *France-
Observateur*, 29 May (the best short account of the early days in Algiers),
12 June, 18 September; *Le Canard Enchaîné*, 2 July; *La Nef*, July-
August (by Moch); *Esprit*, September; *L'Humanité*, 31 October.
Mollet, Moch, Lacoste and the Corsican Casalta spoke informatively at
a party meeting: *Bulletin intérieur* SFIO, 6 July. See also two good
American reports: New York *Herald Tribune*, 16 June; *The Reporter*,
26 June.

5

A Roman Dictatorship

The de Gaulle who looked down on an apprehensive Assembly on 1 June was no longer the virile brigadier of 1940 or the liberator of 1944. Age was making its mark. At 67 the slim, erect body was looking thicker, with the slightest of stoops. The face was more fleshy and the skin hanging looser; the penetrating eyes were dimmed by persistent cataract. But the spirit of the man was unquenched.

There was still the almost mystical belief in the mission of France and his own identification with that mission, still the passionate insistence on the path to greatness lying through the nation state. In one of his most revealing personal comments the General once recalled how he discovered during the war that

> there existed in people's spirits someone named de Gaulle, having a personality separated from my own. From that day forward I knew that I should have to take account of that man, of that General de Gaulle. . . . I became almost his prisoner. Before every speech or decision I questioned myself: is this the way in which the people expect de Gaulle to act? There were many things I should like to have done, but that I did not do because they would not have been what they expected of General de Gaulle.[1]

Yet the de Gaulle who now came to power was no longer temperamentally quite the man who in 1946 abandoned the premiership in a huff, and of whom one of his ministers wrote: 'On the chessboard on which he plays, there can be no friendship between the knight that is moved and the hand that moves it'.[2] The touchy pride, impatience, hauteur and even arrogance were still there. France's N.A.T.O. allies were very soon to recall that the weaker her bargaining position the more intransigent de Gaulle would become. But he had

[1] Quoted from *The Saturday Review* in *Le Monde*, 20 May 1959.
[2] Emmanuel d'Astier de la Vigerie, *Seven Times Seven Days*, p. 125.

mellowed. His charm, less celebrated than his more disagreeable qualities, was now much more in evidence. And there were added a new patience and serenity of spirit, a far greater readiness to listen to others, a willingness to compromise in secondary matters and to cajole and persuade his diverse team. If he still regarded his ministers 'with a certain boredom, like a god looking on the imperfections of his creation',[1] he took more pains to disguise his feelings. Long ago the same critic had described 'his three weapons: prestige, secrecy and cunning. His cunning is mediocre, but his secrecy, supported by a natural, icy prestige, takes him a long way'.[1] The portrait was still recognizable, but manifestly incomplete. More humane weapons had been added to the armoury. And the writer, who in 1943 had 'often wondered what his prestige derives from', had perhaps by 1958 found an answer more convincing than his height or his voice or his aloofness.[1]

Insistence on national unity took first place in the spirit of this new de Gaulle. The General had always looked on himself as an asset belonging to all his countrymen. This alone is enough to explain his refusal to accept power from anyone but the representatives of the nation. Though many democrats regarded the investiture of 1 June as almost a blasphemous fraud, constitutional forms had been preserved. By insisting on legality, de Gaulle had kept his hands free of a faction which hoped to control him. He had also done his utmost to prevent the May insurrection festering into yet another political sore for future generations to quarrel over.

For de Gaulle remembered how his own act of defiance of June 1940 had divided his countrymen. He saw it as his central task to work for the national unity for which so many political leaders have appealed. Even the F.L.N. guerillas were treated as men who had cut themselves temporarily off from France. Other politicians arrogated to themselves the title of 'national', excluding their adversaries from the French community. In 1947 de Gaulle himself had called the Communists 'separatists'; but in 1959 he would not countenance Debré's term 'anti-France'. After the referendum he asked, 'of those who voted NON, how many did it against the dictates of their hearts?' His speeches contained hardly any

[1] *Ibid.*, pp. 160, 132.

Nat. unity

derogatory references to his opponents. Instead the themes of unity were constantly on his lips. Even the invocations at every whistle-stop to join him in the 'Marseillaise'—which became the butt of the humorous press—were basically reminders to his hearers of their membership of a national family with a common heritage.

Only through genuine unity, he believed, could national greatness be restored. Without it France would return to the government by factions he had so caustically denounced. But in the short run his passionate concern for unity and consensus was to impede the exercise of power. On taking office he could have induced public opinion to accept practically anything—at the cost of fracturing the fabric of the nation. Instead, major decisions were suspended until the vote of 1 June had been translated by the electorate into a new constitution and new Assembly. In its early months the government was therefore to give the impression of inaction.

unity

This passion for unity has affected the whole style of the regime in another way. The fundamental issues could not be dismissed as technical, for they were profoundly political. Yet basic problems had to be solved without impairing the mood of unity. The persistent temptation of the new regime was therefore to try to muffle them. Public debate might split the nation; better to eliminate public debate. It was a policy of anaesthesia. Opinion must be lulled and soothed until the decision was announced. Thus, though the Republic was preserved, the Gaullist regime was to put many traditional expressions of democracy to sleep.[1]

[1] 'The Republic imposes another obligation upon us. It is necessary in the national interest to allow our vital problems to escape from partisan discussion—in a sense to "depoliticize" them. The future of Algeria can be claimed by neither Right nor Left . . . [European, social, agricultural policy] in all this neither Right nor Left suffices, but a common effort, first to choose then to follow the road of national interest . . . No democrat must stir up conflicts by clothing the fundamental problems in the glittering but fraudulent cloak of a so-called political vocabulary which in truth is merely partisan. The "depoliticization" of the national essential (*sic*) is a major imperative. No national objective, no social objective, no economic objective has any chance of being achieved if we disregard this rule' (Michel Debré, *Journal Officiel, Débats Parlementaires* (*Assemblée Nationale*) (hereafter *J O*), sitting of 15 January 59, p. 27). The words 'No democrat . . . imperative' appear in *Le Monde* (17 January 1959) but not in *J O*.

DE GAULLE'S REPUBLIC

The tone of the General's rule was set in the first three days; the substance of his policy was cautiously indicated within three weeks. His choice of ministers and his deference towards the Assembly showed that he meant to conciliate the old parties, not to attack them—yet his first words in the Algiers Forum on 4 June ('I have understood you') were received as an acceptance of the crowd's aspirations. The General took care to give no needless offence to Parliament or settlers. But he made no real concessions to either. And while his Algerian intentions remained shrouded in mystery, his actions in Morocco and Tunisia showed how little he shared the outlook of the men who had placed him in power.

Though his investiture was the death-knell of the Fourth Republic, many must have doubted it when the cabinet list was announced. Of the twenty ministers named on 1 and 9 June, only three were devoted Gaullists: André Malraux, and two senators who had never held office under the System, Michel Debré and Edmond Michelet. Five were senior civil servants (two more were added in July).[1] But the rest could well have formed a Fourth Republic cabinet, with its safe *dosage* (three seats for each big party and one for each little one), its leftish M.R.P. Minister of Labour, and its safe anti-clerical Radical at Education. The Ministers of State were Louis Jacquinot (C.N.I.), the inevitable Houphouet-Boigny, Guy Mollet, and Pierre Pflimlin—whom Algiers, only hours before, had been accusing of working hand-in-glove with the Communists. Of the men who had led the insurrection there was no sign.

De Gaulle had not been overwhelmed by the System; he had captured it. The presence in his government of Socialists, Radicals of both orthodox and right-wing brands, M.R.P. and C.N.I. inevitably associated these parties with his actions during the coming months when Parliament was in recess. If his measures were unpopular the older parties would share the responsibility—but not the power. For the ministries vital to his programme were all held by technicians; the General himself would give the orders. The one key post confided to a politician was Finance (Antoine Pinay) and

[1] French ministers have never been required to sit in Parliament. For other comments on the cabinet see below, pp. 96–7.

even that had been offered to a technician first. Yet de Gaulle's
acceptance of the traditional parties was not just a manœuvre
to compromise them. It also indicated his desire for national
unity. It is said that after glancing round the cabinet table
the new prime minister remarked genially to his colleagues,
'Well, gentlemen, there seem to be only three missing faces—
M. Maurice Thorez, M. Pierre Poujade, and M. Ferhat Abbas'.

De Gaulle showed the same tolerance in his dealings with
Parliament. Even at the very end of the eleventh hour, the
deputies could not resist a last-minute manœuvre. They
accepted two of the government's three bills—special powers
for Algeria, and almost unlimited delegated authority in
France for six months—but they jibbed at conceding complete
constitution-making power to de Gaulle. Their Suffrage and
Constitutional Committee voted to insist that the government's proposals should be submitted to Parliament within
three months. It was a flat negation of the terms on which de
Gaulle had agreed to stand for the premiership.

Once again the new premier returned to the chamber he
had once sworn never to revisit. Surrounded by his ministers,
he warned that the government would resign that night if the
Assembly accepted the committee's proposals. And yet he
contrived to present his intransigent position with a charm,
a skill, and an appearance of flexibility which completely
won over a suspicious house. He was ostentatiously polite to
the Communists; only to the extreme Right was he cold.[1]
Members were surprised and then delighted by the sincerity
with which he assured them of his devotion to the Republic
and the skill with which he set aside hostile amendments.
He even unbent to affirm 'the honour and pleasure I feel at
being among you'. 'After Operation Sedition, it's Operation
Seduction,' grumbled a Communist, sourly watching the

[1] When Isorni (Pétain's lawyer) declared courageously 'The defender
of Louis XVI cannot vote for Robespierre,' de Gaulle turned to the
extreme left benches, beaming his delight at this certificate of revolutionary respectability. The crypto-fascist Tixier-Vignancour announced
that he had been disgraced once already, in 1940, for voting away his
parliamentary powers into the hands of a military saviour; how could
he now repeat the offence at the demand of the man who had condemned
him before? When Tixier pointed out that he had voted for de Gaulle
on the previous day, the General raised his arms to the ceiling in a
gesture of helplessness.

79

Assembly succumb. And the majority for constitutional revision was large enough to avoid an immediate referendum.[1]

De Gaulle's apparent endorsement of the Fourth Republican politicians was to be balanced by his apparent acceptance of the insurrection when he arrived at Algiers on 4 June. He greeted and thanked the military and civilian leaders of the revolt, praised the army warmly, and gave prodigal assurances that Moslems and Frenchmen were henceforth equal citizens—integration without the word, which he steadfastly refused to pronounce. Yet Algiers was uneasy. The list of safe, familiar ministers, which spread relief in Parliament, had filled the extremists with fury. Some hot-heads talked wildly of rescuing de Gaulle from the System; cries of 'Soustelle!' repeatedly interrupted his tour. Two ministers, Lejeune and Jacquinot, were locked in a back room to prevent them appearing with de Gaulle on the G.C. balcony. And on 10 June the C.S.P. unanimously demanded the dissolution of the old political parties.

The General's reaction was sharp. The C.S.P. was rebuked for its 'vexatious and untimely' motion, and Salan was reproved for transmitting it. In a broadcast three days later, de Gaulle went out of his way to praise the 'worth, honesty and patriotism' of the leaders of the Fourth Republic. On his next trip to Algeria, in early July, the men who had jibbed at Jacquinot and Lejeune had to accept the presence at the General's side of Guy Mollet himself. The C.S.P.s were not extended, as Delbecque had hoped, to France itself.

During these early days when both sides were playing for prestige and position, one decision of real importance was taken. This was the agreement with Tunisia on 17 June (preceded three days earlier by a similar settlement with Morocco). It was after all Tunisian—and not Algerian—policy which had brought Gaillard down, and which had earned for Pflimlin the suspicion and hatred of the extreme Right in Parliament. Where they had failed to solve the thorny

---

[1] Under the old Article 90, a revision proposal had to go to the country unless it attained a two-thirds majority in the Assembly, or three-fifths in both houses. This one had both: 350–161 in the Assembly, 256–30 in the upper chamber. An immediate referendum would have been dangerous in a country so recently close to civil war.

problem of the French troops in Tunisia, de Gaulle succeeded —by accepting and putting through the very proposals sponsored by the Anglo-American 'good offices' team, for which his predecessors had been condemned. The Right grumbled, but submitted. There was hardly a whisper of public protest even from those who, like Tixier-Vignancour, had wanted Lacoste to 'march straight to Tunis and lie with your boots on in Bourguiba's bed'.

For the General's prestige with the public could not be challenged. All along the political spectrum new groups were springing up to exploit it: Left Gaullists, Right Radicals, the French Christian Democracy (D.C.F.) of Bidault and Tixier. Yet though the general public would have accepted almost anything he proposed, de Gaulle did not enjoy a really free hand. The passions so nearly unloosed in May were not yet appeased, and there were ugly incidents between troops and civilians in a number of provincial towns—Pau, Toulouse, Auxerre, Lyons. The government behaved cautiously. In July the two protagonists of the May crisis in Toulouse— General Miquel and the prefect Périllier—both disappeared from their posts. While generals prominent in the insurrectionary movement were promoted and decorated, normal administration returned to Corsica. But for the most spectacular decision, Soustelle's appointment as Minister of Information, the Left could find no compensation.

There was opposition: from M. Poujade (deserted by his former followers), from the peasant organizations (discontented as always with the government's agricultural price policy), and from the frustrated left-wing groups which had opposed both the Algerian war and the appeal to de Gaulle. The latter formed an optimistically-named Union of Democratic Forces (U.F.D.), which embraced Mendès-France's pathetic Radical remnant, Mitterrand and his followers, the Left Socialist Union (U.G.S.) of fellow-travellers and neutralists and Left Catholics, and the anti-Mollet minority of the Socialist party (who in September were to set up their own Autonomous Socialist Party, P.S.A.). Some other leftish bodies, like the teachers' unions and the League of the Rights of Man, also furnished contingents to the U.F.D.'s stage army. Yet all this activity attracted little attention. Frenchmen

81

G

had committed their problems to the care of the most distinguished of their compatriots, and they were anxious only to approve his handling of them. Even more than is usual in July, the Tour de France outstripped any political development in public interest. But by a strange chance the victor of the famous cycle-race in 1958 was a Luxemburger named Charly Gaul. The opportunity was too good to miss, and politics crept into the sporting pages, ranging from *Libération*'s crude headline, '*Charly Gaul contre les Français*' to *Le Monde*'s more sophisticated analysis of the failure of a rival who, after two opportunities to retrieve his position, has still failed to adapt his style sufficiently to new circumstances. Meanwhile, away from the eye of a public preoccupied with the family's holidays rather than the nation's business, small groups of juridical and political specialists were feverishly constructing the new institutions on which, in the General's eyes, the future of France depended.

New constitution

That de Gaulle's advent spelled the death of the Fourth Republic was never in doubt. From Bayeux in 1946 to his last press conference in 1955, his resolve to bring in a new constitution if he returned to power was unremitting. The brief phrases of his 15 May communiqué found space to recall his insistence: 'For twelve years, at grips with problems too powerful for the *régime des partis*, France has been set on a disastrous course'.[1] Again on 19 May he stated: 'The exclusive *régime de partis* did not, does not, and will not resolve the enormous problems with which we are confronted'.[1] First among the roll-call of dangers facing the country, with which de Gaulle opened his investiture speech, was 'the headlong rush of the State into degradation'.[1]

For the General constitutional reform was more than the observance of the tradition of consecrating—and consolidating—a change of regime. It was an attack on 'the profound cause of our trials. That cause—the Assembly knows and the Nation is convinced—is the confusion and consequent impotence of the powers of government.'[1] Without such a transformation of the country's institutions the appeal to

[1] *L'Année Politique*, 1958, pp. 534, 540.

de Gaulle would be no more than a temporary palliative. Obviously reform was of paramount importance to a man who believed that 'the French nation will flower again or perish according to whether the State has or has not strength, constancy, prestige enough to guide it in the way it should go'.[1]

It was in this spirit that, speaking to the people of Algiers about the call for renovation, the General insisted that it must 'begin at the beginning, that is to say with our institutions'.[1] Not only would a new constitution bring speedy proof of the will to renovation; de Gaulle's hands would be freer to propose the constitution of his choice at a time when the old political forces were discredited, demoralized, and shattered.

It was scarcely surprising that the government concentrated its public activity during the summer on constitution-making rather than on the apparently more pressing economic and Algerian crises. Parliament's last act, before being sent off on its last recess, was to agree to the government drawing up a new constitution and submitting it directly to the nation.

At that moment the parliamentarians lacked both the force and the spirit to exact concessions about the shape the revision should take. However, the government agreed to incorporate in the law five principles which should govern it. These were that the sole source of power should be universal suffrage, from which both legislature and executive should emanate directly or indirectly; that their roles should be strictly separate; that the government should be responsible to Parliament; that the independence of the judiciary should be preserved; that relations with the colonies should be revised. To anyone who believed that de Gaulle meant to preserve democracy these safeguards might appear superfluous. But in the summer of 1958, and against the background of his dangerously ambiguous constitutional utterances over the years, they seemed both necessary and reassuring to many deputies. Moreover, they ruled out the solution the Assembly most expected and dreaded: direct presidential rule. This seemed to be foreshadowed in the Bayeux speech; now de Gaulle categorically confirmed quite freely that there was no question of it. It has never been clear whether this was

[1] *L'Année Politique*, 1958, pp. 551, 544.

because he had never intended to install a directly presidential system, or because he believed that such a head-on clash with Republican traditions could not be risked even now.

Both de Gaulle and Michel Debré (a voluble critic in his own right who had inspired many of the General's constitutional views) had inveighed against the Fourth Republic since before its birth. Yet neither man came to power with a constitution in his pocket. The translation of general conceptions into institutional form had to be begun almost from scratch. Time was short; de Gaulle had promised Algiers that the document would be submitted for approval in 'not more than three months'. This was a far cry from the preparation of the 1946 constitution, which gestated for twelve.

The circumstances could hardly have been more different. The 1946 constitution was the product of months of complicated haggling and argument in Parliament, conducted before the public gaze, always in the hands of the political parties. If the essential compromises were made in the corridors, the opposing conceptions were continuously and openly confronted. By contrast, the Fifth Republic emerged from behind closed doors, the work of a small group of men sheltered almost completely from informed public debate, with the final decision in the hands of the government. One common factor emphasized the gulf: de Gaulle. The first constitution was framed largely against him; this was being made for him.

Michel Debré was de Gaulle's obvious choice to take the new constitution in hand. He had thought and written much about such problems, and his loyalty was unquestionable. After he and the General had discussed the broad outlines of the proposals, Debré set up his first working party while de Gaulle was still on his first visit to Algiers. Debré's passionate certainty about the ideal shape for the new Republic led him to recruit a team of impeccable political loyalty, but little experience of constitutional matters. It is not surprising that the draft they produced had so oddly amateurish an air. The constitution of 1958 has been called by René Capitant 'The worst drafted text in our constitutional history . . . a source of permanent humiliation to those who held the pen'.[1] If it

---

[1] Preface to Léo Hamon, *De Gaulle dans la République*, p. xiv.

bears all the marks of haste and confusion, this is partly because the first working parties were operating under considerable pressure and in unusual turmoil. Split into groups of two or three to draft specific sections, they were scattered in temporary accommodation throughout Paris. Drafts came out of the working party for cabinet scrutiny, were discussed in cabinet and returned for redrafting piecemeal.

The process soon bogged down. One of the three months passed without the cabinet agreeing on the first section— the powers of the President. Even three days of almost uninterrupted sessions failed to clear the arrears of drafts prepared by the working parties. Finally Debré retired with three junior colleagues to the Château St. Cloud to complete the first draft while Paris was enjoying a particularly ceremonious Bastille Day.

The draft which Debré presented to the cabinet on 16 July was shorter, simpler, and starker than the official first draft which was published a fortnight later after discussion in cabinet. But all the essentials were there: greater power for the President, particularly in emergencies; separation of the legislature and the executive; reform of legislative procedure; sharp limitation of Parliament's prerogatives. Only the proposal to create a Federation with the colonies was to undergo fundamental change before final publication.

The many amendments which were agreed in cabinet tended to mitigate the transfer of power from Parliament to the executive. At this stage there appeared some of the more cumbersome rules governing governmental stability, favourite panaceas of the later years of the Fourth Republic. Although Debré showed little enthusiasm for these *gadgets* favoured by the Ministers of State, he was to suffer the ridicule they provoked.

When essentials were at stake both de Gaulle and Debré were inflexible. De Gaulle insisted on maintaining a powerful Presidency and keeping ministers out of the legislature. Debré, sharing these views, was just as determined to defend his proposals for strengthening the executive and separating it from Parliament. He was equally insistent on rationalizing Parliament and creating a body to rule on the constitutionality of laws. The draft emerged from the Council of Ministers on 29 July with the Debré principles almost intact.

Once adopted by the cabinet it was sent to a Constitutional Consultative Committee. De Gaulle had promised the Assembly a consultative body with a majority of members chosen by Parliament. But he was adamant that the government should have the last word. Even so, Debré was uneasy about the effect of a hostile report. He carefully vetted the government's nominees, assiduously courted the parties to appoint sympathetic members, and thoughtfully provided the C.C.C.'s secretary-general from his own working party.[1]

He had little to fear. Despite its majority of 'men of the System', the C.C.C. made no onslaught on the government draft. It secured important additions to the list of subjects with which Parliament might deal, and tried to limit the dangers of the President's new emergency powers. With less success, it attempted to remove some of the changes which most shocked parliamentary susceptibilities.

The C.C.C.'s most significant contribution was in transforming the colonial sections. The Cotonou congress of Senghor's party, the P.R.A., had already denounced the sketchy first draft of the Federation and called for a campaign for immediate independence. Now the C.C.C. met one of the major grievances by proposing that the colonies' right to independence should be written into the constitution. Senghor, Lisette, Lamine-Guèye and Tsiranana, representing the main African political forces, helped the C.C.C. to fill in some of the first draft's omissions. For the first time they outlined the role and composition of the Senate and the Executive Council of what they now agreed, significantly, to call the Community.

The Committee's proposals for metropolitan France had a mixed fate. Many were accepted directly or in some modified form. Others, cutting across the essentials of the government's proposals, were rejected out of hand. During the discussion of the C.C.C. report M. Mollet was able, as the price of assuring the support of his Party congress, to exact some

[1] The C.C.C. had 39 members, 16 from the Assembly, 10 from the Council of the Republic and 13 appointed by the government. It sat from 29 July to 14 August under the chairmanship of M. Paul Reynaud. A summary of the C.C.C.'s proposals and the extent to which they were accepted is included in Chapman and Campbell, *The Constitution of the Fifth Republic*.

minor concessions (notably in the prerogatives of the Senate).

Finally, at the end of August, a further outline of the new Community emerged from de Gaulle's flying tour of Africa. The right of Africans to leave the Community when they pleased was fully spelled out. The form of the Community, though still studiously vague, had evolved consistently in a liberal sense. Few afterthoughts have been more potentially fruitful. Thereafter there remained only the scrutiny by the *Conseil d'Etat* of the document's legal phraseology. Three months to the day after de Gaulle's promise in Algiers, the government's final proposals were published.

In its final form the constitution was as multi-layered as an onion. There was the de Gaulle–African layer, a constitution in itself. Through de Gaulle's own liberal pragmatism and the pressure of the Africans, the original proposals had been completely transformed. There was the de Gaulle layer proper—notably the provision of emergency powers for the President. The C.C.C. and the Ministers of State each modified and softened the original outlines, and filled in some of the sketchier sections. The *Conseil d'Etat* retouched the final version here and there.

But the core of the metropolitan constitution was the work of Michel Debré, the Fifth Republic's spiritual father and physical midwife. Given the events of the intervening years, the final draft bears an astonishing resemblance to the proposals Debré advanced for the future Fourth Republic while he was in the Resistance. It was he who chose and briefed the working parties and presided over their meetings. He was *rapporteur* for their proposals in cabinet, and supervised the subsequent redrafting. When the process bogged down completely it was essentially Debré who completed the first draft and defended it in cabinet. He greatly influenced the C.C.C., presided over the final revisions after it had reported, and made before the *Conseil d'Etat* the only thorough going public defence of his proposals.

From beginning to end Debré was far more intimately concerned in the creation of the constitution than anyone else. By and large the final document is the constitution he wished to create. French history is so strewn with the wreckage of plans for reform that it is scarcely surprising that much of

Debré's text is not 'original'. The rationalization of the work of Parliament—the most solid achievement—was inspired by French political scientists, and perhaps in part by Léon Blum. His ideas of the relationship between government and Parliament owed much to an older Gaullist, René Capitant, and to André Tardieu. But it was Debré, always with one eye across the Channel, who wove the elements together.

. . . .

It is one thing to write a constitution, another to have it ratified by the nation. While a majority was never in doubt, bare acceptance was not enough. Gaullists could never forget the 1946 referendum, with its humiliating majority on a derisory poll. The new constitution must be adopted overwhelmingly, not just to lend a prestige which the Fourth Republic had always lacked, but to show beyond all doubt the legitimacy of the regime. De Gaulle wanted to banish once for all the taunt that his power rested solely on the bayonets of the paratroops.

On paper the opposition was imposing. The hostility of the Communists, with nearly a quarter of the popular vote in 1956, was certain from the start. Throughout the summer there was always the danger that both Radicals and Socialists would also reject the government's draft. If that were to happen the theoretical strength of the opposition forces would cut the majority to an unsatisfactory level. But the probability of such a line-up diminished sharply when Gaston Defferre, who had opposed de Gaulle's investiture, talked over Algerian policy with the General and emerged to say 'I vote Yes'. Thereafter the large majority at the Socialist congress in early September was inevitable. The Radicals also came into line by a narrower majority.

The non-Communist opposition was therefore reduced to the new left-wing coalition, the U.F.D., and a motley crew of right-wing malcontents: Pétainists, M. Poujade, a waning star, diehard colonialists who believed Africa was being abandoned, and militant Catholics who could never accept the *laïcité* of the State. During the campaign little was heard of these right-wing opponents.

A ROMAN DICTATORSHIP

The democratic Left was not only deeply divided; it was still utterly demoralized by the discovery that no one would lift a finger for the Republic. As early as July the U.F.D., realizing the utter discredit into which the 1946 constitution had fallen, called for a constructive alternative to the government's proposals. At once they were denounced by the Communists for stabbing the Republic in the back. But the determination of Thorez and Duclos did not survive the discovery that their own followers would no more work for the System than fight or strike for it. When the referendum campaign got under way in September, they too were advocating a *Contrat des NON* and repudiating the defunct regime.

Communist or democratic, the opposition had some points in common. Their attack took in not only the constitution, but the manner of de Gaulle's coming to power. To vote OUI was to acquiesce in the 'murder of the Republic', and to give way to the blackmail of civil war. It was to say OUI to the hamstringing of democracy—for the new powerless Assembly would be a negation of Republican ideals. It would prepare the way for a new Prince-President who would find in the notorious Article 16 an excuse for assuming direct power.

Yet the opposition had no clear alternative. It proposed the calling of a Constituent Assembly to draft a new constitution in a month. But there was no agreement upon, and little attempt to propose, the form of institutions which might emerge. What suggestions were advanced (such as granting more powers to the Assembly, or biennial Parliaments) showed a total incomprehension of the real problems. The Gaullists' taunt that 'Voting NON is a vote for the void' was justified. Moreover, at that moment few could doubt that if the NONS prevailed the void would be filled by the paras rather than by the promised constituent assembly.

With few exceptions the democratic Left refused to campaign jointly with the Communists. It was usually dispirited, unorganized and impoverished. Prominent leaders like Mitterrand and Mendès-France announced their opposition, then retired to their departments to await the result. The burden of campaigning fell chiefly on the second-rank figures, of whom only Sartre and Bourdet were widely known. Although the U.F.D. militants were active in the towns, vast country areas never saw a poster or had a meeting. Outside Paris the only significant press support they enjoyed was in the great Radical journal, the *Dépêche du Midi* of Toulouse, controlled by Jean Baylet, the 'Glaoui of the South-West'.

It was evident from the most casual inspection of the posters and pamphlets that the overwhelming bulk of the opposition effort was contributed by the Communists. Their output was impressive in quantity by normal political standards, although it was clumsy and unreadable by comparison with the government's expensive professional programme. Although the Communists fought hard, they seemed at times to be seeking desperately to stem the rot in their own ranks rather than to win converts. Even in their campaign (much more in the U.F.D.'s) the signs of the forthcoming débâcle were evident. For all their sniping at the myth of the *homme providentiel*, they rarely attacked de Gaulle frontally even before their own members.

During the campaign in metropolitan France the opposition suffered little infringement of its rights. Policemen were inclined to be a little tougher than usual with bill-posting crews; some prefects ordered the removal of 'seditious inscriptions such as NON *à de Gaulle*', and posters were likely to be torn down here and there. These pin-pricks were never either serious or systematic.

The campaign for the constitution was almost wholly in Gaullist or governmental hands. In preparation for the elections some politicians of the traditional parties jumped on the bandwagon by expensively advertising their views. But scarcely any of them campaigned actively. Commending the new constitution was a job for the government, not for a political party, they declared. And so it proved. Throughout the summer the government had taken no action that might ruffle the mood of national unity. Only the offer of independence to the colonies suggested that under its new management the French State was any more capable of taking difficult decisions than before. On Algeria, de Gaulle had retired into delphic ambiguity; elsewhere decisions were temporarily shelved. The Treasury helped by giving orders that tax prosecutions should be deferred 'because of the political circumstances', and collections should be made 'with a very special tact and discernment'.

Where the opposition had relied on traditional methods, particularly public meetings, the campaign for the constitution was based almost entirely on the mass media. In the whole of Paris there was only one public meeting for the OUI —and that mainly for card holders. There was ample evidence that the government was afraid of opposition activity. When de Gaulle went to the Place de la République, to introduce his constitution from the very citadel of working-class Republicanism, the authorities saw to it that the square was filled with a hand-picked triple-checked bourgeois audience. They felt it necessary to banish the opposition to the dim distance, and surround the meeting with a thick screen of police and Gaullist militants.

Even so there were ugly scuffles, and one man was shot. Plans for the General to tour the provinces were hurriedly trimmed. He finally spoke at only four regional capitals at the close of the campaign. At two of them the zeal of the thousands of police thinned and subdued the crowds. Only at Bordeaux and Strasbourg were there impressive signs of de Gaulle's genuine popular appeal. But meanwhile the campaign's unhappy opening had confirmed the government's determination to take no chances.

There has probably never been such an advertising campaign in France before. Thousands of tricolour posters with their 'OUI à la France' slogans assaulted the senses of the most unpolitical Frenchmen from huge sites dominating city squares, from roadside hoardings, and from suburban walls. Public relations experts added a cascade of tracts and pamphlets for every audience. Cinema-goers found a cunningly-contrived Ministry of Information film tacked on to the newsreels to remind them how often France had lacked leadership in past crises. Even the envelope sent to each elector contained, with a ballot paper and a copy of the constitution, a copy of de Gaulle's case for it—but no opposition statement.

The Gaullist organizations had the same preference for mass media. In an expensive campaign one publication alone, *France-Référendum* (a carbon copy of *France-Soir*), was believed to have been distributed free by the million. Their posters were both numerous and professional. These organizations were granted the same official facilities for campaigning (poster panels and radio time) as the established parties. Their claim for equality was dubious. One or two consisted only of a small team of militants and P.R.O.s with offices in central Paris. They were essentially front organizations for the Social Republicans (the Gaullist party), whose established political position on the centre-right limited its direct appeal. Their executive committees overlapped considerably, and they freely agreed that 90 per cent of their workers were from either the Social Republicans or the R.P.F. Created only a few weeks before the referendum, these mushroom organizations were merged into the Union for the New Republic only a week after the poll. But their fleeting existence enabled them to claim many times the official facilities the Social Republicans alone would have had. It was no secret that the bulk of their funds came from official sources.

The government had another useful ally in *Radiodiffusion Française*. R.T.F. has always echoed government policy, but it was now used even more unremittingly than usual. Since June Gaullists or sympathizers had been moved into almost every key post affecting opinion. Items which favoured the government were played up; less welcome news was glossed over. De Gaulle's tour was followed with dithyrambic enthusiasm; in skilful hands scattered cheers could be amplified into a hero's welcome. Correspondents contrived to show how French prestige was restored and her diplomatic initiatives were succeeding. M. Soustelle was allowed most of a 'news' bulletin for attacks on the motives of the opposition, and misrepresentations of their arguments. It was activities like these, and subtler variations, which led Félix Gaillard (a supporter of the constitution) to suggest that the attempt to 'sell it like a shampoo' was a powerful temptation to vote NON.

Ministry of Information, Gaullist organizations, and the R.T.F. all combined to spread the impression that the opposition was almost entirely Communist or fellow-travelling. R.T.F. scarcely ever reported opposition comment outside *L'Humanité*. The Gaullists handed out stickers reading simply '*OUI—NYET*'. Another poster, distributed through the

Ministry of Information, was cruder still: '*FLN + Communistes = Assassins*'.

The government's final weapon was the Anti-Abstention Front. Created under the nominal presidency of André Maurois, the Front flourished during the referendum, but has been comatose ever since. But for some weeks it was hard to escape its enjoinder, '*Votez OUI, Votez NON—Mais Votez*'. There were even a propaganda *bateau-mouche* plying the Seine, and an aircraft tracing *VOTEZ* in the sky. Laudable though any campaign for civic zeal may be, would the Front have received quite such handsome subsidies if the government had not believed that a high poll was to its advantage?[1]

The press was overwhelmingly OUI. Although the new constitution was explained more or less fairly, there was no real public debate about its merits. The layman had no means of assessing the virtues or defects which polemicists found in the government's proposals. Discussions rarely progressed beyond the shouting of slogans about 'democracy', 'authority', 'stability'. Both sides conceded that few electors actually read the document on which they voted. Most citizens probably decided on grounds irrelevant to the merits or demerits of the constitution itself. As an experiment in direct democracy it was not encouraging.

While Frenchmen were deciding whether to adopt a new Republic, the issue in Africa was between the Community and secession. The doubts of the early summer had been appeased by the final draft. Only in Niger and Guinea did the governing party opt for immediate independence, and in the end only Sekou Touré led his people into the wilderness. While Guinea voted 95 per cent NON, elsewhere the Community was adopted by majorities of 78 per cent in Niger to 99.99 per cent in Houphouet-Boigny's Ivory Coast.

The campaign in Algeria was less satisfactory. 'Ten million Frenchmen of Algeria will decide their destiny', de Gaulle had declared on 4 June. This was a campaign without a single newspaper appearing in the vernacular of the majority of the electors. There was not one opposition broadcast from Radio Algiers. After all, Colonel Lacheroy pointed out, the F.L.N. had

[1] The whole government campaign cost £3,000,000 at the lowest estimate, £8,000,000 at the highest.

all the time they wanted on Cairo Radio. Newspapers from the mainland were seized with even greater frequency than usual. Throughout the length and breadth of the country there was no means of legally proclaiming opposition.

The army was determined to inflict a decisive moral defeat on the rebels by producing a majority which would establish beyond all doubt, in de Gaulle's phrase, 'that in the midst of their trials [the Algerians] show confidence in France and, I must add, myself'.[1] The campaign was a full-scale military operation. Polling was spread over three days so that troops could help voters safely to the polls.

A control commission from the mainland was set up to supervise the preparation of the poll. Under M. Hoppenot it laboured with obvious good faith, against some military hostility, to try to make the mechanics of the operation completely fair, and to discourage excessive official intervention. But although the sincerity of the commission was little recognized abroad, the problem was not the juggling of results—for which past Algerian elections had been notorious—but the dilemma which confronted the voters.

The F.L.N. distributed tracts which contained direct warnings for those who voted. After so much bitter experience of what disobedience had meant to others, no Moslem could wholly disregard such a threat. On the other hand there was the French Army, massively present throughout the vote, and expecting a sign of loyalty, protecting some voters but undoubtedly putting pressure on others. Caught between such forces how could anyone make a free choice? The experiment confirmed the scepticism of those who had held that after four years of war a wholly free vote was unattainable. To this judgment de Gaulle himself seems eventually to have rallied. But the referendum in Algeria could not be dismissed. For the first time Moslems and Europeans went to the polls on an equal footing. For the first time Moslem women had the vote. This step forward might well prove far more significant than the votes they cast. These showed that the army had won its struggle. On an 80 per cent poll Algeria had voted 96 per cent OUI.

In metropolitan France, if some of the campaign methods

[1] *L'Année Politique*, 1958, p. 552.

were dubious, the poll was none the less surprising. Ministers and officials publicly forecast a 65 per cent Oui—hoping for 70 per cent. Like everyone else they were taken aback at getting almost 80 per cent on an 85 per cent poll. The myth of Communist invincibility was cracked. They had won 5,450,000 votes in 1956. Now, on a higher poll, there were only 4,600,000 Nons in France. Although the non-Communist opposition appeared to be routed, the proportion of Nons in the Toulouse region and the fiefs of some other opposition leaders was above the average. When their contribution is allowed for, over the whole country at least one Communist voter in five, perhaps one in three or four, had been faithless. Ironically this revelation of the breach in the Party's ranks silenced a vocal and growing campaign for it to be outlawed.

Reservations can be made. Yet the referendum was an impressive beginning for the new Republic, and a devastating repudiation of its predecessor—which not a single organization defended during the campaign. In one of the most decisive results ever freely recorded in France, 68 per cent of the eligible electorate had assented to the Fifth Republic. Such a striking result cannot be explained away as the product of a propaganda campaign. It suggests that beneath perennial divisions the longing of the French for national unity was unquenched.

6

De Gaulle against the Gaullists

The revolution of 13 May naturally made changes in the governing personnel of France. But they were far fewer than its makers had hoped or its opponents feared. The leaders of the insurrection were furious at the survival of the parties they had hoped to destroy. For de Gaulle's cabinet was very like previous ones, and indeed almost a replica of his own fourteen years before. Once again non-political civil servants, spokesmen of the parties and leading Gaullists sat side by side.

When the list of ministers became known on 1 June, there was one conspicuous omission: Jacques Soustelle. The Socialists were said to have vetoed him; however, he became Minister of Information in July, to the dismay of the opposition and the delight of Algiers. Willingly or not, the General seemed to have opted against the parties and for the men of 13 May. But when he was installed as President of the Republic in January 1959, he chose Debré as his Prime Minister; Soustelle was moved to preside over deserts at the Ministry of the Sahara, instead of to the Interior for which he was believed to hope.

Debré's part in the 13 May coup was less well known than Soustelle's. He had won a reputation as a fiery and aggressive senatorial critic of previous governments, and as a passionate nationalist, but also as a loyal follower of de Gaulle. He was succeeded at the Ministry of Justice by Michelet (hitherto Minister for Ex-Servicemen), who with Malraux—whose governmental role was more decorative than functional—represented liberal Gaullism. Both had criticized the colonial and Algerian policies of the dying regime, and condemned the excesses of the repression.

The Fifth Republic's real innovation was the choice of civil servants, not merely for technical departments (like Health, Housing and Industry) but for Education (a highly political ministry in France) and for most key positions. Foreign Affairs (Couve de Murville) and Defence (Guillaumat) were in their hands from the start; Overseas France (Cornut-Gentille) until the Community was born and the ministry died; Algeria from the appointment of a civilian Delegate-General (Delouvrier) in December; the Interior for all but a few weeks. By mid-1959, though a few Fourth Republican politicians still held secondary posts, only one—Pinay— remained at the very top. De Gaulle's preference for technicians illustrates not so much his limited esteem for the men of the System as his determination to control all essential decisions. Key posts, therefore, must go either to devoted personal followers, or to able executives without political strength of their own.

Below ministerial level the changes were not very extensive, except in the radio and TV which had been subject to government interference throughout the Fourth Republic, notably in Mollet's premiership. Soustelle set out to 'colonize' them thoroughly with Gaullists, and his successor Roger Frey, former party secretary, continued his operations with rather more tact. Many Gaullists—including liberals like Grandval and Sainteny—received high government appointments. The cabinet chooses Paris district mayors, and Conservatives complained that it favoured the U.N.R. But the war-cry of the victorious Left a generation before—'*Toutes les places et tout de suite*'—was not put into effect. There was no 'massacre of prefects'; indeed, good judges claimed that politics affected their selection less than before. The government's restraint aroused protests even from moderate U.N.R. leaders, though they repudiated any self-interested motive. Critics maintained that the administration was full of creatures of the old order who were busy undermining the new.[2] But ministers went their own way, even continuing the amiable Fourth

[1] Here, when de Gaulle's nominee (Pelletier) resigned, Debré chose a Radical Senator, Berthoin. But he left (over the quarrel about Parliament's rights) and another official, Chatenet, took over. Yet another, Joxe, was put in charge of civil service and some foreign questions in July 1959. Even Finance was first offered not to Pinay but to an official, Bloch-Lainé. Most of these civil servants, so often accused of being reactionary technocrats, were in fact liberal and progressive.

[2] Chalandon (U.N.R. general secretary): 'Politicized for fifteen years, the Administration is a stronghold of the old parties. We do not ask

H

Republican tradition of finding jobs for unlucky politicians of the wrong party. When Lacoste lost his seat in the electoral holocaust of November 1958, he promptly reappeared as head of the Gas Council. Another defeated Socialist, Lapie (a critic of the Algerian war but a pro-Gaullist) became French member of the Coal and Steel Community. Conservative, M.R.P., Radical, Socialist and even Poujadist victims were found berths in the Economic Council, just as in the good old days. The *République des Camarades* had not completely succumbed to the *République des Compagnons.*

The most important field for manipulating appointments was of course the Army. De Gaulle (who, since he belongs to History, often speaks of himself in the third person) had reassured the party leaders when he met them on 31 May by asking: 'Do you see de Gaulle governing in a whirlwind of generals?' No one knew better the urgent need to restore military discipline.

He set about it characteristically. Generals wholly loyal to himself naturally received key posts. Ely returned as chief of staff, and his retirement was postponed for a year; his aide Beaufort, who had been prospective commander of Operation Resurrection in Paris, became de Gaulle's chief military adviser. Challe, whom the Pflimlin government had arrested for sending troop-carrying planes to Algiers, was made commander-in-chief in Algeria, where the western sector was put under Gambiez (who had saved the day in Tunisia after Sakiet), and the eastern under another faithful Gaullist. There were no favours for conspicuous liberals like La Bollardière, for these would have offended most of the army. Nor were there any penalties for 13 May leaders whose allegiance was thought doubtful. It was not by courts-martial but by

for a politicization to our advantage, we ask for depoliticization . . . *We certainly count on the prime minister . . . to act wholeheartedly in so fundamental a matter*' (U.N.R. *Bulletin de presse*, no. 5, p. 8, reporting the *conseil national* of 25–26 July 1959; italics in original).

Terrenoire (chairman of U.N.R. deputies): 'We don't want a gulf to open between the U.N.R. in power and the U.N.R. militants. We don't want U.N.R. prefects, that isn't true, we simply want Fifth Republican prefects' (*ibid.*, p. 12).

Stibio, Gaullist journalist: 'Some very high officials . . . are preparing for failure. The Fifth Republic is not yet being betrayed, but it is no longer being served' (quoted *Le Monde*, 29 August 1959).

decorations and honorific promotions that de Gaulle revealed, as he had once promised, his ingratitude. Miquel, of Toulouse and Operation Resurrection, was honoured and retired — under the age limit which was waived for Ely. Colonel Gribius, the tank commander who was to have seized the aerodromes near Paris, was promoted general and sent to Algiers; there he indiscreetly hinted to the press at a possible new 13 May, and was promptly posted. Salan, who had told the cheering Algiers crowd in May 'We shall march down the Champs Elysées and they will cover us with flowers', was rewarded with a private lunch with de Gaulle on 13 May 1959, and with the Military Governorship of Paris, a high-sounding post with few duties (apart from leading ceremonial parades on the Champs Elysées).

For that anniversary, *Le Monde* thoughtfully recorded the subsequent fate of the insurrectionary leaders. Of the many senior officers involved, only two remained in the city: Colonel Godard and General Massu, who before 13 May had been called 'the only Gaullist in Algiers'. Altogether 1,500 officers of field rank had been posted. The civilian ultras, who well knew what was happening, protested furiously but vainly. By September 1959 de Gaulle was able to offer delayed self-determination to Algeria without provoking an explosion, or indeed any reaction at all, from the army.

In eighteen months the improvement was immense. But not even de Gaulle, and still less any other head of government, could count any longer on unconditional obedience from the armed forces. His own policy was not particularly welcome to the army; neither was it repugnant to them. He was at pains to explain it to the officers, and to present it in a manner acceptable to them. For he knew well enough that their new-found political consciousness had not disappeared but developed, especially among the junior officers, in the months that followed May 1958. This did not at all mean that they wished to interfere in the day-to-day government of France; their distaste for that was as great as ever. It did mean that the army believed it should enjoy a kind of veto over certain political possibilities. It would not permit an outright capitulation in Algeria, with the consequent abandonment of the French and the pro-French Moslems to F.L.N. vengeance. Nor would it permit a government in Paris controlled by the Communists, against whom the army believed it was already engaged in the third world war. These exigencies, evidently, are far from precise. What is capitulation? What is Communist-controlled? But though not precise, they are categorical. They seem unlikely to disappear soon. While they last, not only Algeria's future but that of democracy in France will remain in doubt.

If French democracy is precarious, it is because of the Algerian war. The threatened army 'veto' existed before the Fifth Republic and indeed brought it into being. Arbitrary interference with press criticism, especially of the army and police, began under Mollet and Bourgès-Maunoury and was checked by de Gaulle, though it has revived under Debré.[1] If intolerant politicians too often impute treasonable conduct to those who disagree with them, the fault is unhappily an old one in France, and the recent marked worsening of the temper of controversy dates from the attacks on Mendès-France in 1954, not from 1958. Bitter disputes which provoke deep emotions have had these results elsewhere; Korea evoked similar consequences in the United States, and not so long ago Ireland threatened parliamentary government in Britain.

De Gaulle was well aware of the danger. Immediately the referendum was over, he set out to put his overwhelming victory to use. Salan was publicly ordered to ensure free elections in Algeria, and army officers were obliged to quit the Committees of Public Safety. The delight of the entire Left was matched only by the dismay of Algiers, where C.S.P. opposition collapsed in face of the army's loyalty to de Gaulle. For the first time since February 1956 Paris had imposed its will. On 23 October the General announced his offer of a cease-fire, the *paix des braves.* Two days later the F.L.N. rejected it. It was the turn of the Right to triumph, and of the Left to be dismayed.

---

[1] But he has applied these arbitrary measures on a somewhat smaller scale, and to the fascist press as well as to that of the Left. Moreover, prosecutions have usually been announced; whether they will reach a court remains to be seen.

Successful cease-fire talks would of course have embarrassed the friends of Algiers, and encouraged the liberals. The timing of de Gaulle's offer, between the referendum and the elections, indicates how little he desired to see a new Parliament dominated by his own professed followers. But his proposed 'white flag of parley' was a mistake which enabled the Algiers press and Soustelle's radio to misrepresent his intentions. It left sufficient ambiguity about them for politicians of diametrically opposed views to fight the election as champions of de Gaulle's Algerian policy. The General made further efforts to limit the success of the Right, choosing an electoral system they disliked and opposing an alliance between the new Gaullist party, the U.N.R., and the old-style Right. But he failed. Entirely freely, and with no flood of official propaganda such as marked and marred the referendum campaign, the voters chose a reactionary and authoritarian-minded Assembly. They did so because of two mistakes. The first was their own: naturally enough they thought they could best help de Gaulle by voting for Gaullists. The second was the General's: the electoral system confounded all expectations by bringing about the very result it was intended to prevent.

The choice of electoral system is always important, and in a multi-party country like France it is capital. Five times in the last forty years it has been completely altered before an election. De Gaulle inherited a law designed in 1951 to damage Communists and Gaullists; no one now favoured it except politicians who owed their seats to it (and they dared not admit their preference). Everyone agreed it must be changed: but for what? The deputies were so concerned with the answer that the one restriction they put on de Gaulle's constitution-drafting powers was that the Assembly must vote the electoral law. This was evaded. The draft constitution authorized the cabinet to choose the system governing the coming election, and the people voted this provision along with the rest.

The government itself was divided. The 'pure' P.R. of 1945–6 could be restored, unencumbered by the hotly criticized devices for pooling the votes of allied parties which had been introduced in 1951. But this would again ensure a quarter of the seats for the Communists, so that the Fifth Republic like the Fourth would never know a coherent parliamentary majority. Therefore this solution had no chance of adoption. In practice the choice lay between two systems. One would keep the existing big constituencies, usually of three to five members, in which party lists would compete. The other would restore the type of single-member system used before 1940. Given French traditions and multi-party complexities, each required two ballots. At the first only a list (or candidate) winning a clear majority of votes would be elected; at the second, a week later, a simple plurality would suffice as in Britain or the United States.

Soustelle, Debré, and most of the Right ardently advocated large constituencies.[1] The list system was claimed to give a better chance of producing a parliamentary majority. It should give maximum scope to the tide of popular feeling, for de Gaulle and against the System, on which the Gaullist leaders counted. Moreover, the Left was split between Communists and democrats, who would not combine; and hardly a single department would give even a relative (let alone an absolute) majority to either of them separately. Thus under the list system the Right and the Gaullists might well sweep the country.

Their opponents naturally preferred single-member seats. These, they thought, should enable them to save local pockets of party or personal strength, and should favour prominent, entrenched personalities against the Gaullist political unknowns. Mendès-France and Mitterrand had been campaigning for this system for years, and even its critics (such as Mollet and the M.R.P. leaders) reluctantly preferred it to the Right's alternative. So, in opting for the single-member

[1] Gaullist doctrine on the electoral system has not been constant. In 1948, when the R.P.F. was the strongest single party in the electorate, it favoured a large-constituency majority system. When its strength declined, however, P.R. became acceptable as an alternative, and was probably the private choice of most of the leaders. Debré, however, always favoured a single rather than a double ballot (on general and not on party grounds), and accepted the large-constituency majority system only as a transition stage to the Anglo-Saxon type of electoral law. For details of the system finally adopted, see below, p. 252; and for a fuller account of the controversy and the campaign, see our section in D. E. Butler, ed.: *Elections Abroad* (Macmillan, 1959).

system, the General was trying to check too sweeping a surge of opinion away from the traditional leaders and towards his own professed followers, the men of 13 May. But the results contradicted both his expectations and those of every practising politician and independent observer.

Choosing a single-member system did not end the matter. The pre-war constituencies could not simply be restored. Even in 1940 seats had been most unfairly distributed; population had shifted since; and the number of metropolitan seats was to be reduced to give more to Algeria. New boundaries had therefore to be drawn in a hurry. The job was done by the prefects, who are often influenced by the most powerful politician in their area, and local biases were common; but these cancelled out, and only the Communists were generally (not always) discriminated against. Though rural areas gained at the expense of towns, this did not harm the Left. And de Gaulle personally made sure that there was no gerrymandering against his two chief critics, Mendès-France and Mitterrand.

The campaign was naturally dominated by the 80 per cent vote for de Gaulle only two months before. No party or politician dared ignore it. Even the open oppositions, Communist or Mendesist, spared the General and attacked only his entourage. Other Non leaders were embarrassingly sheepish: 'I voted No, but I never urged others to' protested Bourgès-Maunoury. But from the majority, who had supported the new constitution out of conviction or prudence, a deafening chorus arose. De Gaulle himself asked that his name be not exploited in the campaign. Few requests can have been so unanimously disregarded. Candidates pointed to past service under the General's banner, discreetly remaining silent about intervening periods of infidelity. A Socialist who had demonstrated against de Gaulle on 28 May, drew attention to a book he had written praising him in 1945. The astute Bernard Lafay had been one of the very first R.P.F. politicians to discover that that movement had lost its usefulness; his opportunist changes of allegiance were so notorious that one opponent said of him 'he is not the symbol of the System, he is the System'. Now he proudly proclaimed himself France's earliest Gaullist of all, for he had gone to school under the General's father, to whom he had been devoted.

Parties, like individuals, sought to establish titles to Gaullism. 'The General has adopted *our* policy', was the universal cry. There were Socialist posters boasting 'De Gaulle and Mollet saved the Republic'. Conservatives proudly observed that Pinay had been the first leader to visit Colombey in May (naturally not adding that he had gone to dissuade the General from taking power). Defferre, a leading critic of the Algerian war, urged Marseilles voters to elect Socialists to help de Gaulle against the ultras who were trying to capture him; elsewhere the Right appealed for all to join de Gaulle in sweeping out the nefarious parties of the System. In the clamour and confusion it was no surprise that many voters felt the men most loyal to de Gaulle would be those who had always followed him.

In October several bodies—the remnant of the old R.P.F., the shadow organizations set up for the referendum, and Delbecque's newly-created Republican Convention—fused in a new Gaullist party, the U.N.R., Union for the New Republic. Outside it were a handful of liberal Gaullists, lacking funds, organization and leadership, and a group of militants disappointed with the old politicians' grip on the new party, who called themselves *Renouveau et Fidélité*. Neither of these splinter groups won a seat of its own at the election. The U.N.R. had all the best-known names, Michelet on the left of the movement, Soustelle on the right, Debré for the most intransigent politicians, Chaban-Delmas for the compromisers, Delbecque for the rank and file outside Parliament. It had the staff and militants of the old R.P.F. It was lavishly financed, and well advised by commercial publicity experts. It imposed itself everywhere as the authentic party of Gaullism.

The tide was not only flowing in favour of the General, it was also ebbing away from the Fourth Republic. Hostility to the established politicians of the System was familiar in French politics. It had brought votes to the Communists at every election, to the R.P.F. in 1947 and 1951, to Poujade and Mendès-France in 1956. But this time it seemed stronger than ever. A dozen new parties tried to cash in on the demand for a change. There were the Gaullists of various hues. There were their unbending opponents of the U.F.D., critics both of the Algerian war and of the Fifth Republic. Then, over on the Right, there were M.R.P. dissidents led by Bidault (D.C.F.), ex-Radicals following Morice and Lafay (Republican Centre), and even anti-Poujade Poujadists.

The old parties, too, scented danger. Radical and M.R.P. candidates sought shelter under other labels wherever they could. A respected M.R.P. leader from Paris thought it wise to disguise himself as candidate for 'union for democratic reforms and the economic and social revival of the Hautes-Alpes'; indeed M.R.P. seriously considered changing its name. That it survived the election without serious loss makes the panic all the more striking.

Both the appeal of de Gaulle and the demand for change were heard everywhere. But, being so nearly universal, they cannot really be said to have formed ingredients of a national campaign. Issues abounded—Algeria, the Common Market, relations with N.A.T.O., the future of French democracy, the alarming economic situation—but they were hardly discussed seriously. This was the result not only of general conformism, but also of the electoral system, for candidates assumed— perhaps wrongly—that they were expected to concentrate largely on parochial problems and personalities. There were 465 separate contests, but no national head-on clash.

Some order might have come into the chaos but for another decision of de Gaulle's, following his choice of electoral system. This was his intervention in a sharp dispute which nearly split the U.N.R. as soon as it was formed. Soustelle wanted to make the new party the instrument of his old policy, all-out war in Algeria, for which long before 13 May he had made his parliamentary alliance with Duchet, Morice and Bidault. He wished the 'quartet' to sponsor a single candidate in each constituency; this would maximize the chance of a solid right-wing majority in the Assembly, which de Gaulle himself would find it hard to thwart. But within the U.N.R. he found himself isolated. The other leaders insisted, with de Gaulle's approval, that they must not commit themselves to the Right. This decision deprived the Conservatives (with their satellites from the Bidault and Morice groups) of an advantageous alliance with the U.N.R., and instead exposed them to dangerous competition from it. Gaullist officers stood against some of M. Duchet's close friends; he attacked them as '*les colonels de division*'. Feelings were already bitter before the first ballot, and the second was to exacerbate them into hatred.

France went to the polls on 23 November. The vote was high—78 per cent. Among the thirty-nine members who were elected at once, having won over half the total vote in their district, were Pflimlin, Pinay and Soustelle—and a young newcomer, backed by the entire Right, who ousted Mendès-France. Bidault just missed. Over the whole country the traditional parties did better than they had feared. The Right continued its steady advance, Socialists and M.R.P. held their own, and only the Radicals suffered disaster—under the very electoral system for which they had so long clamoured. They were harassed by their dissidents on Right and Left, Morice and Mendès-France; many of their orthodox leaders had voted Non; and they had no hope of holding the (largely Gaullist) votes which Mendès-France had brought them three years before.

The main victims were the previous assailants of the System. Poujadists and Mendesists, in their different geographical and political sectors, had both urged the electorate of 1956 to 'chuck out the old gang'. Now they themselves were *sortants*, and suffered the same fate; under those two labels, not one deputy survived. And the Communists, the great permanent party of protest, dropped to 3,800,000 votes. It was the first time since the war that they had fallen below the five-million mark.

The gainers were the U.N.R. Rival Gaullists cut little ice. Around Bordeaux the mayor, Chaban-Delmas, a U.N.R. leader but an undoubted 'man of the System', was hotly opposed by an extreme Right group led by General Chassin (an associate of the Algiers ultra Martel, and financed, some said, by General Salan). Their slogan CHA-CHA-CHA, short for *Chassin chassera Chaban*, could just as well have been turned round; the mayor and his protégés easily beat off the challenge. Nationally the U.N.R. won 3,700,000 votes—fewer than the R.P.F. in 1951, but then the new movement was not fighting everywhere. Plainly a great many of them came from the Left.

Its leaders drew their conclusions. The wind was in their sails, and their appeal was not confined to the Right. There was less reason than ever to make concessions to M. Duchet's Conservative friends. U.N.R. candidates therefore stayed in the fight, even where a rival had led on the previous ballot, unless there was danger of a Communist winning on a split vote. Where they did withdraw, it was usually in favour of the Right, but the exceptions—notably their second-ballot support of Mollet and Lacoste—were given much publicity (except in the Socialist press). The Conservatives were furious, and with good reason.

For now the bandwagon was really rolling, and on the second ballot the full force of attraction to Gaullism and revulsion from the old politicians became plain. So far, leaders of the System (other than Nons) had rarely lost supporters. But now they went down in droves. Wherever a prominent politician was standing, everyone else (occasionally even including some Communists) combined behind the candidate likeliest to throw him out. Bernard Lafay in Paris, Gaston Defferre in Marseilles each gained 400 votes between ballots. Their two unknown U.N.R. opponents gained 10,000 each, and won both seats. Examples could be multiplied.

For Right and Left voters alike, for both clericals and anti-clericals, the U.N.R.—which had no programme at all and claimed to be a centre party—was preferable to their traditional enemies. For those anxious to vote Gaullist but also worried about wasting their votes, the first ballot had shown that the U.N.R. was a 'serious' party. Thus it emerged triumphant from the second round. Before the first poll it had been expected to win 80 or 90 seats at most. In the next week the shrewdest commentators gave it 120 or 130. When the second ballot votes were counted it had 188, and when unattached and overseas members had surveyed the parliamentary scene, it went above 200. Allied with the 66 Algerians, it had just half the seats. The single-member system, chosen in order to check the tide, had helped swell it instead. No other electoral law would have served the U.N.R. so well. Like Louis XVIII in 1815, de Gaulle found himself faced with a *chambre introuvable* far more royalist than the King.

The Communists were almost wiped out; only ten were

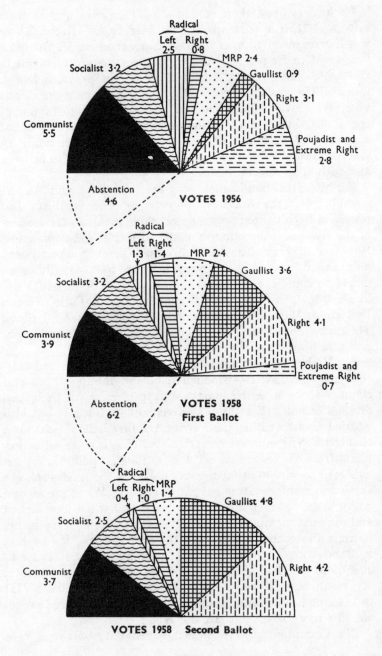

Radical
Left Right
2·5 0·8 MRP 2·4
Socialist 3·2 Gaullist 0·9
Right 3·1
Communist 5·5 Poujadist and Extreme Right 2·8
Abstention 4·6 **VOTES 1956**

Radical
Left Right
1·3 1·4 MRP 2·4
Socialist 3·2 Gaullist 3·6
Right 4·1
Communist 3·9 Poujadist and Extreme Right 0·7
Abstention 6·2 **VOTES 1958 First Ballot**

Radical
Left Right MRP
0·4 1·0 1·4 Gaullist 4·8
Socialist 2·5 Right 4·2
Communist 3·7 **VOTES 1958   Second Ballot**

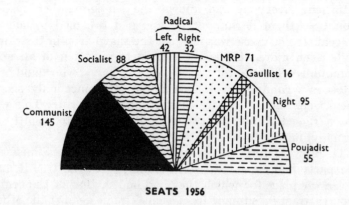

SEATS 1956

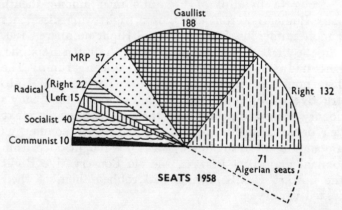

SEATS 1958

Metropolitan France only; 52 overseas members omitted in 1956, and 16 in 1958 (politically diverse). Votes are given in millions. 'Gaullists' means Social Republicans in 1956, U.N.R. in 1958. Many candidates withdrew before the second ballot. For details see *Elections Abroad*, pp. 74–5.

In seats fought both in 1956 and 1958 (first ballot) the votes were:

	Com.	Soc.	Rad., etc.	Right-Rad.	M.R.P.	Gaull.	Right	Pouj., etc.
1956:	5·5	3·2	1·3	0·5	1·7	0·7	2·4	0·8
1958:	3·8	3·1	1·1	0·7	2·2	2·7	3·5	0·2

returned. Everyone had known the single-member system would do them harm, but no one had dreamed of such a holocaust. The cause was not just the sharp drop in their own poll. Even more, it was the grim determination of all non-Communists to vote for anyone, of any party, who could beat 'Moscow's candidate'. In the whole of France only six of them were allowed to slip through on a split vote. This was not a rigged result; it was what the electorate, rightly or wrongly, meant to achieve.

There were forty Socialists. The gloomiest pessimists in the party had expected twice as many; but the U.N.R. had stolen the place for which they had hoped, that of the centre group attracting support from each extreme against the other. M.R.P. did much better than they had feared, returning fifty-seven strong (a handful of Bidault's men among them). Orthodox Radicals were a bare dozen, right-wing dissidents rather more numerous. The traditional Right numbered 130. Thus, in the first National Assembly of the Fifth Republic, the Left had shrivelled into an insignificant rump. The Socialist ministers resigned, and the party went into 'constructive opposition'; the General's option for Pinay's deflationary economic policy gave them an excellent pretext for their departure. But the real parliamentary conflict, as the campaign had foreshadowed, was to be fought out within the nominal majority—between the old Conservative Right and the upstart U.N.R., which had robbed them of their anticipated victory.

. . . .

A prime minister who reflected the outlook of this majority might prove a serious obstacle to de Gaulle's plans. Consequently, some speculated that the General might renounce the Presidency, the office designed for him, and retain the premiership where he could more effectively impose his own policy on a recalcitrant Parliament. They were wrong. In mid-December he confirmed his candidature for the Elysée, which was contested by two opponents: a respected Communist veteran, Marrane, and a distinguished scientist, Chatelet, put up by the U.F.D. to demonstrate the existence of a non-Communist Left opposition. On 21 December the

80,000 local *notables* cast their votes. More than three-quarters supported the General, who had 62,000 to 10,000 for Marrane and 6,700 for Chatelet. Beyond the shores of France his majority was even more overwhelming. On 8 January he began his seven-year term, and chose as his Prime Minister his faithful follower Michel Debré.

But even from the Elysée de Gaulle directed policy on major issues, above all on the crucial question, Algeria. Here he could wait quietly until the moment was ripe for a fresh move. Unlike his President, Debré was obliged to defend his policies constantly, and to face integrationist attempts to tie down a government which, with equal determination, was trying to leave room for manœuvre. Debré, the outspoken opponent of scuttle under the Fourth Republic, was to disarm the suspicions of the Right and to bear the thankless brunt of a tortuous holding operation until de Gaulle revealed his plans. Though he knew de Gaulle's aims when he accepted office, it was nevertheless onerous to defend policies which he had not formed and whose boundaries remained vague. Loyally he avoided the words de Gaulle proscribed. He lacked the President's aptitude for ambiguous phrases, while his juridical and narrowly nationalist temperament had little in common with de Gaulle's lofty vision and liberal humanism. There crept into his speeches a harsh and irritable rigidity, and a passionate resentment against unco-operative allies or anxious liberals. Two contradictory impressions spread: that Debré was simply an office boy; or that he was undermining the liberal policies of the President, now little more than a prisoner in the Elysée. Both views failed to do Debré justice, for he genuinely believed that a strong government could afford to make concessions which would have ruined a weak one. But both criticisms encouraged the growing malaise in either camp. Despite Debré's warm order of the day to the army on taking office, he was greeted by hostile cries in Algiers, and the declaration of the *Mouvement Algérie Française* that his policy was identical with that of Mendès-France and Gaillard.

These suspicions were fully exploited by the Right, who found in Bidault a leader more acceptable than Debré. Their quarrel with the U.N.R. was more a clash of interests and personalities than of policies, for most U.N.R. members were as conservative, clerical and nationalist as their right-wing rivals, and a few were crypto-fascists (though the U.N.R. had supported fewer open anti-democrats than the traditional Conservatives). But the new movement also took quite seriously its responsibilities as a 'party of government'. Usually, deputies of all opinions have been jealous of the prerogatives of their house; but in the bitter quarrel over Parliament's powers, the U.N.R. stood alone (yet virtually united) on the side of the ministry. The attack was violent, and it came not only from the traditionally parliamentary Left and Centre, but also from the Right and the Algerians, who hoped to use the Assembly to impose their own Algerian policy on de Gaulle.

A similar development occurred over the economic policy of the government. A team of Conservative experts had advised it and a Conservative Minister of Finance had adopted it, but the Conservative Right exploited every real hardship and demagogic grievance against the cabinet they nominally supported. Many U.N.R. members disliked the policy itself. The new party secretary, Chalandon (who succeeded Frey when he joined the government in January), had himself been the main advocate of a more expansionist alternative. But when the cabinet decided otherwise the U.N.R. set their teeth and accepted the disagreeable electoral consequences of a policy which was not their own.

Those consequences were serious. The electorate did not stay for long in its November mood. The U.N.R. entered the municipal elections in March 1959 with high hopes that the wave of success which had swept them into Parliament would now carry them forward into the town halls of France. Often they were newcomers who lacked strong local roots; if they were to turn their mushroom movement into a solid party, they needed the local position and patronage which a massive irruption into municipal administration would bring them. But they were grievously disappointed, for these elections became 'the revenge of the Fourth Republic'. The Communists recovered all they had lost in November, and the U.N.R. vote fell off, sometimes spectacularly. Lyons chose a despised Radical for the mayor's seat which Soustelle coveted; he was not even runner-up. Neuwirth, Delbecque's associate on 13 May, won 9 per cent of the vote at St. Etienne—a mere quarter of his share four months before. Politicians beaten for the Assembly four months earlier—like Defferre at Marseilles or Provo at Roubaix—easily held their *mairies*, often against the same opponents. Next month the election of the new Senate underlined the change of mood. Many (twenty-five) Fourth Republican victims of November now entered the upper house—Mitterrand, Edgar Faure, Defferre, Duclos, Lafay— and at once it became the forum for serious criticism and debate which the impatient and intolerant Assembly no longer afforded.

The voters' defection from the U.N.R. was a grave handicap to the integrationist wing in its struggle for control. For the party had become a battlefield on which the divergent forces responsible for 13 May fought for their different conceptions of their movement. The insurrection had been made in de Gaulle's name by ardent advocates of the integration of Algeria into France. What would they do if their standard-bearer decided to march in the wrong direction?

That crucial question exposed the equivocal nature of the U.N.R., and indeed of Gaullism. For the Gaullism of 1958 was a third phase of the movement. The first, Free France, had rallied against Vichy all types of Frenchmen, from intransigent nationalists with right-wing and even anti-republican pasts to patriotic socialists opposed to Nazism and reaction, from reforming administrators like Debré, anxious above all for effective government, to liberal Catholics who hoped that the common struggle would bring about a reconciliation of Church, workers and Republic.

When the General launched the second Gaullism, the R.P.F., he and other leaders wished it to retain similar characteristics: recruitment from all the French 'spiritual families', patriotic intransigence abroad and reformist policies at home. But these intentions were frustrated. Because of the cold war, the violence of the Communist opposition, the suspicions of the democratic Left, and the search by Vichyite voters and conservative politicians for a respectable patriotic covering, the R.P.F. became a right-wing movement (with a few reforming leaders and unconventional policies). Later, as the party shed

113

its conservative opportunists, the liberal views of some of its leaders again mingled and sometimes clashed with the nationalism of others. In 1953 the General himself publicly defended the Sultan of Morocco against the vicious personal attacks by which the Right justified his deposition. And in the Indo-Chinese, Tunisian and Moroccan controversies there were prominent Gaullists on both sides.

This remained true when Algeria came to hold the centre of the stage. In spring 1958 Mendesists were the keenest advocates of an appeal to the General; by autumn 1959 fascist stickers on the walls of Paris were proclaiming, 'De Gaulle = Mendès'. At the same time, intransigent nationalists continued to follow the liberator of 1944, in whom they saw a leader in the Bonapartist tradition, who stood for strong government and a vigorous assertion of France's position in the world. The revival of nationalist feeling over Algeria reinforced this camp with some powerful recruits (especially Soustelle) who before 1956 would have been counted as liberals.

The party leaders were well aware of the dangers of dis-loyalty. The common bond of personal loyalty to de Gaulle was strong, and easy to underestimate; but the fiasco of the R.P.F. had shown that it might not be enough. Precautions were taken. Deserters from the defunct movement were not welcome in the reincarnated organization. All U.N.R. candidates had to sign a written oath of fidelity to the General:

> . . . Respecting the mandate conferred on me by the voters, I pledge myself for the life of the Parliament to join no other parliamentary group. I undertake to remain faithful to the objectives of the U.N.R.; to support the action of General de Gaulle in Parliament and in my constituency; to vote according to the decision of the majority of the group on important questions . . .

How seriously they would take this pledge remained to be seen. Little confidence could be put in extremists like Biaggi, who had bludgeoned himself and a few friends into Parliament by threatening to run opposing candidates and split the vote, or Colonel Thomazo, who had campaigned for

Chassin against Chaban-Delmas. At the other end of the spectrum, some U.N.R. deputies were not men of the Right at all: a few ex-Socialists, a number of anti-clericals, liberals and Left Catholics like Michelet. But the Left was weaker than in the R.P.F. days. The great majority were in between, right-wingers by background and temperament but personally loyal to de Gaulle.

Two interpretations of the party's function competed within the leadership. One group sought to use the U.N.R. to fight for *Algérie française*, to promote integration, in short to press a positive policy upon a de Gaulle reduced to figure-head status. The other section, unconditional loyalists, wanted to make it a 'mass of manœuvre' which the General could manipulate at will. This was the thankless role Chalandon defined for U.N.R. members:

> We have to recognize things as they are. General de Gaulle is our clandestine leader. We are somewhat in the position of secret agents who owe complete obedience to their military chief, a military chief who does not hesitate to disavow them when things are going badly.[1]

The first interpretation pointed to a right-wing alliance. The second would produce a kind of rejuvenated Radical party, a 'party of government' seeking its allies on both sides and willing to support whatever policy the General and his ministers chose.

> We are condemned to support governments whatever they may be, to be the pivot of the majorities which form; perhaps it will be on the Left, perhaps it will be on the Right—in any event we shall always be present.[2]

De Gaulle himself kept up a steady pressure on the party. Soustelle did not become president (none was appointed); he was denied the electoral system he wanted, which would have forced the U.N.R. into a right-wing combination; and his colleagues in the leadership refused the pact with Bidault and Duchet. In all these decisions de Gaulle was believed to have intervened privately. And when in January 1959 a

---

[1] U.N.R. *Bulletin de Presse*, quoted *Le Monde*, 19 May 1959.
[2] Chalandon, *loc. cit.*

U.N.R. deputy committed the Assembly to an integrationist resolution by a procedural trick, the General rebuked Chaban-Delmas (now President of the Assembly) for permitting the rules to be broken.

Soustelle could still hope to stimulate counter-pressure from the rank-and-file U.N.R. members. He could exploit both their right-wing sympathies and their resentment at the sheep-like role to which Chalandon's conception of the party's task reduced them. On the other hand, loyalty to de Gaulle was the mainstay of many members' political lives. For a Debré, and for many less-known figures, to oppose the General openly would mean a real *crise de conscience*. Past records were not always reliable pointers to future conduct: Chalandon's chief supporter was Neuwirth. Where loyalty was not enough, self-interest might tell in the same direction. The new members were well aware that they owed their seats to de Gaulle's popularity and not to their own; the municipal elections drove the lesson home. And they were soon to discover how widespread was support for any move by the General towards peace in Algeria. At the election, the (comparatively few) candidates who were liberal about Algeria without being opposed to de Gaulle had invariably polled well, even when they failed to save their seats. Now, many who might have been against him were deterred by fear that a dissolution of Parliament would smash them.

The struggle for the party's soul went on behind the scenes throughout 1959, occasionally breaking into the open. In April the parliamentary group elected an 'orthodox' chairman, Terrenoire, by 124 votes to 72 for Biaggi. 'Still two-thirds of *beni-oui-oui*', commented Colonel Thomazo. In May, Soustelle supported Sérigny for the Senate; Neuwirth and Chalandon opposed him, and resignations were threatened on both sides.[1] In June the integrationists mounted a vigorous assault against Chalandon, whom they attacked as a rich man without any elective position or contact with the rank and file. Delbecque announced his candidature for the secretaryship, presenting himself as a parliamentarian of working-class origins and a representative of the party militants. In July the two interpretations clashed openly at

[1] See below, p. 202.

the party's first *conseil national*.[1] In September, when de Gaulle offered self-determination to Algeria, both Soustelle and Delbecque urged the party to come out for integration: the executive declined to do so, but eighteen of the sixty-seven members abstained from voting in protest. In October the party required Biaggi to resign from the new *Rassemblement pour l'Algérie française* which he had just founded, along with Bidault and Duchet, to work for the integrationist cause.

Two weeks later the Assembly's debate on de Gaulle's Algerian policy brought matters to a head. There were reports of a new 13 May in preparation: an attempt to drive Debré into resignation by demonstrations in Algiers, a split in the U.N.R., and private pressure by the army on de Gaulle.

[1] From U.N.R. *Bulletin de Presse*, no. 5, reporting the *conseil national* of 25–26 July 1959 (italics in original):

P. 8. *Chalandon:* 'There is a permanent difficulty: General de Gaulle is our creator; from him we derive our existence, our thinking, our unity. *But, if we belong to him, he does not belong to us; his position as arbitrator will always prevent him from confining himself within the bounds of a party, however faithful it may be.* Thus we are in a situation in which we must constantly serve him without directly receiving orders from him. There is the difficulty . . . we must allow General de Gaulle to carry out his policy. Certainly there are anti-Gaullists in the country, but *more dangerous than they are those who are Gaullists on condition that General de Gaulle thinks like them, does as they wish.* There always are and always will be attempts to commit the U.N.R. to a bloc which can force the hand of General de Gaulle and take him prisoner. The U.N.R. must keep out of all these manœuvres; it must remain free, always at the disposal of the President of the Republic. Thus it is our task to be purely and simply Gaullists, and not to seek to embrace the General the better to smother him . . . there ought not to be, in the U.N.R.'s eyes, a Party policy about Algeria. There can be no policy but that of General de Gaulle.'

P. 11. *Delbecque:* 'Stop spreading stories according to which all those who disagree, sometimes with decisions which have not been studied together or decided after a majority vote, are anti-Gaullists or people who want a split in the U.N.R. at any cost . . . an absolute necessity . . . for you to explain yourselves, and to bring out what you want, on the ideological level as well as on the structural . . . . Shall we be the party of the Arbitrator, that is a party that arbitrates? Or shall we rather have our own personality, on the plain understanding that we give unconditional support to Gaullist ideology?'

P. 7. *Soustelle:* 'The party is not the Government; it ought not . . . above all to have the complexes about its action which it would have if it were the Government . . . the party must not be paralysed, as it were, by a kind of respect, however great it may be, for the chief of State and for the Government, in such a way that in the end it brings them no active support. . . .'

Chalandon and Terrenoire confirmed the reports, while Neu-wirth warned that 'killer commandos' had already crossed the Spanish border. (An alleged attack on Mitterrand lent colour to the story.) When tension was at its height, five deputies broke with the U.N.R., among them Arrighi, Biaggi and Thomazo. Delbecque and three others also resigned, but voted for the government and at once applied to rejoin; the Prime Minister came to a U.N.R. political bureau meeting for the first time and successfully insisted that their applications be refused.

Both sides prepared assiduously for the party's first annual congress in mid-November. Though it was carefully held in Chaban-Delmas territory at Bordeaux, the hall was full of partisans of Soustelle, who cheered his demands for stronger action against the 'treasonous press' and for the readmission of Delbecque and his friends. Orthodox speakers were shouted down, leaders' names booed, and blows exchanged in the lobbies. Attempts by the leadership to rig the resolutions com-mittee were repeatedly defeated. One journalist called the U.N.R. 'the party where you should take a bodyguard when you mount the rostrum'. Such was the atmosphere that Ali Mallem (a Moslem deputy whose written report called for negotiations with the F.L.N. and referred to the Moslem de-puties as 'prefabs') made a 'Soustellian' speech which flatly contradicted his own report. The two sides could agree only on the need for a larger share in power for the U.N.R.

But the leaders had taken precautions. Just before the congress the Seine federation, which they controlled, swelled magically in membership—just as loyal Radical federations used to do in the bad old days of the System. The final re-solution on Algeria was harmlessly non-committal; from the overwhelmingly activist congress there somehow emerged an overwhelmingly orthodox central committee. The one concession was Chalandon's voluntary retirement; but his successor was an orthodox senator, Richard. The U.N.R.'s first congress—like other party conferences in France and elsewhere—showed the difficulties facing extremist party workers who try to force the hand of moderate leaders and parliamentarians.

PART III

The New Reign

7. *The Institutions of the Fifth Republic*

The nation needs a régime in which the governing power has strength and continuity.

8. *The New System*

He who holds office is, in fact, responsible to General de Gaulle and to him alone.

9. *'A Government that Governs'*

I take the decision which seems right to me. Thereby it becomes the decision of the Cabinet.

10. *The Algerian Tightrope*

In politics as well as in strategy, it is better to persuade the stronger than to go against them.

11. *The Gaullist Transition: Pre-Fascism or New Deal?*

No man can be a substitute for a people.

Quotations from General de Gaulle, *Le Salut*; pp. 239, 122, 126, 53, 232.

7

The Institutions of the Fifth Republic

'We must rebuild France; that is to say rebuild a democracy, rebuild a State, rebuild a Power.'[1] The aim could scarcely have been more ambitious, even with Debré's cautious reminder that 'texts are texts and nothing more'. Earlier Republics died of their inability to combine democracy and effective government. The electoral system remorselessly translated the opinions of a divided nation into Parliaments with no stable majority. Fleeting cabinets, deadlock and impotence followed inevitably. If the choice had to be made, Republican tradition set democracy before the power to govern.

It was a popular Gaullist contention that the old political parties would disappear with the System, revealing the underlying cohesion of the nation. Debré generally inclined to this view, and de Gaulle, while speaking of a 'profoundly divided people', acts as if the nation were united. Both sentiments can be found in their constitution.

If driven to choose, they place authority before democracy. Debré's object was 'first and before everything else, to try to reconstruct a Power without which there is neither State nor democracy . . . neither France nor Republic'.[2] Nothing more clearly underlines his intention than his declaration that 'because in France governmental stability cannot result from the electoral law, it must result in part at least from making constitutional rules, and that is just what gives this proposal its decisive explanation and its historical justification'.[3]

This determination to give governments the means to govern—even against the pressure of public opinion—is the hallmark of Debré's constitution, linking together his principal reforms. These restrict the competence and privileges of the National Assembly, recast parliamentary procedure, create

[1] M. Debré, *Refaire une Démocratie, Un Etat, Un Pouvoir*, p. 9.
[2] *Revue française de science politique*, IX, 1; January-March 1959, p. 7 (hereafter *R.F.S.P.*). [3] *R.F.S.P.*, p. 17.

a Constitutional Council, amend the powers of the Senate—even transform the Presidency. Scorning both 'extremes', presidential rule and the traditional sovereignty of the assembly, Debré has chosen a hybrid: the *régime parlementaire*.

The keystone, in Debré's term, is the Presidency. With Charles de Gaulle the obvious candidate it could scarcely have been otherwise. For the present the 'weight' of this much-misunderstood office is an enigma. Debré's intentions are relatively clear, but there is a world of difference between what the office has become in the hands of de Gaulle, and the Presidency which, even with his legacy, may evolve under his successors.

Debré clearly does not conceive the President as a day-to-day ruler. He resisted the great temptation to introduce a fully presidential system. The administrative and political problems of imposing it on a multi-racial Community were obvious. De Gaulle had in effect promised the Assembly that he would not make so drastic a break with Republican tradition. Election by universal suffrage raised the distant spectres of a new Bonaparte or Boulanger, or of a Popular Front President.[1] Moreover a President on the American pattern would probably find a divided Assembly even harder to manage than Congress. And from de Gaulle's utterances it seems clear that he has never had any taste for wielding power in the manner of some American Presidents.

Since Debré set out to create a *deus* in *machina*, the traditional dialogue between government and Parliament remains. Yet there are always the dangers of deadlock, or of breaches of the spirit of the constitution. Debré's President is the divine mechanic and moral magistrate who sets the machine on the rails and enforces the sanctity of the constitution, by provoking a solution rather than by imposing his own verdict. Only in the gravest moments does he emerge as a medieval warrior king to lead the nation away from the abyss. Throughout he is to be the 'arbitrator of the nation', 'placed above the parties', who distinguishes disinterestedly the 'interest of the nation' amid the competing cries of the political factions.

[1] With the system of indirect election which was finally adopted, this danger is much less. See below, p. 131.

The result is a Hanoverian monarch masquerading as a Republican President, who is also head of state, guardian of the ark of the covenant, one head of a two-headed executive, mediator within his cabinet and between the government and Parliament, and in a great crisis constitutional dictator. For good measure he is theoretically almost absolute ruler of the colonial Community.[1]

The President's fresh prerogatives are few. As official Head of State his formal duties have altered little, although he should have fewer crises to resolve than his predecessors.[2] Debré has grafted on new prerogatives which permit the President to function as *'arbitre national'*. These amount essentially to a series of checks and initiatives. Thus the President can now dissolve Parliament, appoint a Prime Minister, and address messages to Parliament. He may ask Parliament to reconsider a bill, seek the opinion of the Constitutional Council (one-third of which he appoints) on its constitutionality, or rule on proposals to send a bill to referendum. His last additional power in normal times, the right to negotiate treaties, seems aberrant.[3]

[1] See below (p. 182). Clearly if the President exercises real power in the Community his stature in metropolitan France will grow. But this wholly depends on the form and durability of the Community.

[2] These formal duties include, beyond the customary ceremonial functions, the right of pardon, receiving and accrediting diplomats, signing decrees and ordinances (an innovation), and promulgating laws adopted by Parliament. He presides over the cabinet, certain defence committees, and the High Council of the Judiciary.

The provision that 'he appoints to the civil and military posts of the State' might seem to introduce presidential patronage. In fact de Gaulle has delegated much of his power to the Prime Minister, while most posts are filled by cabinet nomination or routine civil service procedures. The choice of a few posts for direct nomination by presidential decree seems intended to confer on them a special prestige.

[3] The President requires countersignature for all acts but appointment of a Prime Minister, dissolution, emergency powers, messages to Parliament, reference to the Constitutional Council, appointment of three of its members, and decisions whether to hold referenda. Article 19, listing the functions he may perform without countersignature, does not include his powers in relation to the Community. However, it has been assumed that this article is not intended to refer to the President's acts as President of the Community, and his 'decisions' have all appeared without countersignature. If a minister's signature were required, the French government would make the effective decisions, which would be totally contrary to the spirit of the Community.

The most significant of these powers is 'that capital arm of any parliamentary system', the dissolution. It is intended to provoke a solution to deadlocks or to discipline an unruly Assembly. Yet this is a limited weapon. Such a stigma of anti-republicanism has clung to it that, since its misuse by MacMahon in 1877, it has been employed only once (by Edgar Faure in 1955). De Gaulle might make it respectable; making it effective is less simple. Where the electorate is so divided on so many issues, and no party will win a majority, the 'judgment of the sovereign people' may produce no clear-cut verdict. Moreover, an unsuccessful or partisan dissolution can undermine a President's position. But the dissolution may be more potent in prospect than in practice. The mere threat of an appeal to the country by a determined President might be an effective means of knocking politicians' heads together. De Gaulle has already threatened obliquely to dismiss an Assembly which asserts itself too brashly. The weapon cannot be disregarded as a means of presidential influence.

'The President of the Republic appoints the Prime Minister.' If the bare wording of the constitution were believed, Fifth Republic governments would be the nominees of the President rather than Parliament, for all reference to parliamentary investiture has disappeared. De Gaulle certainly seems to take this view of his powers. The Elysée's communiqué on Debré's appointment was couched in the unmistakeable style:

> M. Debré submitted for the approval of General de Gaulle his conceptions concerning general policy, and the names of the persons who would become his collaborators in the government.
> The President of the Republic appointed M. Michel Debré Prime Minister.

Yet Debré at once set a precedent by appearing before Parliament with a declaration of policy. Had it been rejected he would have been obliged to resign. This is the Fourth Republic system in all but words. De Gaulle's own prestige and the U.N.R. victory gave him a free hand to control both the policies and the members of the new government. Future Presidents will not enjoy these advantages; they may be thankful to find anyone who can command a majority before the Assembly. They are unlikely to be able to impose the man of their choice. Moreover the President cannot dismiss his Prime Minister, and even his power to refuse his resignation is doubtful.[1]

Where President and referendum rub shoulders in one French sentence (Art. 11), there is no escaping the historical reflex: Bonapartism. But it is misleading. In the Fifth Republic the referendum strengthens the government more than the President. The danger of a return to presidential government by referendum is slight. He may *refuse* a referendum proposed by the government or the two assemblies, but he cannot initiate one. This detail was apparently overlooked in General de Gaulle's promise of a referendum on the future of Algeria after peace was restored; yet even he needs either the cabinet's or Parliament's formal permission to keep his word. Referenda are sure to be infrequent.[2] But they do allow a government to appeal to the people against a hostile legislature.[3]

Both these extensions of the President's new prerogatives are essentially powers of leverage. So are his subsidiary rights: messages to Parliament, reference to the Constitutional Council, and requests to Parliament to reconsider a bill. The single exception in normal times is his enhanced status in foreign affairs. He can negotiate treaties, where previously he merely formally ratified them (having been 'informed', often tardily, of the negotiations). Any treaties he may conclude must have the countersignature of the Prime Minister and Minister for Foreign Affairs and be accepted by Parliament

[1] See Article 8: The President of the Republic appoints the Prime Minister. He puts an end to his tenure of office when the latter presents the resignation of the Government.

[2] Referenda may be held on any government bill dealing with 'organization of public authorities', approving a Community Agreement, or proposing ratification of a treaty which 'without being contrary to the Constitution would affect the functioning of institutions'. Two of these categories could mean almost anything.

During constitutional revision the President may decide whether to submit the proposal to a joint session of the assemblies or to referendum (but he requires a minister's countersignature).

[3] Therefore referenda requested by the government may be held only during Parliamentary sessions, so that Parliament cannot be muzzled. The referendum can hardly be used against the government since it applies only to government bills, and the President cannot initiate it.

(or by referendum). But, as he can refuse to conclude a treaty, he enjoys an unshakeable veto.[1] However, the decisive acts of modern diplomacy rarely take the form of treaties. If Presidents feel entitled to make declarations of policy and join in international talks, this may ultimately prove more important than treaty-making powers. It has certainly been President de Gaulle's interpretation. And here the President requires no countersignature.

It is the President's duty to see that the constitution is respected, and to be 'guarantor of the nation's independence'. The right to make treaties is one logical consequence of this. Gaullists favoured putting every obstacle in the way of fresh commitments such as the European Defence Community and the Common Market Treaty, which they characterized as flagrantly unconstitutional and damaging to national independence alike.[2] Another consequence is expressed in Article 16 containing the President's emergency powers. This has provoked more heated discussion than any of the other 91 articles. It states:

> When the institutions of the Republic, the independence of the nation, the integrity of its territory or the execution of its international commitments are gravely and immediately threatened and the regular functioning of the constitutional public authorities is interrupted, the President of the Republic takes the measures required by these circumstances after official consultation with the Prime Minister and the Presidents of the assemblies as well as with the Constitutional Council.

[1] The President is simply 'kept informed' of negotiations leading to the conclusion of other forms of diplomatic agreement. In certain circumstances, therefore, the government could circumvent a President's opposition.

[2] The constitution puts several obstacles in the way of accepting supranational commitments. Presidents were expected to be hostile to any extension of supranationalism. But if they are tainted the government or Parliament may still resist. Moreover, if the Constitutional Council rules a proposed treaty unconstitutional it cannot be ratified unless the constitution is amended. This constitution makes derogations of sovereignty more difficult than its predecessor. The latter's idealistic internationalism was expressed in such statements as, 'on condition of reciprocity France will accept those limitations of her sovereignty which are necessary for the organization and defence of peace'. In 1958 the government even refused to countenance the C.C.C.'s proposal that the list of guarantees refer to the United Nations Declaration of Human Rights.

It needs little knowledge of French history to see why Article 16 conjures up spectres of a new Prince-President emerging from a legal *coup d'état*. Some critics allege that a President could use riots in Algiers as a pretext for installing a military junta. De Gaulle may be above suspicion, they say, but what of his successors?

Yet only in the gravest national danger can these powers be legitimately invoked: the 'regular functioning' of the 'constitutional public authorities' must be interrupted, and there must be a 'grave and immediate' threat to the Republic. These terms are hardly precise. They would cover July 1940, but May 1958 is far more doubtful. Plainly very few occasions would be desperate enough to justify resort to these powers. However, the judge of the gravity of the situation is the President himself. He must seek the advice of the Prime Minister, the Presidents of the assemblies, and the Constitutional Council. He is not bound to take it, though the Council's opinion on whether Article 16 is being legitimately used must be published.

Once armed with emergency powers the President can do anything but amend the constitution or dissolve the Assembly. He alone judges when the emergency ends and what is to be done. Again he must consult the Constitutional Council, but he need not take its advice, although he is charged solemnly to restore the normal functioning of government in 'the shortest possible time'.

Parliament meets in special sesson once the emergency is declared—why is not clear. It could support the President, or it could impeach him. Theoretically the presence of Parliament prevents the President from taking the opportunity to impose an unpopular Prime Minister. But once emergency powers are invoked there are no effective legal safeguards. The constitution can only present a succession of opportunities for the legality and popularity of the President's actions to be judged. These provide the clear path of duty for a scrupulous President.

If the President's action proves controversial there is no telling how effective the opposition could be. Parliament met in 1940 and 1958 and on both occasions transferred power with all the trappings of legality. The Constitutional Council might be coerced or silenced. Yet Article 16 is scarcely a Trojan Horse. It presents few fresh dangers even with an unscrupulous President. If the Republic elects a man who will subvert a constitution he has sworn to uphold, no Article 16 need show him the way. The last two Republics died of their failure to command sufficient loyalty to assure their defence.

Debré has half-heartedly tried to present Article 16 as a precaution against nuclear warfare—for which it is grimly insufficient.[1] But it really fights the battles of the last war, not the next. Its inspiration is the General's bitter recollections of 1940. He has never forgotten how President Lebrun declared himself powerless even to leave France in 1940, and how for years his own London Committee was handicapped by having no valid legal status. If any such disaster should again befall France, the constitution must give 'a legitimate basis to the action of the man who represents legitimacy'.[2] De Gaulle could have made good use of Article 16 in 1940—but was this really all that President Lebrun lacked then, and President Coty in 1958?[3]

Speaking of less troubled times Debré summed up these powers of the President as amounting to 'the power to solicit the decision of another power: he solicits the decision of Parliament, he solicits the decision of the Constitutional Council, he solicits the decision of the electorate', but he

---

[1] *R.F.S.P.*, p. 23. These problems are dealt with more realistically in an ordinance of the Debré government on national defence. This contains provisions which, being more readily invoked, might threaten freedom more seriously than Article 16. A clause allowing the government to conscript all necessary men and resources, when necessary for national defence, was used to prevent a threatened national railway strike in June 1959.

[2] *R.F.S.P.*, p. 23.

[3] Article 16 seems inadequate for either nuclear warfare or internal subversion. There are many gaps and uncertainties. What if the President or the Constitutional Council are under duress? Does the seizure of the President by insurgents amount to 'incapacity to act'? Can the Constitutional Council declare the President 'incapable' for mental reasons during the operation of emergency powers? What if the President cannot or will not consult the persons whose opinion he is bound to take: does this invalidate his decisions? What if he suppresses the opinion of the Constitutional Council? These are all pedantries, yet such gaps are surprising in an article which seeks to set legitimacy beyond all doubt.

never has the final word.[1] These were ingenuous words for so experienced a politician. To turn a phrase of Mendès-France, *choisir, c'est gouverner*. The power to indicate options may often go well beyond simple leverage. Yet Debré was right to stress in how few matters the President alone can decide.

All his prerogatives except that of giving advice must be exercised discontinuously, either by direct provision of the constitution (dissolution, allowed only once a year), or by the need not to devalue them (messages to Parliament), or by their very nature (appointment of Prime Minister, references to Constitutional Council, choice of procedure for constitutional revision, and reference back of bills). Prudence also counsels the President to use his powers sparingly. The constitution may declare him an arbitrator, but only he can win acceptance for his impartiality. The more he commits himself on controversial issues, the more he risks political debate on his actions, clashes between presidential and anti-presidential camps, and his own decline from 'national arbiter' to simple politician. Some of the bitterest debates have been on foreign policy (e.g. E.D.C.). Can the President both publicly commit himself to a controversial treaty and arbitrate in the dispute over it?

In normal times the President's powers are meant to initiate a moral magistracy. Both Debré and de Gaulle repeatedly insist that he will be 'above the parties', speaking for the nation amid the political factions. He incarnates the national will, or at least intuitively divines it. He is an *arbitre national* in two senses—both referee and arbitrator.

The idea of the President as referee is not new. Such was Vincent Auriol's interpretation of his office when he defended the Fourth Republic against Communist and Gaullist attacks in 1948. It was as defender of the constitution that de Gaulle reprimanded the President of the National Assembly, Chaban-Delmas, for countenancing a procedural subterfuge which circumvented the spirit of the new constitution.[2]

Debré's President is not intended to make personal policies. He is to enforce political morality, notably by maintaining

[1] *R.F.S.P.*, p. 22.
[2] See below, p. 155.

the balance of the constitution, above all today by supporting the government against any attempt to restore the Assembly's former ascendancy. His new powers could be employed against the government, but they are more suitable for defending it.

The contrast between this influential yet secondary figure and President de Gaulle need not be emphasized. For all the allegations that this was simply a constitution made to measure for him, his tenure of the Elysée has been in a sense unconstitutional. This is not the simple arbitrator who merely solicits decisions, so passionately advocated by Debré. Instead de Gaulle seeks to be 'guide of France and chief of the republican State, exercising the supreme power in all the breadth it carries'.[1] De Gaulle has so dominated his cabinet that Professor Duverger could ask, 'Does M. Debré exist?'[2] Since December 1958 France has had a largely presidential regime which is complicated by operating in the guise of parliamentary democracy.

De Gaulle's pre-eminence depends on his personality and prestige more than on his direct prerogatives. He has made even his most formal duties elevate the dignity of his office. Ministers have accepted his arbitration of their everyday differences, and as chairman of the cabinet he has settled all major policies. Nothing suggests that future Presidents will have such a position. Not only are de Gaulle's character and record altogether exceptional; his Prime Minister's whole political career has been an expression of personal loyalty; and would-be dissidents know that he still enjoys the confidence of the electorate.

No future President can look for such abdication by his ministers. They will accept his arbitration and counsel only if they trust his wisdom, experience or expertise. If some refuse he is impotent. His one weapon against the cabinet is to dissolve the Assembly. A lesser man than de Gaulle may well hesitate before using a weapon which might boomerang, producing an Assembly elected against him and a cabinet over which he would have no influence. Failure would con-

---

[1] *L'Année Politique 1958*, p. 567. Yet in his speech of 4 September 1958, de Gaulle seemed to accept Debré's views. See *ibid.*, p. 551.
[2] *La Nef*, no. 30 (July 1959), p. 3.

demn him to political sterility. MacMahon remains the awful warning.[1]

The President will also lack political weight. In the event of his clashing with the Assembly, he is challenging men who emanate from the electorate. Yet he is chosen by only 80,000 presidential electors, mostly provincial notables. In 1958 the 16,000,000 people living in rural communes of under 2,000 inhabitants had 39,000 electors. The 27,000,000 living in communes of over 2,000 had only 33,500. A mere 33 per cent of the population had 51 per cent of the presidential votes. No wonder Professor Vedel calls the President 'the choice of corn and chestnut'.[2] Election by this college can give him none of the prestige an American President draws from being elected by the entire country. Moreover, these electors are unlikely to choose a man who would use his powers to the full. Their choice would normally fall more readily on a Pinay or a Coty than on an Auriol or a de Gaulle. Once de Gaulle leaves the scene, therefore, the presidency may well assume less importance than Debré expected. A powerful yet indirectly-elected President is an anachronism in a democratic age. Although future occupants of the Elysée should count for rather more than their predecessors, there will be constant pressure on them to take the easy way of a constitutional monarch, accepting the advice of their ministers and bowing to the electorate's will.

.   .   .   .

Another institution which is intended to guarantee the working of the new system, to protect the national interest against partisan passions, and to moralize politics is the

[1] The President is clearly weaker in a clash with the government than in a conflict with the Assembly. Theoretically he might ally himself with the Assembly and dissolve to get rid of his government, but this seems unlikely.

[2] Debré replied to this accusation: 'How far removed from the evergreen tree of life is this grey theory. . . . This strong participation of peasants in the electoral body . . . attaches us to the earth . . . which is also, and everywhere, the earth of our Country, the earth of the generations which have made France. What better electoral body than that which reflects the earth from which is born the Nation?' (*Refaire une Démocratie, un Etat, un Pouvoir*, pp. 15–16). For further details of the system of presidential elections see below, p. 250.

Constitutional Council. Although the Council is a judicial body, the spirit in which it was created was not entirely judicial. Safely insulated from political pressure, it exists largely to help the cabinet and the President resist Parliament's efforts to regain its lost rights. As well as being an 'arm against the deviation of the parliamentary system', the Council is to be a watchdog against surrender of sovereignty to international organizations. It is also given wide powers to supervise elections and referenda.

This Council is far more powerful than the Constitutional Committee of the Fourth Republic. Even so its jurisdiction and access to it are more limited than is common in constitutional courts. As Debré explained, 'It is neither in the spirit of parliamentary government nor in the French tradition to give justice—that is, the individual citizen—the right to examine the value of the law'.[1] He gave the right to refer bills to the Council only to the President of the Republic, the Prime Minister, and the Presidents of the two assemblies. The Council has no independent initiative in constitutional matters.

Obviously Debré intended to fill the embarrassing gap which was revealed when he among others denounced the E.D.C. treaty as unconstitutional, only to find that no authority could give a ruling. On that occasion the Presidents of the Republic (Auriol) and Assembly (Herriot) were both opposed to E.D.C. But Debré in 1958 refused the C.C.C.'s proposal to give access to the Council to one-third of the deputies, so that unless the dissidents have the support of one of the four authorities, they are as powerless now as Debré himself was in 1953. The minority has no redress if the majority flouts the constitution.[2]

The Council is essentially a domestic tribunal for a limited range of disputes between Parliament and the executive over the interpretation of the constitution.[3] It has no

[1] *R.F.S.P.*, p. 16.

[2] Bills may be referred at any stage before promulgation (see below, p. 139). If Parliament has voted them, they cannot be promulgated until the Council so rules. If not, a reference to the Council suspends the debate. Debré may have feared that a minority, given the right of access, would use it obstructively.

[3] Although the Council's decisions are couched in conventional legal phraseology, it is technically part of the executive. It meets in camera and decides on the basis of documents only, without hearing argument,

jurisdiction over the relations of either arm of government with the judiciary, or over the actions of the President (except in declared national emergencies). Thus there seems little chance that the Fifth Republic's constitution will be 'what the eleven old men in the Palais Royal say it is'.

Yet the Council's first ruling (on the assemblies' standing orders) showed how influential it may be within its restricted jurisdiction. Before amendments to these standing orders go into force, or organic laws are promulgated, the Council will automatically be called on to decide whether they conform to the constitution. Acting on reference, it rules on the constitutionality of any bill, amendment or treaty. Thus it may decide whether a treaty abdicates national sovereignty to an unconstitutional degree, or whether a bill or amendment falls in the domain of the law (see below, p. 139). It may also rule on the government's proposals to amend Fifth Republic laws by decree on the ground that they intervene in the executive domain. In all these matters its decisions are subject to no appeal. They are enforced automatically, since provisions which it finds unconstitutional cannot be put into operation or proceeded with, although the remainder of the measure may be (unless the Council indicates to the contrary).

The Council may give the President of the Community advisory opinions on Community Agreements. It may also be called on to declare the Presidency vacant on grounds of the President's incapacity; this requires an absolute majority. Its least controversial role is to ensure the regularity of referenda and elections. Aided by qualified legal assistants, it has full power to investigate complaints by electors and candidates, and even to annul a result in part or whole. Again its decision is final. During a referendum it is also consulted by the government about the arrangements, and may 'present observations' about the list of organizations allowed to use official campaign facilities.[1] Without waiting for complaints to come in, it can send observers to investigate any aspect of the referendum it pleases. It is responsible for

within a month of reference being made to it (a week if the matter is urgent). Decisions require a majority of the membership. No dissenting or concurring opinion is published.

[1] The need for such control was clear in September 1958. See above, p. 92.

the count and for proclaiming the result of both referenda and presidential elections.

The removal of electoral disputes from Parliament is welcome. Few features of the System were less attractive than the squalid debates and partisan decisions on demands for invalidation. Unfortunately the Council is asked to administer an electoral law so outdated and so disregarded that if it were enforced a large fraction of the Assembly would be unseated. In 1958 the provisional Constitutional Commission thought it better to overlook innumerable infringements which it considered had not been decisive. Even so there were cries of outrage from the five deputies it unseated, and they were promptly returned with increased majorities. The way of the moralizer is not easy.[1]

Debré was clearly at pains to have his Council accepted and respected. Protocol assigns Councillors an elevated place, and they must take a solemn oath of secrecy and fidelity to the constitution. They are sternly enjoined not to take position publicly or professionally on any matter within their jurisdiction (yet they are automatically granted leave of absence to contest an election). Their President is appointed by the President of the Republic. Former Presidents serve ex-officio, are exempt from taking the oath, and (unlike their colleagues) may make public statements if they resign. The Presidents of the assemblies and the President of the Republic each appoint three of the nine ordinary members. These have the security of a nine-year term, and their stipends are assured by being linked to a stated civil service grade.

In the long term the Council's moral authority depends on the ability and integrity of its members. The first appointments did little to lull suspicions that it was a partisan body in judicial form. It was alleged that the cost of ensuring a narrow Gaullist majority on the Council was that it was elderly and insufficiently qualified. One or two appointments were perhaps ill-advised, but the general criticism was unfair. If the average age of the first Council (65) was high, the unexacting volume of business is well within the powers of

---

[1] Such is also the opinion of the *Conseil d'Etat*, which remembered its unhappy experiences with elections to the old Algerian Assembly, and would not hear of Debré's original idea of giving it this jurisdiction.

men of advancing years but undiminished mental vigour. None had been a professor of political or economic science (such men are also rare in the United States Supreme Court), and none had had an exclusively legal career, but eight of the nine were legally qualified. In fact the Council has an impressive proportion of men with wide and varied experience of executive-legislative problems.[1]

They should be well equipped to judge the political consequences of their decisions. Their first major ruling, on the assemblies' standing orders, reflected their Gaullist majority — and perhaps also an inclination to legalistic rigidity. There is no certainty, however, that the Council will always be so ready to enforce the constitution to the letter. Since six of its members are nominated by the Presidents of the assemblies they may take a more liberal view of Parliament's prerogatives once the Gaullist phase is past. Moreover, councillors may, like Justices of the United States Supreme Court, develop in a fashion which surprises those who nominated them. In this case Debré's other measures for strengthening the executive against the legislature may assume more importance.

. . . .

A determined Prime Minister, as we have seen, need have little to fear from his President. The root of the problem is still his relations with Parliament. The heart of the constitution is the quest for a 'government made to govern'.

[1] De Gaulle chose the President, Léon Noël, who has been *maître de requêtes*, prefect, secretary-general of the Ministry of the Interior, ambassador to Poland, R.P.F. deputy, and member of the C.C.C.; Patin, ex-President of the criminal chamber of the *Cour de Cassation*, who is also President of the Safeguard Commission investigating abuses in Algeria; and Pompidou, a former *maître de requêtes* and a banker, who was director of de Gaulle's cabinet. Monnerville nominated Gilbert-Jules, Radical senator, ex-minister and ex-member of the C.C.C., a constitutional specialist; and two men who had served on the High Council of the Judiciary (respectively as M.R.P. and Socialist choices): Le Coq de Kerland, a lawyer, and Delépine, former *conseiller d'état*, *chef de cabinet* to Auriol, and technical counsellor in government departments. Chaban-Delmas chose Michard-Pélissier, a lawyer, former technical counsellor and pre-war deputy; Chatenay, an R.P.F. deputy and ex-senator who had legal training; and Pasteur Vallery-Radot, a distinguished professor of medicine and former R.P.F. deputy. Ex-Presidents Coty and Auriol serve *ex-officio*.

The brave affirmation that 'the government determines and guides the policy of the nation' was more than a pious hope; it was a call for a political revolution. Debré had a vision of a cabinet emerging from an election to enact its programme for its full term, safe from both President and Parliament.

There are many signs that Debré was looking enviously across the Channel. His government is even headed by a *Premier Ministre* instead of a *Président du Conseil*. Yet continuity is not won so readily in Paris as at Westminster. Accordingly Debré set out to put a succession of rules and procedures in place of the social homogeneity, the electoral system, and the party machines in Britain. This may amount to 'government by gimmick', but there is no clear alternative pending some realignment of social forces which may in time produce genuine stability. To achieve these purposes, the powers of members of Parliament must obviously be limited —as they are in Britain.

The most popular of Debré's measures to strengthen cabinets was the provision that members of Parliament must give up their seats within a month of taking office.[1] '*Une constitution, c'est aussi une morale,*' remarked Debré primly. He was convinced that ambition led deputies to overthrow the cabinet in the hope of gaining office in the next. Governmental stability would be improved, and unsavoury portfolio-grubbing suppressed, if a sure seat in Parliament had to be relinquished as the price of office.

Debré's general approach to the constitutional problem was to insist on a clear separation of the executive from the legislature, even at the risk of sharpening their antagonism. He also believed that banishing ministers from the Assembly was essential to restore its full independence. Recalling that in the early years of the Third Republic ministers who sat in Parliament did not vote (even when their abstention caused their own defeat), he cried 'What a fall in our morals since those days!'[2] Gaullist theory seems to put a minister who votes for himself in Parliament on a level with a card-sharper. In

[1] Other provisions which lay down incompatibilities between ministerial office and retaining outside interests confirm and extend Fourth Republic practice, and are similar to 'conflict of interest' rules in other countries. See p. 251.

[2] *R.F.S.P.*, p. 15.

de Gaulle's dictum, 'No one should be member of Parliament and minister at once—that is, judge and party, controller and controlled'.[1]

In a climate of anti-parliamentarianism this attempt to check the excesses of the System enjoyed a great demagogic success; many politicians, who privately thought it folly, dared not publicly attack the proposal. Yet it may well turn out a cure worse than the disease. If cabinet stability is not attained, it may soon become intolerable. Parliamentarians will hesitate to accept office if they know that in a few months they may be stranded with neither portfolio nor seat. And if recruitment of ministers from the two houses were to tend to dry up, so before long would recruitment of able men into Parliament.

State employees, who can revert to their former grade on leaving the government, suffer no such disincentives. De Gaulle and Debré have appointed many technician-ministers. Understandably the practice is unpopular with Parliament and may not last. If it does, the civil service and nationalized industries (and the armed forces) might suffer more political interference. Some ministries are already prone to factional disputes; choosing one civil servant rather than another for promotion to office might embitter them. Relations between the ex-minister, his new superior, and his former subordinates would be very delicate. Moreover, he might be identified with the policies he had supported, and his usefulness as a non-political public servant gravely compromised. It is strange that a regime which insists on a rigid separation of the executive from Parliament should blur the distinction between a neutral public service and the politicians. In any event, problems of political choice cannot be conjured away by handing them over to technicians. The belief that they can is one of the commonest political illusions; but it is surprising that it should survive in France, and among Gaullists, after the conclusive experience of Vichy.

Even if stable government is achieved, and parliamentary recruitment maintained, the advantages of the new system seem outweighed by its drawbacks. It may well deter those strange beings who (it is said) entered the race for portfolios

[1] Quoted by Léon Noël, *Notre Dernière Chance*, p. 184.

merely in order to be called *Monsieur le Ministre* for life. But few of them can have wielded enough parliamentary influence to threaten ministries. More important, members of an existing cabinet may now be more cautious about intriguing against it in the hope of higher office in the next combination. On the other hand, if the prospects for a new government seem bright, ambitious deputies may still be tempted to upset the present one in order to try their luck. And what is to become of the misfits, the sick, and the jaded? Incompetents were easily disposed of when cabinets fell every few months. But now, if they are dropped, they have no hope of returning to politics before the next election. They must be carried as passengers, thrown on the scrap heap, or found a cosy billet in the best Fourth Republic tradition.

If 'jobs for the boys' become accepted as an established practice (which seems the likeliest solution), ministers will not need to worry about their personal or family finances.[1] But surely this will not satisfy those of them who seek political influence. In the Fourth Republic, a defeated minister remained a powerful deputy; yet many a cabinet clung to office, bending to every parliamentary breeze, eschewing decisive actions or positive policies for fear these would endanger their survival. Fifth Republican ex-ministers will disappear without trace from the political scene, even if convenient cushions are provided to break their fall. Will cabinets so uncertain of their future be more resolute in face of parliamentary criticism, more courageous in taking decisions than their predecessors whose stake in survival was smaller?

On a technical level, at any rate, every effort has been made to strengthen their hand. The Assembly's teeth have been drawn. The constitution makes a root and branch attack on the '*impossible régime d'assemblée*', the traditional omnicompetent legislature suspicious of executive power. Parliament can now legislate on a limited range of subjects only, and has few opportunities of putting the government in jeopardy.

---

[1] In the first relevant case, M. Pelletier, a prefect who became de Gaulle's Minister of the Interior, was made French representative in Monaco on leaving office. See also below, p. 251.

The idea that certain matters are inherently 'executive' in nature, while others are the proper stuff of politics, is a favourite juridical notion. The constitution now defines a 'domain of the law' to which Parliament is restricted. Parliament may pass laws on every 'detail' of certain subjects, but is confined to the 'principles' of others.[1] The Assembly has no power to legislate on anything outside its domain, although it may debate or put questions.

Few innovations have been more resented. But the government has an impressive range of weapons against poachers. Its newly-acquired control of Parliament's *ordre du jour*, reinforced by the standing orders, should keep most bills which invade the executive domain off the agenda. If there is any question whether a bill or amendment is within the Assembly's domain, the government can ask for it to be ruled out of order. If that fails it may ask the Constitutional Council for a ruling, against which there is no appeal. If ever a cabinet proves craven or absent-minded about these prerogatives, the President of the Republic can consult the Constitutional Council. And if Parliament still slips somehow into forbidden territory, the government can amend the law by decree at any time in the future, provided the Constitutional Council agrees that the question is executive.

How restrictive these provisions will be depends on the Constitutional Council's interpretation of those vague terms detail and principle.[2] This breach of parliamentary sovereignty shocked many constitutional purists, but it made political sense. During the Fourth Republic Parliament had obstinately insisted on burying itself in trivia, often shirking the discussion of pressing national issues. M. Debré did not exaggerate in condemning

> . . . a Parliament overwhelmed with bills, galloping in disorder into the proliferation of interventions in points of detail, with

[1] For lists of subjects in each category see below, p. 238.
[2] The government may, by decree, modify laws voted during the Fourth Republic, after asking the *Conseil d'Etat* whether they cover executive questions. The *Conseil's* advice need not be followed. No duplication of its jurisdiction with that of the Constitutional Council is possible, but they might unhappily interpret detail and principle quite differently in parallel cases. And on the right to strike, or education, one man's detail is legitimately another man's principle.

a government dealing with the gravest international problems without parliamentary intervention.[1]

Continually clogged, the legislative machine was incapable of accommodating any government programme. Periodically the log-jam had to be exploded, the deputies abdicating to the government the power to legislate by decree.[2] Debré insisted that the Assembly put first things first by brutally seeing to it that the rest were nowhere. The immediate consequence has been to slacken the former torrent of private members' bills to a trickle.[3] The government can now monopolize the time of Parliament as effectively as in Britain. Yet Parliament is still competent to legislate on almost every question which caused serious controversy under the Fourth Republic.

The price is heavy. A whole range of activity is sealed off from the reach of legislators. They may argue or interrogate, but short of bringing the full weight of a motion of censure against the government there is no way by which Parliament can remedy an abuse of power by the executive. Yet the success of this attempt to erect a screen around the civil service hangs on the future of the whole bid for stable government. If cabinets become weak or transitory again, Parliament will possibly find some way to burst its bounds and wrest concessions from the government in matters where it cannot constitutionally intervene directly. Moreover, the provisions

[1] *R.F.S.P.*, p. 11.

[2] The constitution guards against a recurrence of this paralysis by providing that Parliament may delegate to the government the right to legislate by ordinance (subject to subsequent parliamentary ratification) for a stated period in matters assigned to the domain of the law.

[3] At the end of the Fourth Republic an average of 2,200 private members' bills per year were laid before the Assembly. There were only 211 during the first parliamentary year of the Fifth Republic. The fall has also come about because the old provision, that deputies cannot propose increases in expenditure or cuts in revenue, is now being enforced. The new rule applied to motions as well as bills, and was at first interpreted so severely that a motion for repressing prostitution was ruled out because it would require more police and therefore more expense. Pleven remarked that an attempt to abolish capital punishment would be disallowed because it cost more to jail prisoners than to execute them. The government agreed to limit the ban to motions *directly* intended to increase expenditure or reduce revenue. But the Constitutional Council disallowed all but procedural motions.

of the article defining the domain of the law 'may be clarified and completed (*précisées et complétées*) by an organic law'. While the Constitutional Council may prevent Parliament from exploiting the remarkable ambiguity of this phrase too exuberantly, once the Gaullist phase is over Parliament may well be able to widen its jurisdiction.

Even within its shrunken domain Parliament's power to harass the government is undermined. It now meets for less than six months in the autumn and spring, instead of eight or more.[1] Its procedure has been 'rationalized' to the point where critics allege that Parliament can be no more than a rubber stamp or a talking shop. Lest Parliament try to regain its former privileges, most of this 'rationalization' is firmly embedded in the constitution itself, rather than in the assemblies' standing orders where it more readily belongs. Yet if Debré's first thought is to protect the government, his second is to give Parliament the chance to work efficiently at last. These two aims are expressed in a series of changes which reverse the Fourth Republic's systematic discrimination against the government—bringing to the Palais Bourbon procedures which have been accepted at Westminster for decades.

Only now has the government won the right to decide the agenda of Parliament. Formerly it had to take its chance in a Conference of Presidents where, despite a theoretical majority, it might be outvoted. Government bills might vanish without trace, suppressed by partisan committees or simply kept from the agenda. Responsibility in the Fifth Republic falls directly on the government. Fourth Republic governments, while publicly blaming Parliament, were sometimes privately glad to let it bury bills which pressure groups had imposed on them. Now the government controls the date when its bills shall come up for discussion, and the committee to which they shall be referred.

The revolution in the committee system is much the most important change in parliamentary organization. The old Assembly had a ramshackle system of nineteen specialist committees. Some had so little to do that they turned to multiplying insignificant bills to justify their existence.

[1] See below, p. 253.

141

Others were bridgeheads of important interest groups, which could easily block measures which displeased them. Debré would have preferred to sweep away the specialist committees and set up four non-specialized permanent committees in the British tradition. Finally the constitution limited the number of committees to six. Their composition is so broad that no single interest can dominate them.

The government can choose whether its bill will be sent to a standing committee or to an *ad hoc* committee. The latter is likely to be used for bills which overlap the spheres of several standing committees. Special committees, numbering thirty members, are far more efficient working bodies than the standing committees, which suffer from the Assembly's traditionalist insistence on assigning every member to a committee. They have swollen into monstrously unwieldy sub-Parliaments of from 60 to 120 members which cannot work effectively.[1] Standing orders do not allow the creation of sub-committees, but they let the committees decide their own working methods. At once 'working groups' sprang up, with fields of interest corresponding roughly to the old specialist committees.[2] However, their recommendations are at present scrutinized by the full committee, on which other interests have their say.

Large committees may thus dilute the pressure groups which so often dominated their smaller predecessors. In any case, shorn of their powers, they are less dangerous to the government. Today the minister responsible for a bill may rise to introduce it. In the Fourth Republic a *rapporteur* opened the debate on the bill—presented in the form adopted by his committee. Often it had been mangled beyond all recognition. The government only rarely risked the unpopularity of insisting on a return to its original text. If it wanted to repair

[1] The committees are Finance, Foreign Affairs, Defence, Legislation, Social Affairs, and Production. See also pp. 156 and 253–4.

[2] The Production Committee alone appointed eighteen advisory *rapporteurs* for the 1960 budget. Nearly all their subjects corresponded to those of committees or sub-committees in the Fourth Republic. Agriculture was reported on by two former Vice-Presidents of the old Agriculture Committee, and Building by a former President of the old Housing and Reconstruction Committee (*J. O.*, 4 November 1959, p. 2184).

the damage it had to call on a friendly deputy to move its amendments; now ministers may move their own. They can also block those proposed from the floor which have not been through committee. This should put an end to the extemporized suggestions from the floor (which used to make debates so confused and fruitless) while safeguarding the government from surprise attacks.[1] None of these privileges is unreasonable. Much more dubious is the new provision allowing ministers to demand in one single sweeping vote the rejection of every amendment they dislike.

The government has even stronger powers over the budget. Budget debates were an annual guerilla under the Fourth Republic, often destroying a government and resulting in mangled and dismembered legislation. Now the government has special procedural advantages. It can stop all proposals by members of Parliament to cut taxes or to increase expenditure. (They had all but lost this right under earlier legislation, while a proposal for its final suppression was among the reforms accepted by the tottering Pflimlin government.) But deputies could often force the government to introduce the changes they were unable to propose directly, by repeatedly adjourning the vote on sections of the budget, or rejecting them altogether, and so forcing the government to its knees.[2] Now, if the budget bill has not received its first reading after forty days it goes automatically to the Senate. The Senate must vote on the first reading within two weeks, otherwise the bill returns to the Assembly for accelerated discussion. If the two houses cannot agree, or try to obstruct to a point where the final vote has not been taken in seventy days, the government has the trump card. It can impose the budget by decree.

It has one more weapon, even more draconian: the question of confidence. If a bill gets into difficulties it may make its adoption an issue of confidence. The Assembly must then take up the challenge. The bill is carried automatically unless the opposition can muster one-tenth of the deputies within

[1] But see below, p. 155.
[2] The Finance and Social Affairs Committees both rejected the Ex-Servicemen's budget for 1960 (see below, p. 144 n.). But rejection in committee is now simply a political demonstration, which does not prevent the government bringing the budget before the Assembly.

twenty-four hours to sign a motion of censure, and can then get an absolute majority to vote it. Only votes for the censure motion are counted. All the outside world will learn is that there were, say, 250 hostile votes—less than the requisite majority. No one will know how many members would have voted for the government, and how many would have abstained. But if nearly half the members vote a censure motion, will any government have the audacity to promulgate a law which Parliament would have rejected?[1]

Once through the Assembly bills go to the Senate. The second chamber has regained its pre-war title, and with it much of its Third Republic status and privilege. Its President is now the third personage in the State, ranking only after the President of the Republic and the Prime Minister. He nominates one-third of the Constitutional Council, and is consulted about the introduction of emergency powers on equal terms with his colleague of the Assembly. If the President of the Republic becomes incapacitated the President of the Senate temporarily takes his place. (Formerly he was replaced by the President of the National Assembly.) Eventually the chair of the Senate may again be the natural stepping-stone to the Elysée. The strengthening of the Senate might seem strange in a constitution which hopes for dynamic yet stable government; between the wars the Senate was both a scourge of governments and the very symbol of dreary conservatism. Debré explained this with commendable candour: 'If there was the possibility of producing a clear and constant majority [in the Assembly] there would be no need to provide a Senate whose chief role is to support, when necessary, a government against too encroaching an Assembly.'[2]

Its most significant power lies in constitutional revision. Here it is a trifle more than the Assembly's equal. Proposals

---

[1] They may. This dubious clause was foisted on Debré by the Fourth Republican leaders in the de Gaulle government. They were perhaps justified by the first vote of censure. Debré had demanded a vote of confidence on the 1960 budget, because the Assembly was almost unanimous in condemning his refusal to restore ex-service bonuses. The government survived, and passed the budget, because the Left's censure motion was drafted to ensure failure (it alienated the Right by approving de Gaulle's Algerian policy).   [2] *R.F.S.P.*, p. 17.

from either Parliament or the government must be adopted in identical terms by both houses. (Thus the Senate has complete power to block all constitutional change. Not only does the Assembly lose its customary last word, but the Senate is immune from the threat of dissolution.) Thereafter, unless the President of the Republic lets the proposals go to referendum, the final decision is made by a Congress of both houses, at which a three-fifths majority is necessary.[1] Debré obviously hoped that, with the improvement in its status and its traditional conservatism, the upper house would become, with the President and Constitutional Council, a bulwark against popular revisionist zeal. Although the Senate has as much reason as the Assembly to attack the eviction of ministers from Parliament, widen the domain of the law, and dismantle some of the government's defences against Parliament, it will be sensitive to any tampering with the presidential electorate, which is so close to its own, and it will obviously be hostile to any attempt to diminish its own privileges.

Even so, the new Senate by no means enjoys the power of its Third Republican namesake. It can overthrow no governments.[2] If ever a left-wing government backed by the Assembly comes to power, it should have none of the difficulties

[1] The drafting of the relevant article is more than usually inept. It grants initiative of a revision concurrently to Parliament, and to 'the President of the Republic on the proposal of the Prime Minister'. This is apparently a clumsy means of associating the President with revision. It plainly does not grant him a veto over governmental initiatives, since ministers could still call on a member of Parliament to help them. It specifies no way in which a presidential bill could be brought before Parliament. By implication only, the amending bill is debated under normal legislative procedure, including the use of conference committees and the exceptional procedure for forcing bills through without a majority. No procedure is laid down for the Congress of the two houses. By accident or design only government proposals may be submitted to such a Congress; bills originating in Parliament must be sent to referendum. A provision that the constitution may not be amended when the 'integrity of the territory is impaired' might be termed a 1958 clause, replacing the Fourth Republic's '1940 clause' forbidding revision during occupation by *foreign* troops.

[2] This point is slightly doubtful. Article 20 of the constitution says that the government is responsible to 'Parliament' but refers explicitly to Articles 49 and 50 which deal only with responsibility to the Assembly. Article 49 lets the Prime Minister demand the Assembly's approval of a declaration of general policy without binding him to resign if it is rejected. It was probably intended to allow governments to seek the

with the Senate which frustrated Léon Blum in 1937. The upper house may delay, but it cannot sabotage. It can thwart the Assembly but not the government.

This explains the intricate procedure for resolving differences between the two houses. If they adopt different versions of a bill, the government may call a conference committee drawn equally from both chambers. This immediately gives it the right to consign any bill it opposes to limbo, simply by refusing to call the committee. Similarly it can pigeonhole the committee's findings if they are not acceptable. If the committee does not agree on a compromise reading of the bill, then after a further reading in each house the government may (but need not) let the Assembly have the last word.[1] Thus the government not only keeps the whip hand throughout, it can use support in either house to defeat a hostile majority in the other.

There are only two ways in which the Assembly can force the government from office (except by challenging it during the discussion of a bill in the complicated way already described). The 'normal' procedure is just as complicated and even more limited. The Assembly may move a motion of censure on its own initiative. However, deputies are limited to a single motion in any session. Even this modest ration is hard to claim in the present Assembly. The bizarre consequence of the electoral system is that no opposition group can alone muster the requisite fifty-six signatures. However, once made the challenge must be faced. Under the Fourth Republic censure motions might be treated with contempt or adjourned *sine die*. Now they must be debated within three sitting days.[2]

support of the Senate, as Mollet did (with doubtful constitutionality) at the time of Suez. It is not explicitly ruled out that a government would resign on an adverse vote, but it is probably still 'un-Republican' to ask for a vote which might be refused.

[1] The conference committee can be convoked only after the bill has been read twice (once if the government declares it urgent) in both houses without a common text being agreed. When the committee's proposals are under discussion amendments may be proposed only if the government agrees.

[2] A censure motion cannot be withdrawn once the debate has opened. Otherwise the same group of members could enforce prompt debates on a series of motions, reserving the vote for the last of the session or the occasion when the government was weakest.

There is one simple means of ousting the government. This is to reject a statement of its policy by a simple majority. It seems generally assumed that these statements will normally be made when a cabinet is first formed. But nothing limits them to such occasions. Debré made one in October 1959, as a means of obtaining parliamentary endorsement for the new policy for Algeria. Even though it is the government which decides whether there shall be a vote, there is no certainty that such declarations will not sometimes prove fatal.[1]

Throughout the debate on the Assembly's standing orders Debré was adamant that these three ways of attacking the government should not be supplemented. There must be no chance of an 'indicative' vote, no hostile motions; every loophole must be closed. His success is still uncertain. The constitution-makers optimistically assume that governments will not be foolish enough to expose themselves to defeat by a simple majority. They assume that it will be much harder to muster a majority for a vote of censure, although this is far from sure.[2] Stability may be harder to achieve than they thought.

The 1946 constitution also demanded an absolute majority for the overthrow of governments. Yet only six of the twenty Fourth Republic governments fell in such a way. The rest went down without formal defeat or on a minority vote. They resigned because their position had become politically impossible, not because it was constitutionally untenable. Once they had been put in a minority the game was up; the Assembly could hamstring every move. Many of the new rules are aimed at allowing governments which find themselves

[1] In making a statement of general rather than Algerian policy, Debré increased the risks by acting with scrupulous constitutionality. His adversaries hoped that the Left would vote against the government's economic policies, and therefore 'plotted' to add to the opposition a large dissident integrationist fraction of the U.N.R., in order to undermine a government they still could not hope to overthrow.

[2] Only the total vote cast against the government is published. Thus absentees and abstainers are in effect reckoned as voting for the government. Hitherto a deputy, afraid of losing votes by supporting the government yet reluctant to turn it out, could take refuge in a friendly abstention. Now he may feel he must protect himself by a hostile vote.

in such a position to cling to office. But a prime minister of the Third or Fourth Republics who hoped to hold office again would not wantonly offend the deputies by trying to stay in power after they had indicated that he had outstayed his welcome. Not merely was his armoury inadequate; in the long-term interests of his career, he dared not use even the weapons he had. If this outlook persists, restocking the armoury will make little difference. For governments to stay in office there must be a change in political attitudes as well as in the rules.

.   .   .   .

In the long term only the emergence of a coherent majority party or coalition can create stability. If the elements which form and support governments are as fissiparous and incompatible as in the past the improvement may be remarkably small. No constitution can keep a cabinet from collapsing from its internal dissensions. Nothing can preserve a divided government from masterly inactivity. If the Fifth Republic could only replace unstable *immobilisme* by immobile stability the gain would be small indeed. The improvement in the efficiency of the administration would be welcome—but France also needs dynamic policies. Next to the struggle for simple survival, the search for a true majority is among the Republic's gravest challenges.

Debré's campaign against the Assembly is often dismissed as nothing but a punitive expedition. What, after all, is a Parliament which almost never overthrows a government, which rejects no bills, and carries no amendments against the government, and where private members have little chance of legislating? In spirit the constitution certainly spells the demise of traditional French parliamentarianism—but not of Parliament. Debré set himself a second, more difficult task: the renaissance of a Parliament capable of making a positive contribution to political life.

Some of this desire to encourage a new tradition is evident in the constitution itself. In its zeal for dignity it has a vaguely puritanical air. Ministers are banished from the assemblies, a healthy cure—it was hoped—for ambition. Members are forbidden to read their speeches, and are summoned to attend diligently on pain of losing part of their salary.[1] They must vote in person. The old practice of confiding a voting card to the party *boîtier* (which could lead to six men casting the votes of six hundred) is now abolished. Debré was under the astonishing illusion that the House of Commons votes infrequently, and his intention was to ensure that 'a vote is as serious a matter for a parliamentarian as it is for a minister to put his signature to a decree'.[2]

Other modifications are in the same spirit. If the government fails to respect Parliament by putting down its budget in due time, the Assembly is permitted to remain in session longer. If the opposition can muster the signatures for a vote of censure, the government is obliged to find the time to face the challenge. The reforms of the work of both chambers offer Parliament a genuine chance to escape from its former impotent confusion.

The strengthening of the position of the President of the Assembly (against strong C.C.C. opposition) is clearly intended to raise the Assembly's status. He is elected for the duration of the legislature, so that he need not fear that unpopular rulings on the new standing orders might lead to his defeat in an annual contest. In matters of internal discipline and in the arrangement of business (such as 'organized' debates), he acquires on paper the role of leadership for which Léon Blum appealed forty years ago. The change has been justified by appeal to the British example. But Mr. Speaker wields wide authority only because the traditions of his office impose rigorous political impartiality. No such tradition prevails in France; the President of the Assembly remains a politician with a career ahead of him. Chaban-Delmas has continued to take an active part in the U.N.R.'s internal politics. It remains doubtful whether the chair's new authority can be sustained without a change in this respect.

Debré himself set great store on the weekly sitting at which members' questions take priority over government business. (Questions are short discussions midway between a question at Westminster and an adjournment debate.) In this cautious

---

[1] This was interpreted so rigidly that 'fines' were inflicted on members who were in their departments to receive President de Gaulle, and on Mollet when he went to Israel on an official mission. In reaction against these excesses it quickly became a near dead-letter. See below, pp. 154n. and 254.　　　　[2] *J.O.*, 27 May 1959, p. 559.

imitation of House of Commons practice Debré saw 'the decisive mark of the parliamentary regime, and of the recognition of the rights of the opposition within it'.[1]

The eventual balance of power between government and Parliament is quite uncertain. Theoretically the cabinet is bound to emerge stronger than it was (or is). After surveying the succession of innovations intended to protect governments, it is hard to believe that they can ever again be as impotent and transitory as their predecessors. And yet the attempt to construct a truly independent governmental power runs counter to the entire democratic tradition in France. It is also undermined by the deep divisions within the electorate. So long as these persist, bringing divided Parliaments and coalition cabinets as their consequence, it is difficult to see how governments can be as stable and forceful as Debré hoped, for all their new prerogatives.

There is only one sound maxim about French constitutions: they invariably confound their authors—and their critics. From the beginning the distribution of power between the various organs of the Fifth Republic has differed appreciably from the pattern Debré envisaged in his proposals for a régime parlementaire. So long as de Gaulle is at the Elysée, the present ascendancy of the President over cabinet and Parliament will probably endure. (While his term might end at any moment, he could well survive to be re-elected.) No future occupant of the Elysée can hope to hold the same position. Although future Presidents will exercise more power than their predecessors, just how much of his strength the General can transmit to them is one of the constitution's enigmas.

Even now the social, economic and religious realignments which might close the political divisions may be under way, but the emergence of anything approaching a coherent majority party is unlikely to be rapid. While these differences remain, the success of the present experiment must be in doubt. Yet almost every possibility remains open—even the régime parlementaire. The final balance may well not be exactly what Debré intended. What it will be no one can tell. The only conclusion the commentator can prudently reach is Sir Winston Churchill's: 'The future is veiled in obscurity.'

[1] *R.F.S.P.*, p. 27.

8

The New System

Gaullist criticism of the Fourth Republic was directed against the System in general even more than against specific policies. Debré charged the 'princes who rule us' with dividing the country, with diverting attention from real problems to false ones, and with a passion for conservatism. 'Our princes, some quite deliberately, others blindly and uncomprehendingly, vigilantly maintain this division, this diversion, this conservatism. Usually they claim to be the victims of tendencies which they denounce while attentively protecting them.'[1] Their selfish and egotistical disputes had reduced Parliament to an arena for disorderly factional squabbles. Government was paralysed by a bad constitution and internal quarrels; 'no one can say precisely where the government of France is'.[1] Pressure groups had excessive influence. 'The parties are thus the representatives, not of the nation at the service of the State, but of fractions of the nation within the State.'[1] Weak ministers, never daring to risk any real reforms, were always tempted to leave uncomfortable problems to their successors. 'Our princes have adopted a system which camouflages responsibility as much as possible';[1] much energy was spent on trying to conceal it, transfer it, or evade it.

The new regime would change all that. It was mere evasion and special pleading to blame the ordinary citizen for the faults of government. The irresponsibility and selfishness of the 'princes' had left both average Frenchmen and potential national leaders disgusted with public life. New institutions, designed to encourage men of authority and character, new leaders, genuinely anxious for the public good, would call forth an instant response from the nation, and revolutionize the tone and mood of politics.[1] These were the hopes held out by the critics. Yet neither in the working of Parliament, nor

[1] *Ces Princes qui nous gouvernent*, pp. 20, 27, 29, 37, 196.

in the organization and functioning of the executive, nor in the government's relations with the interest groups in society have these promises been fulfilled.

Debré was genuinely anxious to organize a constructive 'collaboration of the powers' between executive and legislature. 'What we must avoid', he said, 'is disequilibrium. There are two sorts: arbitrary government, and the crushing of the government by the omnicompetence of the assemblies.'[1] If his constitution works as it stands on paper the first danger is undoubtedly the greater. Unbalance can be avoided only if the government willingly defers to the Assembly. Such a relationship would demand profound readjustments from both sides, for co-operation cannot be instituted by constitutional fiat. Since the government had conceived the constitution and held the whip hand, the initiative had to be Gaullist. But Parliament too had to reconcile itself to a new role— less influential though not necessarily less useful. Finding such a role should have been the first task of the new institutions.

The problem was to devise a procedure enabling Parliament to criticize without dominating the government. At least cabinets would be free from continuous legislative interference now that the new monster committees could no longer exercise effective control (especially since ministers could at will remove a bill from their competence). But governments had really been feeble because majorities were incoherent. The deputies could upset the cabinet at any time, and all procedural attempts to restrain them proved vain. Ministers found their credit exhausted by repeated minor setbacks, and were harried into resignations which were not constitutionally obligatory. Both de Gaulle and Debré were determined that the new standing orders must prevent any revival of these practices.

They met strong resistance. Parliament's one weapon, the motion of censure, was so unwieldy that no single opposition party could use it.[2] Moreover, many responsible members wanted some less drastic means of impressing their views on the government (and the country)—a demand which Debré did not contest in theory, but refused in practice because of the need to break the bad habits of the past. The U.N.R. alone supported him. When the provisional standing orders were

[1] *J.O.*, 27 May 1959, p. 558. [2] See above, p. 146.

debated in January, they blocked several attempts to rein-
troduce interpellations and unofficial confidence votes by the
back door. But the constitution gives 'questions' priority on
Fridays. A Conservative member persuaded the Assembly to
permit 'oral questions with debate', and then—on a Communist motion—it adopted a standing order (copied from the
Senate rules) which allowed them to be followed by a vote.

Violent controversy raged round these decisions when they
came up for final approval in the summer. The U.N.R. warned
that the 'Friday guerilla' would once again allow members to
straddle the fence between majority and opposition, and to
harass ministers into resignation while evading responsibility
for their actions. Debré claimed that he was pleading for his
successors: 'in ten years M. Mollet will thank me'. Mollet
answered that when his friends came to power they would at
once change the rules. Left and Right alike warned against
closing every safety-valve for members' discontent; protested
against reducing Parliament to 'a democratic umbrella covering the reality of bureaucratic dictatorship'; and pointed out
that it was Debré himself who in the Fourth Republic had
made the 'oral question' a dangerous parliamentary weapon.
Nevertheless the deputies, who feared an adverse ruling from
the Constitutional Council, were induced to accept a compromise (so ingenious that both sides thought it a victory).

The senators were less amenable. They were not entitled
even to censure the government; besides, their benches were
full of newly-elected Fourth Republican leaders. Refusing the
slightest concession, they insisted on their right to vote resolutions criticizing the cabinet. Debré retaliated by forbidding his ministers to appear before them.[1] The new relationship between government and Parliament could hardly have
got off to a worse start.

At the very same moment both houses were behaving—
imprudently enough—in a way which justified all the government's fears. The Senate passed by 210 to 0 a resolution
demanding the full restoration of the ex-service bonus, lately

---

[1] Two, MM. Berthoin (Interior) and Houdet (Agriculture) had just
been re-elected senators. They had been expected to prefer office to
Parliament, but in fact resigned their ministerial posts, partly for
reasons of health.

withdrawn. The Assembly was asked to pronounce on the ownership of the Polish Library in Paris; the motion, two years old, was exhumed because the courts were about to decide the case. The anti-Communist demagogy of Bidault and Pleven easily swept aside the feeble resistance of the U.N.R. and the Minister, Frey, and a resolution which plainly sought to deflect the course of justice was voted by 467 to 10.[1] These instances of irresponsibility may perhaps have affected the verdict of the Constitutional Council, which (allegedly by a narrow majority) accepted the most restrictive possible view of Parliament's rights. The senators raged impotently. Neither house could now vote to criticize the government, except by passing a vote of censure, or rejecting a motion of confidence demanded by it.

During these months there were bitter complaints that the government was ignoring and neglecting its parliamentary supporters. Meetings between ministers and the leaders of the majority parties did little to appease the discontent, which was vigorously expressed in the Conservative and M.R.P. ranks. U.N.R. members were no less dissatisfied, but were more inhibited about complaining publicly. For while their rivals could freely denounce the lowly status of Parliament, they were obliged to proclaim the superiority of the new regime. Critics maintained that difficult problems—such as church schools or wage claims—were dealt with, just as in the past, by postponement. But the government and the U.N.R. could point to a good deal of useful secondary legislation passed through an Assembly which certainly wasted far less time purposelessly than in the Fourth Republic.

Apologists dilated freely on the efficiency and dignity of the 'new-style Parliament'. But these virtues were less apparent to outsiders. Attendance was as bad as ever; but since voting was the criterion, formal votes were avoided when many members were absent.[2] Standing orders continued to be

[1] The deputies were in good company. See below, p. 162n.

[2] A division taken at random, on Article 16 of the 1960 Budget Bill, shows how little has changed. The voting was: For the Article 200; Against 62; Abstentions 131; 'Did not take part in the vote' 110; Absent 47; Proxies 94; Excused 29. Of the last two groups 27 were engaged at international assemblies and on government missions, 12 had a 'grave family event', and 84 were 'ill'. *J.O.*, 9 November 1959, pp. 2325–6. But attendance in the Senate has improved.

evaded or flouted when inconvenient.[1] In the amnesty debate in July 1959, right-wing extremists like Le Pen and Biaggi extended the scope of the bill to cover 'patriotic' crimes; their amendments from the floor, without reference to the committee, caused complete chaos until the Minister reluctantly had them ruled out of order. Before some of the most important debates, committee reports were distributed too late to be assimilated. The government itself sent the 1960 budget to the Assembly two weeks late.[2] Confusion in minor matters had never been worse.[3]

On the score of dignity matters were little better. Demagogy was as rife as ever, though not as effective. Of the first 150 bills proposed, nearly two-thirds were out of order.[4] During the budget debate a tax on 'automatic games' was rejected almost unanimously on a show of hands. When a bill for increasing certain life annuities was under discussion, the Finance Committee refused to invoke Article 40 (preventing new expenditure) against it as the government

[1] Thus Chaban-Delmas connived at a vote after the session was closed: see above, pp. 116, 129.

[2] The government laid the budget by instalments. There was dispute whether the first instalment or the last counted for reckoning the seventy (calendar) days allowed for discussion by the constitution. The constitution and the organic law on budget procedure were in contradiction. Moreover, less than seventy days of the session remained, and although the constitution provides that if the budget is laid late the Assembly still has its full seventy days, it also states categorically that the session ends on the third Friday in December. This apparently confronted the government with the dilemma of calling a special session or waiting until the next session in the spring to vote the budget. It took the former course. Both houses protested because the government made them sit right through the weekends, and used its control of the agenda to take a large slice of the seventy days for other business. See also Epilogue.

[3] During the standing orders debate, André Marie (a right-wing Radical ex-premier) complained that no one not represented on the Presidents' Conference had been told the proposal on which they were voting. Early in the new session M.R.P.'s chairman (Bosson) protested that the government had put an important bill on the agenda without distributing the text to members. For the first major debate, standing orders had to be specially modified; the government wanted a foreign affairs discussion in which all points of view could be expressed, but the drafters, in their restrictive zeal, had permitted only one member to reply to a declaration of government policy.

[4] *J.O.*, 27 May 1959, pp. 600–1. Of 151 bills, only 58 (including government bills) were in order.

demanded. Socialist, Conservative and U.N.R. deputies approved the Committee's stand.

The debate on fiscal reform displayed as much demagogy, confusion and disorder as the Fourth Republic had ever shown. An amendment favouring agriculture was supported by spokesmen for the peasantry and the Production Committee, opposed by the government and the *rapporteur-général*—and carried by 443 to 27. Town and country, expanding and declining areas, engaged in a classic wrangle over local taxes. The Assembly voted by 296 votes to 120 to amend an article it had previously suppressed. 'An extraordinary agitation seized the deputies.' The losers demanded a vote on a previous amendment which had been abandoned (but not technically withdrawn). A member attempted to speak, 'but the uproar was such that he could not make himself heard'. The President warned the Assembly that he would suspend the sitting if the disorder continued; and as it took no notice of this warning, he left the chair.[1]

Petty-mindedness was more widespread than before. No Fourth Republican politician would have demanded the punishment of a *chansonnier* for treating deputies as ridiculous (he would have realized that he was merely proving the *chansonnier*'s point). Intolerance was far worse. In the past Communists had been kept from key posts (committee chairs and some defence functions). Now it was carefully arranged that they (but no one else) should be kept off all committees. And a Centre leader (M. Claudius Petit) brought protests from the U.N.R. by suggesting that a parliamentarian should defend 'everyone's liberty, and our opponents' first of all'.

Shouting opponents down had not—despite the popular myth—been common in the old Parliament. When it did occur, the Communists were almost always the aggressors or the victims. Now that they were reduced from a large party to a tiny group of ten, to stop them speaking became less excusable—and more common. The habit spread. In the Algerian debate in June the victims included the Socialist spokesmen Mollet and Leenhardt, and the young M.R.P. deputy Lambert (who had been decorated in Algeria). Colonel Thomazo's contribution to the dignity of the new Parliament

[1] *Le Monde*, 30 October 1959.

was an attempt to deny 'soldier Lambert's' right to discuss the problem. Appeals by Mollet and Debré were disregarded.

Intolerance was common in the Assembly. Ministers were attacked for laxity towards the 'treasonous press', and influential deputies proposed hard labour for anyone in France (including foreigners) who demoralized the army by criticizing the French cause.[1] Yet this illiberal house had not the courage of its reactionary convictions. For when de Gaulle promised self-determination to Algeria, the members who had refused to allow Lambert to pronounce the word four months before gave their approval by 441 to 23—a vote notoriously reflecting not their views, but their awareness of the General's popularity.

One surprise of the new regime was the Senate. Many front-rank political leaders, defeated in the November election, found refuge—and revenge—in the upper house. For the first time since the war the senators were equal or superior to the deputies in political talent. Where the latter seemed unable to find questions to raise or bills to introduce which were at once in order and genuinely important, the former were more skilful and effective in working the new system. They were also, since far more of them belonged to the official opposition, more openly critical of the government (though sometimes their hostility took the form of mere sulkiness). The Senate had often been obstructive and unimaginative in the past, and it remained a stronghold of the despised politicians of the Fourth Republic. But in decorum in debate and tolerance towards minorities it set a useful example to the renovators of the Assembly.

The new constitution has not doomed Parliament to frustration and futility. But circumstances have so far conspired against it: the unrepresentative political composition

[1] The 'tendentious presentation of a true fact' was to be considered culpable. Editors, managers, directors, printers and distributors were to be equally liable for journalistic matter 'of a kind to threaten the morale, unity, discipline, hierarchy of the army or to cast doubt on the legitimacy of the cause it serves by order of the government'. Among the men to whom the army's morale, etc., seemed so fragile were Biaggi, Béraudier (formerly Soustelle's *chef de cabinet*) and La Malène (formerly Debré's). It therefore seems unlikely that their bill (which was not debated) was directed—as it might seem on the face of it—against the leaders of the 13 May.

of the Assembly, the low proportion of experienced members, the dominance of dynamic but aggressive and intolerant extremists, and the personality of the Prime Minister. Debré was honest and well-intentioned, and in opposition he had been a formidable critic. But he was a fighter, not a conciliator. Despising ministers who gave way to pressure, he was perhaps too ready to reject advice, even from well-wishers. The leader of his own party warned him when Parliament first met: 'Equilibrium would be broken if the notions of governmental responsibility and, consequentially, parliamentary control were not as loyally respected as the independence and the authority of the executive . . . the people [would] condemn an impotent Assembly as scornfully as the former omnipotent one. [Applause.] Our young Republic will march neither straight nor far if one of its legs is shorter than the other.'[1]

The Prime Minister did not heed the warning. He was haunted by fears of a return of past abuses, and determined to check any parliamentary encroachment; but he lacked the skill to coax members into the more constructive activity he would genuinely have welcomed. His position was desperately difficult, for he took responsibility for policies he had not chosen and sometimes manifestly disliked. But his tactlessness sometimes annoyed Parliament unnecessarily, and he rarely won its ear.

A more flexible personality might have smoothed over the minor irritations which Debré only inflamed. But any first Parliament of the Fifth Republic would have found difficulty in accepting its diminished status. The interests of the Right, the doctrine of the Left, and the *esprit de corps* of the whole body led deputies to press for more effective powers of criticism. Though U.N.R. members resisted these demands, their public discipline did not overcome—indeed perhaps exacerbated—their private discontent. Debates on major problems in the Assembly of the Fifth Republic were hardly more frequent or more frank than in the Fourth, and were less representative of opinion in the country. Politicians who still seemed unable to attract public respect by raising the great questions and discussing them freely, had now suffered even

[1] Terrenoire, *J.O.*, 15 January 1959, p. 36.

in their secondary function of channelling the private grievances of their constituents. For a government less dependent on them paid less attention to them, as pressure groups soon found and ordinary citizens more slowly discovered. The Assembly elected in November 1958, nominally devoted to de Gaulle but at heart opposed to his policies, was particularly bound to come into conflict with the government. The regime was still too precarious for any premier loyal to the General to risk concessions which would play into the hands of those right-wing critics with whom part of the army (though few of the people) sympathized. In the circumstances ministers were bound to be intransigent about the rights of Parliament, and members were bound to feel frustrated and discontented.

.   .   .   .

Friction and irritation between government and Parliament were thus inevitable. Compensation might however be hoped for in better harmony within the executive itself, and greater authority in its dealings with outside interests. The creation of an inviolable executive domain should have allowed the administration to work with none of the uncertainty which complicated its life under the Fourth Republic. Ministers have the time to master their departments; some were already experts. They should need to worry far less than their predecessors about political appeasement—or so the authors of the constitution assumed.

Debré's search for a new style of government set great store on routing the 'feudal powers', as he called the vested interests which 'divide the State and live on it with scarcely a thought for the nation or its citizens'.[1] He believed that they were part of the System itself, conspiring with the politicians to prolong *immobilisme* and social injustice. De Gaulle himself has never had patience with anything which troubles his mystical communion with his people, considering pressure groups and parties as unrepresentative and egotistical factions. In the early months both men seemed determined to govern without, and even against the pressure groups. Debré sounded the advance in splendidly Jacobin terms: 'In the

[1] *Ces Princes qui nous Gouvernent*, p. 50.

measure in which we wish to return to the flame of the Republicans of '89 or '48, to want, with a firm and united nation a State which takes orders from no source but universal suffrage, we are (let us realize) in contradiction with fifty bad years of French history in which, as in the eighteenth century, a series of intermediary forces cut off the people of the nation from the public authorities'.[1] From the beginning this bold declaration of the independence of the State was compromised by the regime's inability to control completely the strongest 'intermediary force' of all—the army.

However, both de Gaulle and Debré dealt more sternly with lesser forces. De Gaulle's reply to students' protests about the inadequacy of the 1959 education budget had a note of unparalleled imperiousness:

> I have no intention of allowing the President of the French National Union of Students to come and talk to me about 'total bankruptcy' in this matter. The demonstrations in which the students are indulging are perhaps such as to enable them to deceive themselves about what is desirable in relation to what is possible. But that is not the slightest contribution to solving the problem.[2]

Several ministers, free at last of parliamentary interference, were determined to break the grip of the pressure groups. Organizations which had formerly been consulted about every shift in policy now learned of important decisions only through the newspapers. Even if they were given a hearing, their advice was often rejected uncompromisingly. Professor Debré (the Prime Minister's father) drafted a hospital reform which pleased the medical students but made no concessions to their outraged seniors. Michel Debré tried to set a pattern for the new regime by refusing to sacrifice a line of his judiciary reform to its many critics.

But the revolutionary ardour soon flagged. Although the Ministry of Finance has welcomed the chance to keep the groups at arm's length, other ministries have resumed their normal contacts with all the 'serious' interests. Such ministries as Agriculture, Industry and Commerce, and Labour

---

[1] U.N.R. *Bulletin de Presse*, no. 5, August 1959, p. 5.
[2] *Le Monde*, 14–15 December 1958.

were not easily won away from their established relations with the groups. They saw consultation as a mutually useful exercise, more necessary than ever when the role of Parliament was reduced. Though the ex-servicemen's associations were furious at the cabinet's pensions policy, the Minister's relations with them were as warm as ever—for M. Triboulet has shown a capacity for dissociating himself from his colleagues which would have been noteworthy even in the System.

There have indeed been moments worse than the Fourth Republic. For, after their energetic use of their transitional powers, the new rulers have proved surprisingly inefficient. Something is clearly amiss when ministers have to ask journalists what the next cabinet meeting will discuss,[1] and when the Minister for Ex-Servicemen confesses to Parliament that he learned through the newspapers that the Minister of Finance was ready to restore bonus cuts. These are not isolated instances of muddle and confusion. The Ministry of Armed Forces announced sweeping restrictions on deferments of military service. While there were many abuses under the existing system, the remedy not only caught dodgers, but threatened to wreck scientific and medical research and the graduate training programme. The regulations were apparently drawn up by experts in the Ministry of Armed Forces who did not consult the Ministry of Education. The outcry by the educational world—backed by its Ministry— resulted in a stream of explanations and 'correctives', and even an attempt to explain that the Ministry's circular was not meant as a binding instruction.[2]

Other sections of the government pursued contradictory or unrelated policies. While in Madagascar, de Gaulle indicated that three Malagasy deputies convicted of complicity in the 1947 rebellion, and subsequently assigned to residence in France, were now free to return to the island. One of them set off at once with the consent of the Ministry

---

[1] *Le Monde*, 23 July 1959.

[2] A reasonable compromise was found. Having won concessions, the Ministry—it is said—persuaded the students not to press their opposition because they might rouse the Assembly to pass a law restricting deferment more tightly. This threat to turn Parliament on a disgruntled pressure group must be without parallel.

of the Interior, only to be arrested at Djibouti and bundled back to France on the direction of the Prime Minister's office. Michelet, the liberal Minister of Justice, declared in the presence of the Israeli Ambassador that there would be no seizure of *La Gangrène*, a book describing alleged tortures of Algerian students. 'We're not under Bourgès-Maunoury now!' he exclaimed proudly. The book was seized that afternoon.[1] The investigation of the Mitterrand affair revealed that the traditional feuds between the *Sûreté Nationale* and the Paris Prefecture of Police were still intense. Even agreed policies might be advocated in quite contradictory ways. The Prime Minister once tried to drum up foreign support for Algerian policy by insisting that 'the world balance of forces' turned on Algeria (though he still claimed it as an exclusively internal matter), and by warning that criticism of France's action by her allies would lead to a collapse of N.A.T.O. and all the European institutions; meanwhile his Foreign Minister was publicly denying that there was any problem of disloyalty, and trying desperately to mend the broken fences.

Co-ordination and authority are poor because of the complicated way decisions are made. Responsibility for Community affairs lies partly with the President, partly with M. Janot, the Secretary-General for the Community, partly with M. Robert Lecourt, Minister of State for the Community (whose functions remain obscure). The old Ministry of Overseas France has been scattered into a dozen fragments in almost every other ministry. Similarly Algerian affairs were dealt with by de Gaulle, Debré, and at least seven other ministries and *bureaux*. Three distinct foreign offices serve the President, the Prime Minister and the Foreign Minister, while the former Secretary-General of the Quai d'Orsay, Louis

---

[1] Debré justified the seizure by calling the book 'a fabrication from beginning to end, put together by two members of the Communist party'; the defence lawyers tried to sue him for infringing his own new penal code by putting pressure on judges. Frey merely called the charges 'plainly false or exaggerated'. Neither tried to answer the detailed accusations, or rebut the abundant circumstantial evidence. The students' suit against the police was dismissed by the very examining magistrate who—they had alleged—had ignored their marks showing physical ill-treatment. But Michelet, at least, tried hard to have the case thoroughly investigated. (And see Epilogue).

Joxe, was brought into the government with ill-defined responsibilities in foreign affairs. The increased importance of the President and Prime Minister has led to an expansion of their staffs. Not content with co-ordinating and controlling, these experts tend to generate their own policies, exercising power without responsibility. Decisions are delayed even further, and uncertainty is deepened.

In minor matters too the regime has often been indecisive. One pressing reform was the award of a charter to the French radio (R.T.F.). While everyone except ministers in office had always agreed that R.T.F. should have a 'B.B.C.' status, every government had wanted to keep it as a political instrument. Soustelle promised action, and indeed introduced by ordinance something termed a charter. This granted much-needed financial and administrative autonomy, but confirmed the R.T.F.'s political subjection to the government. The unions opposed the continued political exploitation of R.T.F. and were indignant at the failure to provide guarantees for the staff. They were promised that these would follow rapidly. In June they wrote to de Gaulle to protest at the continued delay. In August they were on the verge of striking when Debré intervened. Having discovered that (despite the R.T.F.'s 'autonomy') the proposal had been pigeon-holed in the Ministry of Finance for two months, he promised that it would definitely be published by October. But the year ended with a strike instead of a *statut*.

On the other hand the energetic Minister of Construction, Pierre Sudreau, launched the first real attack in decades on the housing shortage. Plans were pushed forward to solve a problem which symbolized the impotence of the Fourth Republic, the gross inefficiency and congestion of the Paris Halles, on which was concentrated most of the nation's food marketing. An even distribution of food supplies was to be ensured through 'national' markets in the provinces. At least the costly and senseless routing of almost all produce through Paris would be eliminated, and middlemen's profits might be reduced—although this was expecting much of any regime.

There was a steady stream of useful if unspectacular legislation on adoption, colonial penal law, school and university building, vocational training, 'social' investment, hospitals and public health. The government also simplified the structure of the prefectoral corps and set about remedying its serious over-staffing. It gave more serious attention to research and technology. It even tackled the *bouilleurs de cru* —the private distillers whose fiscal frauds are legendary. There is no better indication of a cabinet's determination than its policy towards the *bouilleurs*. Mendès-France made an all-out attack on them in 1954, but the *bouilleurs'* lobby was powerful enough to prevent the law becoming operative. Now Debré proposed a modest but realistic solution: that the privilege of distilling a quantity of tax-free spirit should die with the holder.[1]

By Fourth Republic standards these were substantial achievements. Nevertheless they fell well short of the dynamic decision-making promised by opponents of the System, who had encouraged the belief that only the meaningless haggling of the parties, the venality or cowardice of the politicians, and the weakness of institutions stood in the way of dramatic progress. Before coming to power, Debré had maintained that the divisions of opinion, the attention to unreal problems and the conservatism of French society were mere by-products of self-seeking politicians trying to perpetuate their power at the country's expense, and of ill-organized institutions which drove able and honest men out of public life. Now new institutions were in place, and new men in power. Yet, to his intense irritation, his well-intentioned efforts were opposed and criticized. The country remained divided on social, economic, educational, foreign, colonial and constitutional questions, just as in the days of the System. 'False issues'— the schools problem or the ex-servicemen's bonus—plagued Debré no less than the 'princes' he had denounced. The deputies of the new System defended conservatism as staunchly as those of the old; they too wanted to be re-elected. The Gaullists were learning for themselves how intractable many of France's problems were, and how little room for manœuvre even a strong government commanded.

[1] The Assembly blocked it. See Epilogue.

9

'A Government which Governs'

There was little point in changing the country's institutions and rulers unless her policies were changed too. Even before the Algerian war diverted its attention (and resources) the Fourth Republic had been drifting gradually into *immobilisme.* Problem after problem was left unresolved because a solution would upset powerful interests, or because the Assembly was too sunk in cabinet crises and outmoded procedures to act. Many of the country's institutions were slowly corroding through the neglect of problems which were neither politically profitable nor desperately urgent. This unenviable burden of unfinished business passed to the Fifth Republic. To make up the arrears of years would take all the dynamism which the new regime claimed.

It was fortunate in having a golden chance in the four months which followed the promulgation of the constitution, in which the government held unlimited powers. This produced a cascade of some 300 ordinances and decrees, of which the scope and consequence are even now uncertain, but which collectively influence practically every aspect of French life. Without any reference to Parliament or the electorate, the government filled in the constitution's sketchy outline of the new institutions.[1] It used another series of ordinances to impose the 1959 budget and the Constantine Plan, and to attack the economic and financial crises. Such measures were obviously conceived under the new regime, but many others had been gathering dust for years in the ministries. The

[1] By this means the government decided almost all details of the institutions of the Community, the Economic and Social Council, the High Court of Justice, the High Council of the Judiciary, and the Constitutional Council. It laid down the electoral system for every office from President to local councillor, and settled many questions concerning the operation of Parliament, budget procedure, ministerial incompatibilities, and parliamentary salaries.

ordinance authorizing the construction of an aqueduct bringing Loire water to Paris may have ended a battle which began in 1931.

The range of these ordinances was strikingly wide. One stroke of the pen closed almost the whole Corsican railway system,[1] another reformed the Stock Exchange, a third modified hospital administration and the training of medical students, and a fourth sought to stop sharp practice among house-agents. Secondary measures introduced a new road-safety code and reformed the laws of adoption and child care, encouraged the co-ordination of urban local government and the decentralization of the Paris region, revised cinema subsidies, modified the conditions of service of state employees and of reservists, raised rents, introduced profit-sharing and closer association of labour and management, and extended unemployment insurance. There were fourteen ordinances dealing with building construction and landlord and tenant law. And these were only a few. A handful of ordinances were of major importance; they reformed the educational system, the administration of justice, the conditions of service of the judiciary, the code of criminal procedure, and the organization of national defence.

The educational reform is intended to encourage the production of more scientists and technicians, and to reduce the excessive emphasis on formal literary education. All children entering school after October 1959 will remain until they are 16 (in place of 14). An 'observation period' is created for children of 11 to 13, to help in allocating them to the most appropriate secondary schools. The syllabus for the *baccalauréat* is modified to put less emphasis on book-work and oral examinations and more on classroom teaching.

The defence reform tries to meet the problems of nuclear and subversive warfare. It provides for a sweeping reorganization of the armed services to fight the new-style wars, establishes the succession of political authority, and allows considerable decentralization of military and civil powers

[1] But the Corsican roads could not carry the burden. The closure was postponed after the islanders had threatened a general strike and the Minister had been besieged by all the many Corsicans in the Assembly from the Communists to Biaggi.

when communications break down. The government now has the power, in ill-defined circumstances, to declare a 'state of alert' without reference to Parliament. This gives it wide discretionary powers over persons and property, including the right to call a partial mobilization. (These were the powers that the government proposed to use against railway strikers in June 1959.) The reorganization of the central defence administration clearly establishes the Prime Minister's authority to lay down military policy, while allowing the Chief of the General Staff at the Ministry of National Defence (the highest military authority) a greater say in the formation of military and civil policy.

In reorganizing the administration of justice, Debré was reforming a structure which had changed little since 1790. The distribution of the civil courts had failed to keep pace with urbanization. Consequently, while many rural magistrates were under-employed, justice in the towns was painfully slow because the urban courts were overloaded. Debré set out to correct this by concentrating the civil courts in the more populous areas. Thus 3,000 *juges de paix* were replaced by only 455 *tribunaux d'instance* (dealing with minor cases and with a jurisdiction corresponding roughly to an *arrondissement*); and instead of 351 *tribunaux de première instance*, 172 *tribunaux de grande instance* deal with more important cases. The abolition of that familiar rural figure, the *juge de paix*, was a hard blow to the pride of the hundreds of small towns which now lost their tribunal. The location and duties of the higher courts were unchanged.

Another group of measures provided better pay, training and working conditions for judges, magistrates and public prosecutors. (The bench is not recruited from the bar in France.) Although these go far to remedy the steady decline in the attractiveness of the profession in recent years, they do not solve the problem of political interference with judges' promotion.[1]

The new criminal code was coolly received by the bar. Its defect was to open the door to even longer detention of a suspect by the police. But it reduced the danger of abuse by guaranteeing his right to medical examination, and providing

[1] See also below, p. 256.

a more effective form of appeal against detention before trial. Changes in trial procedure tended to speed justice and to favour the accused. The rules regarding judges' impartiality were tightened and the judges were no longer to discuss the *dossier* with the jury behind closed doors. The press was outraged by regulations enforcing stricter secrecy in inquiries conducted by investigating magistrates, and forbidding 'throwing discredit on a judgment' or making comments which might put pressure on judges and witnesses. Much press criticism derived from the fear of being deprived of lurid stories, and it was often overlooked that secrecy was intended to protect the accused. But there were dangers in limiting press criticism in a country where justice has been so painfully slow, and where the administration of justice has not invariably been above suspicion.

The breathtaking speed of these reforms had its price. Mollet has said that the cabinet was 'unable for lack of time and documentation to give proposals the thorough study they demanded'. Since one cabinet meeting dealt with fifty ordinances, this seems an understatement. Not surprisingly, some ordinances were ineptly drafted, imperfectly understood by the cabinet, or—despite their 'expert' origin—irrelevant, incomplete or unworkable.

Understandably they had a mixed reception. Some were inherently unpopular. But the government had only itself to blame when the public gave it little credit. Few ministers attempted to explain (even to the press) what they were doing and why, or to answer the spate of anxious questions the measures provoked. They even failed to introduce their ordinances with the customary explanatory *exposé des motifs*. The press was overwhelmed by the torrent of complicated and diverse legislation, which it was quite unable to communicate and explain to its readers. The public therefore had little idea of the government's achievements, and it did not much like the little it knew. The experience was alarming, less as a classic case of inept public relations than because

---

[1] Juries were to be drawn from wider sections of the population, and a full jury was now nine (sitting with three judges) instead of seven (with three judges). Eight votes instead of six were required for conviction.

it gave an impression of a government which acted arbitrarily, unconcerned whether the public either knew or accepted its policies.

Many minor problems were settled and some major ones attacked. The new regime achieved in weeks what would have taken the Fourth Republic years. Many of the secondary measures were valuable. But there was little sign of wider thinking about the really important and essential structural changes. Only a handful of ordinances—notably the introduction of profit-sharing—were distinctively Gaullist. In both its R.P.F. and U.N.R. phases Gaullism had often preferred to 'straddle' domestic issues in an attempt to appeal to both Right and Left. Ministers were now supplementing their own limited range of policies by turning to technicians for new ideas. But there was disturbing evidence that the Fourth Republic's *immobilisme* had constricted even the horizons of the technicians, for almost all the really important ordinances had been in the parliamentary pipeline in some form in May 1958.

.   .   .   .

The differing approach of the politicians and the technocrats was evident in the handling of the most pressing of all domestic problems—the search for economic stability. While the Fourth Republic bequeathed to de Gaulle an economic base firmer than was generally recognized, at its death it was pursuing a familiar financial rake's progess. Until de Gaulle's return, no one dared to admit the crypto-devaluation of 1957, which had been squandered fruitlessly. Inflation was mounting and the exchange reserves were inexorably dwindling. France seemed certain to break her pledges to the Common Market and need yet another injection of foreign aid— compromising still further her freedom of action. To cure the fever, de Gaulle chose as Minister of Finance the very symbol of unsentimental financial orthodoxy, Antoine Pinay. He was advised by a group of liberal economists headed by Rueff, formerly a senior Finance Ministry official.

Even the revival of confidence and Pinay's highly successful loan in the summer could be only palliatives. But since drastic surgery was needed, and would shatter the mood of euphoric unity, Pinay had to wait until all the national elections were over. (The U.N.R.'s poor showing in the local elections was to prove how prudent the delay had been.) With authority under the constitution's transitional clauses to 'take in all matters. the measures it judges necessary to the life of the nation', the government could impose by ordinance both the budget and its proposals for economic recovery. However, there were already wide divergences over what the policy should be. The U.N.R., and notably Chalandon, favoured a more 'popuiar' programme of reflation to counter the spread of the slight depression. Pinay accepted Rueff's insistence on discipline and deflation.

Remembering his error in deciding against Mendès-France in 1945, de Gaulle arbitrated in favour of Rueff, Pinay and austerity—but the U.N.R. reaped the unpopularity. The budget, and the measures announced at the close of December, attacked a series of economic and financial ailments in a self-consciously spectacular demonstration of the gravity of the crisis, and of the regime's determination to govern whatever the cost in popularity.

The franc was devalued by $17\frac{1}{2}$ per cent and external convertibility was restored in common with other Western European nations. This first group of measures was clearly intended to enable France to compete both within the Common Market and elsewhere. A second group, which de Gaulle termed *vérité et sévérité*, amounted to an all-out attack on inflation, that arch-enemy of sound finance and economic stability. A new franc, worth a hundred of the old, was introduced in an attempt to underline the new prestige and stability of the currency. Income tax, corporation taxes and sales tax (except on luxuries) were all raised, nationalized industries put up their prices, and subsidies on public services, agricultural *matériel*, and items of mass consumption were cut drastically or suppressed. Although social security contributions were raised, benefits were reduced—notably by making insured persons pay the first 3,000 francs (£2 2s.) of medical expenses in any half year. More important for the attack on inflation, the government annulled all escalator clauses linking agricultural prices and wage contracts (except the standard minimum wage itself) to the cost of living.

Economy

(Previously these had frustrated attempts to curb the inflationary spiral.) Finally, the token bonuses paid to ex-servicemen (other than the disabled or very poor) were suppressed. This measure, of negligible financial consequence, seems to have been included simply for its psychological value; few interest groups exercised more power under the Fourth Republic than the ex-servicemen. This was a symbolic challenge.

Rueff and his colleagues were determined that this devaluation should not be squandered like its predecessors. They believed that the economy must be restored to sanity by scrapping the patchwork of subsidies which governments had adopted to quieten noisy interest groups or to manipulate the cost-of-living index. The way to economic realism was to free the price mechanism. Despite a genuflection towards stricter tax collection, *vérité et sévérité* amounted essentially to 'soaking the poor'. For while the standard minimum wage, civil service salaries and some pensions were increased, the incidence of the higher taxes and prices and of the cuts in social benefits was strongly regressive. Economic stability was to be reached by a reduction in real wages, reinforced by a wage-freeze for up to two years. This policy was the signal for Mollet to refuse Socialist participation in the Debré government and lead his party into opposition. By apparently identifying Gaullism with the economic views of the Right, it also undermined the U.N.R.'s universal electoral appeal, and sent back to the Communists those who had been wooed away at the elections. The chance of breaking decisively the Communist grip on the working-class vote had vanished.

If the policy was controversial, there was no denying its energy or its courage. The air was loud with the fury of offended groups like farmers and ex-servicemen (who were still boycotting official ceremonies a year later). In earlier days their opposition would surely have been fatal to any cabinet which was rash enough to attack them head on. Now, despite strong pressure even within its own ranks, the government stood its ground impressively. In February 1959 it announced that the success of its policies already justified an increase in family allowances and the full reimbursement of medical expenses.[1] In autumn 1959 the continuing improvement in the economic situation permitted a partial restoration of the ex-servicemens' bonus, which still left their associations dissatisfied.

In the short run the new policies seemed successful. The unions' bargaining power was undermined by the continuing stagnation of some sectors of the economy, and by their perpetual divisions. They could no longer rely on escalator clauses, and they had few friends in Parliament. When they threatened a railway strike which might have triggered off a general wage rise, the government deterred them by the menace of using its emergency powers. Stable internal prices in turn enabled the devaluation to earn its full reward; the foreign trade balance became healthier than it had been for years.

But even strong government must bow to the elements. The long drought of 1959 put the new policies to the test. Although the government was now leaning more on the Left as a consequence of its Algerian policy, it remained—despite a steady rise in food prices—hostile to wage increases. As real wages fell, *sévérité* was maintained but *vérité* took a rough handling. All the old weapons which the Fourth Republic had used to manipulate the price index were brought out—price cuts in the nationalized industries, *ad hoc* subsidies on 'key' items, even the threat to prosecute profiteering butchers. Whether a new Republic had really turned over a new leaf was still in doubt.

Pinay was able to enforce austerity during 1959 despite such prolonged disagreements with his colleagues that the budget could not be published on time. His determination to limit the deficit again forced drastic pruning of the estimates. Housing, which enjoyed de Gaulle's special protection, kept its privileged place. But lack of funds was now hampering desperately urgent school and university building, the expansion of research, and much-needed improvements in the social services. If stability was to be achieved, these must

[1] The latter was probably less a result of pressure than of the discovery that the measure cost more to enforce than it saved. Similarly the technicians produced a spectacular extension of the tax on 'external signs of wealth', which had to be whittled away steadily as unworkable.

be sacrificed—so long as the country also pressed forward with its generosity to the Community, its onerous Algerian commitments, and its quest for nuclear grandeur.

Among problems which were universally accepted as urgent was reform of the outmoded and inequitable taxation system. For years this had figured prominently in every government's programme; but it was invariably shirked because Finance Ministers dared not contemplate the (apparently inevitable) transitional fall in revenue. What was needed (and promised) was a thorough overhaul of the labyrinthine taxation codes. What emerged from a committee of experts was so modest that the U.N.R. parliamentary group refused to recognize it as fiscal reform at all. The government surprisingly allowed Parliament to water down these proposals still further. The final version contained a useful minor rationalization of the structure of taxation in several ways (such as fighting tax dodgers by increasing tax-free allowances), but its revised taxation rates made one of the world's most regressive fiscal systems more regressive still. Further reform was promised.

One problem that the government did not expect was the question of aid to church schools. This old battle had apparently been losing much of its bitterness; during the election Mollet had even envisaged a *curé* becoming secretary of his local Socialist party. But the election brought to the Assembly 380 pledged supporters of aid to church schools, who at once launched a violent campaign for much bigger subsidies. These extravagant demands certainly did not have their origin in the Hierarchy, which saw beyond the majority of the moment to a time when the Left might retaliate by suppressing the subsidies completely. The real instigators were apparently the militant pressure group for the *école libre*, and a number of C.N.I. deputies. The latter saw their opportunity to embarrass the government, which wanted to retain contact with the Left and keep the U.N.R. as a centre party. Determined to break the U.N.R. if they could, they chose the very weapon that the R.P.F. itself had so mercilessly used against the M.R.P. and the C.N.I. in 1951.

Like many Gaullists, Debré (himself a former Radical) considered the quarrel over church schools outdated. Yet, although its revival could hardly have been less opportune, his position was secure. Since Parliament no longer had the right to propose new expenditure, the supporters of higher subsidies must persuade the government to introduce them. Fortified by the support of de Gaulle and the threat of dissolution, fired with a determination to resist the tyranny of the pressure groups, Debré had a golden opportunity to defy the constant lobbying. Instead he temporized by trying to reassure the Right without alienating the Left. While Mollet was willing to be understanding at first, the anger of his followers soon made him change his tone. The crowded meetings denouncing the threat to *laïcité* were the only—and impressive—exceptions to the general public apathy about politics. As both sides became more intransigent, Debré gave a token increase in subsidies which merely aroused suspicion all round. Then he sought refuge in a committee of enquiry. He genuinely believed he could present 'not simply a proposed subsidy—however large the majority it would win, however great the applause it would receive'—but a bill which would find a final solution to the problem.[1] He must have been speedily disillusioned by the spontaneous passions which this ancient quarrel aroused, when no contemporary problem stirred the slightest interest. Meanwhile there was little sign of dynamic and decisive government.

. . . .

Sir Winston Churchill once remarked that of all his wartime crosses the heaviest was the Cross of Lorraine. The phrase must have echoed wryly in many a chancellery since June 1958, and for much the same reasons. For during the war de Gaulle was striving (almost as much against his allies as against the enemy) to save France's status as a great power, to maintain her identity and sovereignty inviolate, and to assert her right to share in decisions made in her name. In a world which at least spoke increasingly of internationalism and interdependence, de Gaulle clung to the belief that France could realize her 'destiny as a great nation' by exercising fully the traditional freedom of action of the nation state. He believed these principles to be threatened almost as gravely in 1958 as during the war. For the Fourth Republic's

[1] U.N.R. *Bulletin de Presse*, no. 5, August 1959, p. 5. See Epilogue.

political and economic weaknesses had undermined her ability
to get her own way in foreign affairs; some of her sovereignty
had been signed away to supranational organizations; and
in de Gaulle's eyes the Atlantic alliance perpetuated the wartime ascendancy of the Anglo-Saxons.

In practice the reversal of Fourth Republic policies was
less dramatic than the General's convictions appeared to
foreshadow. Contemporary international relations leave
even a de Gaulle relatively little freedom of manœuvre.
Moreover, the General is a man of his word; engagements
must be kept, even to the supranational organizations he had
opposed so caustically. Thus on 1 January 1959, France met
in full her obligations under the first stage of application of
the Common Market Treaty—although, in the previous spring,
inflation and a deteriorating commercial balance had made it
doubtful whether the 'Europeans' of the Fourth Republic
would honour their commitments. France was thus committed to *Europe à six* even under Gaullism, despite de
Gaulle's lack of enthusiasm for more comprehensive schemes
or closer political unity.

The negotiations over the Free Trade Area seemed more in
the style of the old de Gaulle, for it was under his premiership that attempts to associate the F.T.A. with the Common
Market collapsed. Yet de Gaulle was really responsible neither
for the failure of this belated expedient, nor for the acrimony
of the negotiations, in which he took little interest. Only a
handful of 'Europeans' were prepared to consider it in order
to preserve some link with Britain. Adenauer was against it,
and French business, believing that the Common Market was
all it could reasonably digest, was violently hostile. De Gaulle
simply gave the *coup de grâce* to a scheme which no other
conceivable French government would have supported at
that time.

Surprisingly in view of the R.P.F.'s anti-German past, the
rapprochement with West Germany developed even more
rapidly than before. Perhaps indeed de Gaulle and Adenauer
found themselves kindred spirits. Though neither was likely
to let visions of fraternity make him lose sight of his idea of
national interest, both hoped to lay the German problem to
rest. They shared a common suspicion of Britain, and also

of the super-powers which, they feared, were ready to negotiate over their heads and would treat them as pawns in
the diplomatic game. Adenauer, the more exposed, was
always the keener for a closer relationship. He was even
willing to overlook de Gaulle's recognition of the Oder-
Neisse frontier which, coming from Washington or London,
would have provoked a major crisis. De Gaulle found in the
link with Germany welcome support for his action in Algeria.
For the moment he had to share the limelight in 'little
Europe' with Adenauer; but the Chancellor was 82, and he
only 67. Meanwhile France could magnify her importance
among the western powers and the Big Four by claiming to
speak for Western Europe.

It was in East–West relations and within N.A.T.O. that the
wartime de Gaulle revealed himself most clearly. He risked
no major initiatives immediately, but he was determined to
establish France's right to be consulted as an equal and to
assert every French prerogative to the full. No opportunity
was too small; it was no coincidence that Paris became increasingly the centre of international meetings, and that
Eisenhower, Khrushchev and Macmillan all made the pil-
grimage to the General before he went to them. If Britain
hoped to seize the diplomatic initiative after the death of
Dulles, de Gaulle (with Adenauer) soon disillusioned her.
They made it clear that while American leadership must be
tolerated, Britain could have no hope of such a role.

The General was at his wiliest when a summit conference
was in the air. Here he had to be treated as something approaching an equal. Just as Washington, Moscow and London
were publicly congratulating themselves on the imminence
of a summit meeting, de Gaulle let it be known that the time
was not ripe, and that his conceptions of such a meeting
differed profoundly from that of all the other participants.
Having forced one postponement, he commandeered the
planning of the West's preparations and of the conference
itself. He had shown yet again that France was a force which
even super-powers must take into account.

The General's reassertion of French rights was most marked
in N.A.T.O. He has always believed that N.A.T.O. makes
France a dependent nation deprived of her freedom of action.

The war ingrained in him the conviction that an allied high command would deploy its forces in British and American interests at the expense of France. He lost little time in demanding that France should be admitted to the Anglo-American directory of N.A.T.O. in recognition of her 'special role'; that she should be awarded more N.A.T.O. commands; and that the Americans should share their atomic secrets with him. Since the Algerian war had cut her N.A.T.O. contribution to a purely nominal level, it was not altogether the most opportune moment to demand more privileges. This did not deter the General. He backed his demands by administrative obstruction, and by insisting that France should control missile bases on her territory, withdrawing the French Mediterranean fleet from N.A.T.O. command in wartime, halting integration of the French Air Force in N.A.T.O. and, in the summer of 1959, demanding control of aircraft carrying nuclear weapons from French bases. Meanwhile he pushed forward with the Fourth Republic's policy of making the atomic bomb, without which he believed that France was doomed to permanent subservience.

The questions implied in de Gaulle's policies could not be brushed aside by his allies. N.A.T.O.'s sense of purpose had been weakening for years. Britain of all countries should have recognized that de Gaulle was not alone in putting his national interest first. Conversion to nuclear weapons raised more acutely than ever the problem of civilian control; while the American refusal to give their allies atomic warheads made it less plausible than ever to portray N.A.T.O. as an association of equals. Some nations might accept military dependence, but not France. Even before de Gaulle's return she had been tending towards military autarky. A handful of bombs and a token strike force may have been a wasteful duplication of effort which would neither make her militarily independent, nor turn her into a first-class power—nor even give her a strong bargaining position with the Americans. But de Gaulle refused to accept this view, and when supporters of the British deterrent dismissed the French bomb as vainglorious or militarily irrelevant, the French could hardly fail to scent the hypocrisy of perfidious Albion.

Unfortunately de Gaulle's proposed three-power directory

of N.A.T.O. was no solution at all. It was based on his belief that the British and Americans were running N.A.T.O., which sprang from his imperfect understanding of their wartime relationship, and from Britain's addiction to taking credit for American decisions. The 'directory' which the General so resented was largely a fig-leaf, covering the decline in British power but irritating continentals. If there was a genuine case for giving the French a greater say in N.A.T.O., this was because her government had previously been too unstable to claim its due. But now any tripartite directory would plainly be unacceptable to the powers which were left outside.

De Gaulle declared on returning to power that he did not intend to dismantle N.A.T.O. But he has never hidden his belief that 'the system called integration . . . has had its day'[1] and that France should eventually control her forces within a system of national coalitions. Consequently he was unruffled when N.A.T.O. retaliated to his demands for control of missile bases and aircraft on atomic patrol by siting the bases in Italy and flying the aircraft off to less obstreperous countries. This accorded with his general preference for independence. Whether the clashes with N.A.T.O. were steps towards this goal, or prestige points, or both, is far from clear; for the General's objectives were veiled in characteristic ambiguity. Even in his re-assertion of the French position within N.A.T.O., it was hard to see whether he seriously believed that France could equal the super-powers, or whether he felt his real rival was Britain and was set on wresting for France a position comparable to hers. The illusions and pretensions of each country were a challenge to the other, which went far to explain the development under de Gaulle of the malaise in their relations.

Although the prospect of France exercising full sovereignty might seem an extraordinary anachronism, it brought dividends. De Gaulle's indefatigable readiness to insist on French rights was in harmony with the resurgent nationalism of his countrymen. Significantly, no campaign for nuclear disarmament grew up in France; foreign criticism seemed part of a general conspiracy to cheat France of her position in the

[1] *Le Monde*, 6 November 1959.

world. Every Frenchman had at some time been infuriated by his country's impotence or by her tactless allies. The Right had always encouraged extravagant hopes of the weight that strong institutions would give France in international affairs, and blamed foreign scheming for the collapse of untenable policies. Debré himself once attributed the Algerian problem to 'world-wide greed' for strategic bases and Saharan wealth.[1] The national mood was favourable to the emergence of a champion.

De Gaulle could therefore use a vigorous foreign policy to help make his actions in Algeria acceptable to the nationalist wing of his supporters. Just as strong government and economic recovery strengthened his hand abroad, approval of his Algerian policy by almost every international figure from Eisenhower to Khrushchev bolstered his position at home. Chaban-Delmas spoke for many with his cry, 'At last, under de Gaulle, we are respected again'. Repeatedly news of some diplomatic success, or a fresh blow to defend French interests, was timed to coincide with a new move in Algeria. This was most important in de Gaulle's handling of the army, which was also soothed by the prospect of a modernized service equipped with nuclear weapons. In making and testing the bomb in the teeth of foreign opposition, he was again able to rally patriotic feelings while promoting his views on military independence. He was never a man to kill only one bird with a stone.

. . . .

Obscurity, contended Napoleon, is one of the hallmarks of a good constitution. He would surely have approved the articles on the Community, the constitution within a constitution which outlines the relationship between the Republic and her colonies. Seldom has ambiguity in constitution-making been carried so far—or to such purpose. De Gaulle took power with the authority to propose a fresh colonial policy, and the conviction that this came next in importance only to reconstructing the Republic itself. There was still time to find a way of conciliating national honour with African aspirations, but without a quick and liberal initiative Black

[1] *Le Monde*, 18 August 1959.

179

Africa might move along the same bleak course as Indo-China and North Africa. From this conviction came the decision to let the colonies choose at the referendum between immediate secession and continued association with France.

In declaring 'if they want independence, let them take it on 28 September', de Gaulle had already imposed a silent revolution in colonial policy. But to find the formula which would rally the Africans to remain with France was infinitely more complex. The first draft abolished colonial representation in the National Assembly without granting compensation in the federal machinery. It offered the Africans less power than they had been exercising *de facto* since the Defferre *loi-cadre*. There was not the least recognition of the right to independence. 'An unequivocal setback,' Senghor cried. It was so manifestly inadequate that it was tacitly shelved. Despite his preference for a federation, de Gaulle proved ready to listen to both the C.C.C. and the leaders he met during his African tour. Manifestly the gulf between federalists and decentralizers could not be bridged so quickly. The battle was postponed by a compromise. The Community, meaning all things to all men to a degree remarkable even by Fifth Republic standards, was so adroitly phrased that once the referendum was over it could evolve in any of the directions the rival camps were demanding.

The bid succeeded. Majorities for the Community ranged from impressive to overwhelming everywhere but in Guinea, which proclaimed her promised independence on 2 October. The remaining colonies could now choose between remaining overseas territories under the Defferre *loi-cadre*, or becoming full French departments, or members of the new Community. The five smallest territories, with no hope of surviving on their own, opted for the *status quo*.[1] The remainder chose to be member states. Thus at its inauguration the Community comprised the French Republic (France, Algeria, overseas departments and territories) and the twelve Republics of Black Africa and Madagascar.

These were months of effervescence and recrimination as

[1] These are Polynesia, New Caledonia, Somali Coast, Comoro Is., and St. Pierre-and-Miquelon; also the Austral and Antarctic Lands, which made no choice (having no inhabitants).

the battle of the primary federations reopened.[1] Grandiose
plans for a United States of Africa, a 'Centrafrican' Federation, or a renaissance of the medieval Mali Empire were
aired and shelved. For the moment support for pan-Africanism all but evaporated. The Mali Federation finally united
only Sudan and Senegal. Dahomey and Upper Volta, both
dependent on trade with Ivory Coast, withdrew in face of
Houphouet-Boigny's bitter hostility to Mali. The old regional
groupings based on Dakar and Brazzaville disappeared. Yet
the trend to balkanization was never complete; technical and
economic co-operation (Houphouet-Boigny's alternative to
primary federations) had a strong appeal. Technical agreements and joint development schemes multiplied steadily,
while the customs unions of West and Equatorial Africa were
retained. But the doubt remained. Were these new states
(Ivory Coast excepted) strong enough to stand alone, and
eventually to claim independence for themselves, despite the
attraction of an independent Nigeria?

Whatever relationship with the Republic the states choose,
constitutionally they 'enjoy autonomy, administer themselves,
and manage their own affairs democratically and freely'.
However, the Community as a whole deals with foreign policy,
defence, currency, common economic and financial policies,
supervision of justice, higher education, strategic materials
policy, and the general organization of common and external
transport and telecommunications. This leaves the states—
excepting the French Republic, whose rights remain intact—
with limited internal autonomy.[2] This distribution of powers
would be conventional if the Community were a *fédération*

[1] See above, p. 31.

[2] That the French Republic is a member of the Community is clearly
implied by Articles 1 and 83. Moreover it has transferred the external
signs of sovereignty to the Community (although, anomalously, nationality and diplomatic representation are those of 'the French Republic
and of the Community'). Theoretically France should have lost to the
Community her powers over such questions as foreign policy and
defence. However, she continues to exercise directly all the powers
which Article 78 assigns to the Community as a whole. This privileged
position apparently rests on Article 79 which provides that 'questions
of common competence are settled by the Republic', 'until the entry
into vigour of the measures necessary to the application of the present
Title'. The extent to which ministers responsible for 'common com-
petences' are responsible to the French Parliament is far from certain.

égalitaire, but theoretically at least the constitution gives ultimate power to France alone.

The Senate of the Community is far less than a federal parliament. Normally it is merely an advisory chamber like the defunct Assembly of the French Union, meeting for brief sessions twice a year. It has powers of decision only when the constitution is being revised, when it is the equal of the Parliament of the Republic. It promises to be an obscure sounding board. It could become more important if the member states wished, for their legislatures may delegate their own powers of decision to the Senate.[1] But they are scarcely encouraged to do so by its composition. Of the 284 members, appointed by the parliaments of the states, 186 come from the French Republic; the other member states send a third (98)—which is nevertheless more than their share of population.

The Executive Council of the Community has at least an African majority.[1] Its members, all *ex-officio*, are the President of the Community, the heads of government of all the twelve member states, and the ministers responsible for Community affairs (at present seven, all French). But the Council is in no way a responsible cabinet. It is simply the 'supreme organ of co-operation of the member states', with the right to 'know' and to 'deliberate'—but not to decide.

Decision is the prerogative of the President, the Community's absolute and irresponsible ruler. It is he who presides over and represents the Community, who assures respect for treaties, constitutional laws affecting the Community, and decisions of the Court of Arbitration.[1] He convokes the Executive Council, fixes its agenda, and presides over it. He 'formulates and notifies the measures necessary for the direction of common affairs' and 'sees to their execution'. In short, the President is theoretically legislature and executive rolled into one. His actions need no countersignature, and short of impeachment for treason he is responsible to no one.

If this were the full picture the Community would never have been formed. It would be the camouflaged prolongation of colonial rule that nationalists had been warning against for years. And yet it provides a framework within

[1] The Senate, Executive Council and Court of Arbitration are further described at pp. 256–7.

which France has a real hope of resolving her colonial problem with honour and dignity. Three things transform this apparently inequitable federation: the right of secession, the possibility of altering the initial allocation of powers to the states, and de Gaulle.

What rallied almost every African leader to the Community was the provision that 'a member state of the Community may become independent'. (It may also become an overseas department or territory.) All this needs is a vote by the local legislature, confirmed by a referendum organized and supervised by the Community. The 'detailed arrangements' for the transfer of power must then be determined by an Agreement approved by the Parliaments of the French Republic and the state concerned. Last-ditch colonialists might turn a peaceful transition into a bitter wrangle, but they could not thwart it.[1] No African would call these onerous terms. Sekou Touré's bitter declaration 'we prefer poverty in freedom to riches in slavery' presented a false antithesis. This right to decide whether and when they wish to leave the Community clearly raises the states above the level of simple colonies. The declaration of an F.L.N. spokesman that 'We are free men who refuse to enter into that concentration camp, the French Community, whose head warder is in Paris' is obvious nonsense.[2]

In the short term the freedom to leave has been one of the strongest forces for cohesion in the Community. Its other great virtue in African eyes is that it can become as loose or as tight as they wish. This was the crux of the pre-referendum compromise. If they want closer links with France the constitution permits fresh questions to be confided to the whole Community and the transfer of powers from the local legislatures to the Senate of the Community. Alternatively questions can be transferred from the competence of the Community

[1] The constitution is not wholly precise, but de Gaulle gave his personal pledge (at Brazzaville in August 1958) that 'the Community will take note of its decision, and an Agreement will settle the conditions of transfer between this territory, which will take its independence and follow its own road, and the Community itself. I guarantee in advance that in this case . . . [France] will not oppose it' (*L'Année Politique* 1958, p. 547).

[2] *Le Monde*, 9 June 1959.

to the states. Thus the way is open for a wide variety of relationships between France and the overseas Republics — possibly even a slightly different relationship for each member.

The Community owes this flexibility to the pragmatic vision of de Gaulle, who, when pressed to remain Prime Minister, gave the need to install and shape the Community as his reason for insisting on taking the Presidency. As President he has always been aware that the Community will survive only as long as it satisfies the Africans. This recognition that France may lead but not command has transformed the unpromising institutional structure. Executive Council meetings have been far closer to debates among equals than has the French cabinet. While decisions are promulgated in the President's name, they are rarely made without the consent of the states. On questions which divide the Africans, de Gaulle has renounced his arbitral role and retreated into strict neutrality, letting them concentrate on their own disagreements rather than risking their resentment focusing on France. The Community's pomp and protocol show a shrewd eye for African susceptibilities. The sight of the President and Prime Minister of France and half the French government arriving in an African capital for consultations has made a deep impression. De Gaulle has flattered his African chiefs of government by calling in Couve de Murville to outline foreign policy, and by consulting them on Berlin.[1] He asked their approval of his Algerian initiative of September 1959 even before informing the cabinet of the Republic. Four African Ministers-Counsellor have been appointed to advise the French cabinet and speak for France at the United Nations.

While the Africans were digesting their gains the problem was simple. The Executive Council was busy drawing the lines between the sphere of the Community and the competence of the states, and sharing out the assets of French West and Equatorial Africa. The Community was recognized by receiving seats on the Economic and Social Council, membership of major international organizations and several

[1] An attempt was made to counter African hostility to atomic tests in the Sahara by giving the Bomb to the Community; though not wholly successful, it helped keep criticism of the French atomic programme within the Community to negligible proportions.

expert committees (such as the Monetary Committee of the Franc Zone), and inclusion in the French delegation to the United Nations. Africans may be seconded to embassies in the major capitals and the independent African states.

Since appetite comes by eating, each meeting of the Executive Council brought new requests. Some states wanted direct diplomatic representation, others pressed for their own citizenship—although foreign affairs is a Community question and the constitution permits only Community citizenship. (The recognition of distinct nationalities, announced by Debré in October 1959, circumnavigated this difficulty.) Some chiefs of government challenged the choice of Frenchmen for all the ministries for common affairs. Growing friction was caused by the system of High Commissioners, who represent the President and execute Community policy within each overseas Republic. Although strictly enjoined to keep out of domestic affairs, they are suspect as agents of Paris and relics of colonialism. Pressure has grown for their nomination to be subordinate to the approval of the local governments. Other members want them to be ceremonial figureheads, with responsibility for executing Community decisions transferred to the governments of the overseas Republics.

Such demands are naturally anathema to the federalists. 'We refuse to be part of a Community which would be no more than a Commonwealth', declared Houphouet-Boigny bitterly.[1] Yet there was never any hope of metropolitan opinion accepting his scheme for a multinational state in which Africans would arbitrate the fortunes of ordinary Frenchmen and the President of the Republic himself might be an African.[2] Even in Africa Houphouet's views were out of favour except on his own Ivory Coast. The predominance of France in the Community's institutions scarcely encourages Africans to increase its powers, even if this were not counter to the whole tide of nationalism. Thus in less than a year the confederalists won the ascendancy. Their demands pointed logically to the states having something akin to dominion

[1] *Le Monde*, 7 July 1959.
[2] For one of the few bravely thoroughgoing metropolitan expositions of this view, see Gagliardi and Rossillon, *Survivre à de Gaulle*, p. 19.

status, directly exercising all but the least attractive of the Community's powers. (Black Africans had noted that full independence had cost Ghana some 10 per cent of her income for foreign affairs and defence, without counting the judiciary, telecommunications and higher education.)

It is hard for France to resist such pressures, since a thwarted member can simply resign from the club. Yet, while she has renounced any attempt to constrain him, she might be tempted to rely on cash to deter him. Many Africans believe, like Houphouet-Boigny, that 'rare are the loves which blossom in poverty'.[1] Some might be tempted to suggest that only a healthy injection of economic aid would put independence out of their minds for the time being. Houphouet-Boigny himself has denounced such 'blackmail' because it prevents the final clarification of the relationship between France and the 'genuine' members of the Community. Yet such attempts at 'blackmail' could succeed only if France is misguided enough to set out to buy allegiance to the Community. The right to independence is not unilateral; France is entitled (Art. 86) to divest herself of any colony which becomes too importunate or expensive.

The difficulty of taking sanctions against a seceding state was underlined by the example of Guinea. France cut her off without a shilling and withdrew her administrators on the morrow of the referendum with frighteningly systematic pettiness. The word went out that softness to Touré might cause the rot to set in right through the Community. Britain and the United States were firmly told that loyal allies would know better than to come to Guinea's aid. Guinea's overtures were snubbed, and France was one of the last major powers to grant full recognition. She even broke custom by refusing to sponsor Guinea at the United Nations. French industrialists were allowed to understand that they would incur no disapproval from the government if they abandoned plans to invest in Guinea. But the vacuum left by the French was quickly filled. Iron-curtain embassies sprouted in Conakry, and a Czech ship speedily supplied the arms that the Americans had declined to give. China promised economic aid, and Touré concluded a much-trumpeted (and little imple-

[1] *Le Monde*, 5 September 1958.

mented) association with Ghana. France risked losing Guinea completely from her orbit. After second thoughts she agreed to supply cultural and technical aid. Guinea was expendable, but to pursue a policy of *l'absence française* throughout Black Africa was unthinkable. France would doubtless be more generous to states remaining within the Community, but in the competitive conditions of modern Africa she scarcely dared risk using the economic sanction ruthlessly.

However gracefully France swims with the tide, the future of the Community is uncertain. Many Gaullists—but not de Gaulle—have encouraged grandiose ideas of a unique experiment, 'an *ensemble* destined to forge the political solidarity of all the participants'.[1] Yet the referendum results had scarcely been announced when M. Apithy, Premier of Dahomey, forecast a rapid accession to independence, and Moktar Ould Daddah, later Premier of Mauritania, made it clear that 'when the moment comes we shall leave the Community'.[2] It was a welcome half-way house, but the goal was never in doubt. Several leaders warned against undue haste. Senghor had pointed out in September, 'Voting for independence means voting for selling your peanuts in the world market'.[3] In March 1959 Mamadou Dia urged, 'political independence can only be real if it is based on solid social and economic independence'.[4] Such a prudent resolve was not easily maintained with the thirty-five million Nigerians preparing for independence in 1960. Keita, the Mali Premier, flew off to Tananarive in July declaring that Mali's independence was imminent. For the moment he was apparently quietened by de Gaulle's tact and his own manifest isolation. But the fiery statements were resumed on his return. In September Mali formally demanded her independence—but not by the 'normal' procedure (which would have led to her eventual exclusion from the Community). She asked instead for the transfer to Mali jurisdiction of all matters decided by

[1] *R.F.S.P*, p. 19.
[2] *Le Monde*, 11 October 1958, and 3 October 1958.
[3] *African Affairs*, January 1959. The President of the Senegal Constituent Assembly said, 'We did not vote OUI for the love of General de Gaulle's *beaux yeux*, but because we are afraid of independence now' (*West Africa*, 7 March 1959).
[4] *West Africa*, 7 March 1959.

the Community; once self-governing, she was ready to keep her membership and confederal links with France.

The Community may eventually become a loose association of independent states, or purely symbolic, or even completely memberless. None of these courses need constitute failure. The promise of the Community, even if its life is transitory, is that France can liquidate her colonial problems with dignity. Like the Commonwealth, it can camouflage or sublimate the ebbing of real power from the mother country. Within this framework there is the chance for the Africans of having what they really want, and for France of achieving what has always eluded her: making the loss of a colonial possession a matter of pride rather than humiliation.

10

The Algerian Tightrope

'The future of Algeria lies in Algeria', General de Gaulle has declared.[1] So, he might have added, does that of the Fifth Republic. In providing France with new institutions de Gaulle may indeed have attacked 'the profound cause of our trials', and seized the 'last chance of the Republic'. But unless he can also cure the Algerian gangrene the Fifth Republic can scarcely escape the fate of the Fourth. Before 13 May it was a commonplace in France that de Gaulle alone could impose the necessary treatment or surgery. But when the call came the chances looked slim: an army in revolt against a government without authority, nascent fascism threatening to spread to metropolitan France, a war without prospect of decision, and a Moslem population caught between the fanaticism of the ultras of both sides, European and F.L.N. As if this were not daunting enough, de Gaulle set out to achieve a settlement while maintaining national unity.

This determination to square the circle ruled out any immediate miracle. De Gaulle was to impose on himself so painfully cautious a gradualism, such a patient readiness to accept reverses, that even supporters came to believe he was drifting. But he was not the man to gamble on one desperate throw. In June 1958 even he could have dared to propose only one solution: integration. This he refused to do. He was both doubtful whether integration appealed to the Moslems, and unwilling to split the nation by identifying himself with the insurrection. He had no ready-made plan. Until now he had considered Algeria largely, in Soustelle's phrase, as a 'philosopher-historian'. Now, instead of accepting the *simpliste* slogans of integration or independence, he set out to see

[1] Unattributed quotations from de Gaulle in this chapter are from *L'Année Politique* 1958, pp. 544–50 and 561–6.

what might still be salvaged for France from the wreckage—
always realizing that no solution could succeed without the
genuine assent of the Moslems.

De Gaulle therefore played a waiting game—taking the
calculated risk that, when the moment came to reveal the
final *arbitrage*, his authority might have fatally eroded.
Within weeks he was to discern the shape of his favoured
solution, but it was fifteen months before he clearly revealed
his mind. The delphic utterances of the intervening months
required an exegesis formerly reserved for communiqués from
the Kremlin. Read with historical hindsight, they trace a
consistent and persevering course, but they invariably contained phrases calculated to bolster the hopes of all rival
camps. While buying time with ambiguity, de Gaulle was
preparing the ground in other ways. He was able to establish
himself both as independent of the forces which brought him
to power (against those who contested his legitimacy), and
as a ruler by popular consent (against those who proposed
to play 'Who made you king?'). Before he could announce his
plans the passions of May must be quenched, the extremists
disarmed and isolated, the reliability of the army assured,
and both soldiers and administrators brought back to the
forgotten path of obedience. Most important, the bases
had to be laid for a social and economic transformation of
Algeria which, with the eventual political solution, could
appeal to the Moslem majority.

This pattern was set from the beginning. While in Paris
the Fourth Republic was initialling its death warrant, in
Algiers de Gaulle's cabinet was a bitter pill for the men of
13 May. Only a few days earlier Pflimlin had been rotating in
moth-eaten effigy from a tree in the main square of Algiers.
Now (with other men of the System) he reappeared as Minister of State, while Soustelle was nowhere. Some claimed that
de Gaulle was playing a dark game, and that the politicians
would be dropped when they had served his purposes; others
contended that the System had cheated Algiers of its victory.
Col. Lacheroy remarked with the stiffest of upper lips, 'When
you call in the doctor you don't question his treatment'; but
already Sérigny was writing of the activists' 'disappointment,
bitterness and indignation'. Even while Algiers was being

urged to put out flags to give the General a hero's welcome, Delbecque was flying off to protest in Paris. The first modest steps to isolate the ultras had begun.

The 300,000 *algérois* who filled the Forum came to be thanked, flattered, praised. But the General's compliments were diabolically noncommittal:

> I have understood you. I know what has happened here. I see what you wished to do. I see that the road you have opened in Algeria is that of renovation and fraternity. I say renovation in every respect. But very rightly you wished that this should begin at the beginning; that is to say by our institutions, and that is why I am here.

The homage to the army was warmer, yet limited: 'coherent, ardent, disciplined under the orders of its chiefs', it had 'accomplished a magnificent work of comprehension' in Algeria, and had been 'the witness and guarantor of the movement'.

What his audience did not expect was an appeal aimed almost wholly at the Moslems. 'From today', he promised, 'there is only one category of inhabitant: there are only whole-share Frenchmen, . . . with the same rights, and the same duties.' They must 'open paths which until now were closed to many . . . give the means of living to those who did not have them . . . recognize the dignity of those in whom dignity has been contested . . . assure a motherland to those who could have doubted having one.' Moslems would join equally with Europeans in the referendum, and in forthcoming elections he would introduce the single college, that symbol of integration which the ultras had so violently rejected in the past. 'With those elected representatives, we shall see how to do what remains.' Most audacious of all: 'May there even participate those who, through despair, felt it their duty to conduct on this soil a struggle which is courageous, I recognize, . . . but which is no less cruel and fratricidal for that. I, de Gaulle, open to them the doors of reconciliation.'

If de Gaulle had a message for the Europeans it was his warm reference to 'this magnificent spectacle of men who, whatever their community, commune in the same ardour and hold each other by the hand'. No one knew better than he how untypical that 'communion' was. But he was reminding the Europeans that their future could lie only in creating a genuine partnership.

Not suprisingly the reactions were wildly diverse. Activists noted the General's manifest failure to approve May 13th, while liberals disapproved of his determination to leave the generals unpunished and to press forward with pacification. While the ultras fumed, the F.L.N. declared 'de Gaulle has rallied to the ultras'; *L'Aurore* hailed 'integration of the Moslems in the nation', and the Algerian writer Amrouche announced 'General, I take you at your word', believing that the way was open to negotiation and independence.[1]

By turning a blind eye to the army's breach of discipline, and announcing the social reforms for which it had struggled in vain, the General was winning his first battle, that against the Committees of Public Safety (C.S.P.s). Resisting left-wing demands for their dissolution, he frigidly told the C.S.P.s that their role was to obey legal authority and to work for the 'integration of souls'. 'We did not cross the Rubicon merely to fish in it' retorted Delbecque. Believing themselves the expression of revolutionary popular sovereignty, the C.S.P.s proclaimed their intention of spreading to the mainland to fight the 'princes of the System, [who] will hope to smother the revolution'. Already they were occupying Radio Algiers by force, transmitting totalitarian propaganda in defiance of Paris, and seizing the metropolitan press at will.

De Gaulle countered by making Salan delegate-general and confirming full civil power in army hands. The Left was incensed at this further recognition of a rebel, but since civil administration had collapsed the army was the only immediate alternative to the C.S.P.s. Even control over the army was precarious. Massu was co-chairman of the Algeria-Sahara C.S.P., which on 10 June voted a violent motion attacking the proposed municipal elections, calling for the abrogation of the *loi-cadre*, and demanding the dissolution of all political

---

[1] The confusion de Gaulle had already sown is manifest in this leaflet: 'Everyone to the Forum to show our confidence in General de Gaulle and to recall that the profound desire of the population of Algeria is the constitution of a Government of Public Safety. That is to say, the resignation of all the ministers and the end of the System. Long live de Gaulle! Down with the System!'

parties. De Gaulle at once forced Salan to repudiate it, and frigidly reminded the C.S.P. of its subordinate role.

Returning to Algeria in early July the General talked with Moslems and those administering them, sub-prefects and S.A.S. officers, and saw the terrain for himself. But he was 'too busy' to meet delegations from the C.S.P.s. He promised further industrialization, modernization, votes for women, and the preparation of electoral lists—measures which satisfied the army by granting overdue reforms to the Moslems, yet which were compatible with integration. Still that word— at once a programme and a *mystique*—did not pass his lips; the ultras had to be content with the promise that from Dunkirk to Tamanrasset they might buy the same postage stamps. The volatile ex-servicemen's organization in Algiers spoke darkly of the 'deep malaise'. This was only partly dissipated by the honours and promotions showered on the military on Bastille Day, the shelving of the plan to hold municipal elections (never popular with the army), and the inclusion of Soustelle in the government. The strain within the activist movement grew until the C.S.P. of 13 May split, its Gaullists refusing to join the Poujadist core in reasserting the demand for the abolition of political parties and the establishment of a corporative state. Increasingly isolated from the army, the C.S.P.'s were to drift into noisy and ineffective virulence.

The government was determined to restore its authority, although its methods were sometimes devious.[1] The Safeguard Commission which had fallen into impotence at the end of the Fourth Republic was resurrected with greater powers. In September a special Control Commission was sent from the mainland to encourage freedom of expression and the regularity of the vote. The F.L.N. chose to demand abstention on pain of death instead of coming into the open to contest the referendum. The army was enthusiastically and expensively carrying out Salan's order to 'win the battle of the referendum' with an integrationist appeal for *Algérie française*

---

[1] It raised the petrol tax less in metropolitan France than in Algeria, where taxation had always been kept lower. The Europeans, who own most of the cars, greeted this maliciously logical move towards integration with fury. Nevertheless the government insisted on its rise, though less than it originally proposed.

which often went well beyond de Gaulle's cautious ambiguity. In such an atmosphere no choice could be wholly free. The Right won its expected triumph, and claimed thereafter that the Moslems had decided their future once and for all. It was the Left's turn to be bitter. It had heard little of the Control Commission's numerous but limited successes against military suspicion and civilian fraud; it minimized the significance of universal Moslem suffrage. All its suspicions of de Gaulle were reinforced by his claim that the electors 'did it simply, and without any constraint. . . . That is a fact as clear as the dazzling light of day. . . . That fact is capital, for the reason that it engages Algeria and France to each other for ever . . .'

Yet this referendum also gave de Gaulle the authority to take his first major initiative—an attack on racial discrimination and poverty. This was essential to any political solution which could give France the hope of remaining in Algeria, but it did not commit de Gaulle to any of the rival formulae. The Constantine Plan, revealed on 3 October, promised that over five years 400,000 new jobs would be created, a million people rehoused, and industry expanded. Wages would be raised to metropolitan levels, one-tenth of civil service posts reserved for Algerians, 250,000 hectares of land redistributed to Moslems and (over eight years) elementary education made universal. Moreover, elections were to be held in Algeria at the same time as on the mainland, with two-thirds of the seats allotted to Moslems.

Again de Gaulle spoke principally to the latter. Taking the promise of a transformed Algeria for reality, he called for an 'end to these absurd combats', promising not only that would 'hope flower again', but that 'we shall see the prisons empty.' Proposals for a political solution must wait; 'I think it useless to congeal in advance in words what the enterprise will in any case mark out little by little'. However, 'the future of Algeria will, in any case because it is in the nature of things, be built on a double base: her personality and her close solidarity with the mainland'. Now the General's listeners had become 'Algerians' and his final cry was, '*Vive l'Algérie et la France!*'

· · · · · ·

Both camps again reacted with mingled pleasure and hostility. Furious at de Gaulle's flat refusal to proclaim that Algeria was a province such as Brittany or Burgundy, the Europeans could console themselves with a Plan which was 'integration in deeds if not in words'.[1] While the Left was pleased at the Plan's modest liberalism, it was outraged at the bland declaration that the elections would be held in Algeria 'in the same conditions as in France' itself. It believed he was compounding the fraud of the referendum by bringing to Paris seventy deputies, prefabricated by the ultras and the army, who would sabotage any liberal solution.

They were mollified by de Gaulle's next move. Salan received, publicly, peremptory orders to see that the election took place in 'absolute liberty and sincerity'. The authorities must remain strictly neutral, and above all refrain from sponsoring single 'official' lists. Terrorists apart, candidates of all shades ('I repeat, all shades') must be allowed to campaign, 'whatever their programmes, even regarding the status or political destiny of Algeria'. Civil servants and army officers (who were ordered to quit the C.S.P.s forthwith) were forbidden to stand in Algeria. The aim of the election, de Gaulle insisted, was to encourage the emergence of a Moslem elite to fill the political void created by the rebellion. De Gaulle had not ignored the lessons of the referendum, and though even now his instructions were to be honoured only in part, there was no doubt he intended to be master. While the Left hailed 'the return to Republican legality', the activists were indignant at this 'disavowal of the fraternal action that the army has conducted throughout Algeria'. The Algeria-Sahara

[1] The Plan (costing about £1,500,000,000) is an accelerated version of a ten-year development plan prepared for Lacoste but never implemented. A serious attempt is being made to meet the objectives, but even if they are entirely fulfilled they will scarcely enable the Algerian economy to keep pace with the demographic 'explosion', which is doubling the population every twenty-five years. Before the revolt there were estimated to be about 1,000,000 unemployed in Algeria, almost all Moslem, while Lacoste told the Algerian Assembly in February 1956 that 'five million people live with the utmost precariousness, on an average income which, when account has been taken of what they consume themselves, does not exceed £14 per head per year'. Fewer than one in six Moslem children had any schooling in 1954 (Germaine Tillion, *L'Algérie en 1957*, p. 70, and N. Barbour, *A Survey of North-West Africa* [*The Maghrib*], pp. 237 and 250).

C.S.P. called a general strike, split yet again between Gaullists and activists, and finally renounced its strike in face of the hostility of the army and the reserve of the population. In so far as the army was loyal, the ultras were impotent.

So far the F.L.N. had professed itself unimpressed by de Gaulle's initiatives. During the summer it launched a succession of sabotage attacks on industrial installations in France (including the Eiffel Tower) which collapsed under mass arrests and its own incompetence. On the eve of the referendum it announced the formation of a 'Provisional Government of the Algerian Republic' (G.P.R.A.) with Ferhat Abbas as 'Prime Minister', and it was now launching the customary pre-United Nations offensive. But de Gaulle's message to Salan and his reference to an 'Algerian personality' were moving the 'G.P.R.A.'s' more flexible leaders to recall that it was always ready to negotiate a cease-fire, without insisting on the recognition in advance of the right to independence. Salan and the F.L.N. both released small groups of prisoners. The sky had brightened.

Against this background de Gaulle pressed his campaign further still. Calling a special press conference he pointed to the 'decisive manifestation' of the referendum of 28 September, the appalling human cost of the war, notably to the Moslems, and the promise of a new Algeria as reasons to call for the 'peace of the brave'. Admitting that 'for the most part the men of the insurrection have fought courageously', he proposed that local commanders should come forward under the traditional 'white flag of parley' and negotiate their 'return without humiliation to their family and their work'. The members of 'the external organization of the rebellion' could come to Paris in freedom 'to settle with the authorities the end of hostilities'—but not to discuss political conditions. De Gaulle was refusing to compound with the rebellion, but he was ready to challenge the rebels to combat at the ballot box.

The 'G.P.R.A.' was caught off balance, even though it seems to have had advance knowledge of the proposals. After two days of manifest indecision and contradictory pronouncements, the rebels, whose leadership since Ben Bella's capture had been mediocre, simply struck a familiar attitude. The F.L.N. also has its ultras; they accepted the humiliating construction that the French Right was giving to the white-flag conditions, and discounted Bourguiba's insistence that de Gaulle had admitted that they represented a force, and that if talks began it would be hard to keep them strictly to military matters. They announced a flat refusal. Yet the initiative was not a total failure; in France a seed had been sown, while the F.L.N. was confronted with its political immaturity. Next time it would be more supple.

But in Algeria the talk of negotiations and the F.L.N.'s refusal threw back into *attentisme* the moderates whom de Gaulle had been coaxing into the open. Why a second consultation was being held so soon after the referendum was little understood. The intransigents again had the field; the F.L.N. to call for abstention, and the Europeans to turn the election into a festival of integration. It all but collapsed completely. A few hours before nominations closed there were only eighteen lists spread over twenty constituencies. Even when the authorities coaxed more candidates forward, liberals were few and destined to have little success. The army, caught between its own preferences and the strict order to remain neutral, yet canvassed by many Moslems to help them make their choice, was far more delicately placed than at the referendum. In places its interpretation of de Gaulle's orders was decidedly cavalier, while in Oran particularly the grand tradition of Algerian electoral fraud was not forgotten.

The main contest (where there was one) was between moderate and extreme integrationists. The campaign was drab, and the vote half-hearted; only sixty-four per cent went to the polls. The experiment was not an entire failure; for the first time Algeria returned a majority of Moslem deputies, for the first time Moslem and European votes counted equally. But the worst fears of the Left were realized. To help him 'do what remains', de Gaulle had a group of seventy-one *mal élus*, most of whom formed an Algerian group in the Assembly and swore to work for the triumph of integration. Yet even among these some (as de Gaulle was hoping) were to evolve on reaching Paris.

Again de Gaulle seized the moment for a further advance, visiting Algeria for the fifth time since coming to power.

Twice Salan's posting had been announced; twice it had been withdrawn, to the anguish of the Left, who saw this as proof that the army could defy even de Gaulle. Now Salan went, covered with roses, for a post which was to be suppressed only three weeks later.[1] The quiet removal of the military men of 13 May to less sensitive posts was well under way. Elsewhere civil administrators resumed control from the army wherever possible (though Massu remained as super-prefect in Algiers, while in the combat regions administration often necessarily remained in military hands). Meanwhile, now that the army was free from its long electoral task, de Gaulle reassured the military by charging his new Commander-in-Chief, Challe, to employ fresh methods to exploit the deteriorating morale of the F.L.N. Pacification must be continued. But yet again de Gaulle insisted that 'the page of combats has been turned', and looked to the future 'to reveal better the living personality of Algeria, and the nature of things which unites it to France. It is then that practically and reasonably the political solution will appear.'

Despite the deepening malaise on the Right, de Gaulle won the vote of every Algerian deputy in the presidential election (they were the only electors, as local councils had not yet been chosen). The election gave him a chance to move forward again. Using the incoming President's traditional right of clemency (but in agreement with the new cabinet) he reprieved every Algerian awaiting execution, cut sentences on all others, and ordered the release of 7,000 from internment. The five captured rebel leaders were transferred from the Santé prison to a fortress in Brittany. As was his custom at such moments, de Gaulle carefully congratulated the army on recent successes—irking the Left without calming the Right. Dronne, now a U.N.R. deputy, declared that such acts of clemency risked throwing the Moslems into the arms of the F.L.N., while the *Mouvement Algérie Française* laid the whole blame for a recrudescence of rebel activity on the President's reprieves and his refusal to pronounce the key

[1] On 12 December 1958 the government created for him the office of Inspector-General of Defence, with imprecise responsibilities. After its suppression under the defence reform of 30 December he became Military Governor of Paris. See above, p. 99.

words 'integration' or '*Algérie française*'. Clemency was simply a 'bonus for assassination'.

But Paris no longer shivered when Algiers frowned. Delouvrier sternly told a delegation that demonstrations would not be tolerated. Sadly the ex-servicemen's committees concluded that 'all unconsidered action would be inopportune for the moment'. Speaking to the nation as President for the first time, de Gaulle was to go further still. Again the finality of the referendum was put in doubt: 'The truth is that the destiny of Algeria is being forged at this moment; that this destiny is essentially in the Algerians themselves. . .'[1] Why should not the possibility of an honourable end to hostilities be seized? Once again the F.L.N. refused to be impressed with talk of peace; so far all de Gaulle had brought them was fine words, twisted elections, and mounting military pressure.

The Right had no monopoly of disquiet. While de Gaulle's policy gave liberals grounds for hope, the consequences of the war filled them with dismay. Hundreds of thousands of Moslems from outlying areas were 'regrouped'. Some villages were merely shifted to new locations, with reasonably satis- factory results; the young S.A.S. officers administering them often gave selfless assistance to their Moslem charges (some even voluntarily prolonged their military service to continue with this work). But, elsewhere, peasants were put in camps, sometimes in conditions of appalling misery. Thousands were living for months in squalor, with inadequate nourishment and no employment. The senior dignitaries of the Catholic and Protestant Churches were moved to issue on their behalf the first joint appeal they had ever made.

If some tales of torture and police brutality were fabricated to F.L.N. orders, the continued existence of torture was ad- mitted by Malraux—who in 1958 had announced its sup- pression.[2] A group of priests serving with the army in Algeria declared that summary execution or torture of prisoners was 'very widespread but not universal'. The reply of the Army Chaplain's Office amounted to an admission.[3] The

[1] *Le Monde*, 1–2 February 1959.   [2] *Le Monde*, 29 August 1959.

[3] 'Is there not in Algeria, beyond the pressure of the necessities of military and public security, a certain ideological intolerance which wants, through torture, to make rebels renounce their nationalist convictions?' (quoted in *Le Monde*, 25 April 1959).

National Synod of the Reformed Church was equally alarmed at 'the excesses of repression', while the Archbishop of Algiers denounced the army's use of psychological methods derived from those of the Communists. Thousands of Moslems were arrested on suspicion and disappeared; usually their families could learn nothing of their whereabouts or fate. Officialdom still seemed to regard the disclosure of arbitrary violence as more heinous than the practice—and to compound the degradation by seizing newspapers. Maurice Audin's murderers remained at large (though Michelet prevented the case being hushed up completely). Kovacs, whose bazooka killed Salan's A.D.C. in mistake for Salan himself, was allowed to escape from custody. The Fifth Republic seemed little closer to a remedy than the Fourth.[1]

De Gaulle could claim to have isolated the activists. But he still seemed powerless against the army, while within the administration there was clear evidence of attempts to sabotage his policies.[2] Some soldiers had acquired a taste for political pronouncements: Massu, Salan, Allard and, inevitably, Juin, all came out with declarations deviating from the government's line—Salan explaining that de Gaulle

[1] Nevertheless there were many who tried to stamp out arbitrary violence. They included the army commander in Algeria who revealed both the size of the problem and his own attempts to fight it in these remarks to one of the authors. 'I think I can honestly say that there is no torture now in this command: perhaps one case in a thousand when a junior officer disobeys his instructions. When I came here, I made it my first job to stamp it out—mostly by persuading officers not only that it was dishonourable but that it didn't even pay, for one got information that was unreliable. We have had to take disciplinary action too, but we never make these cases public. We are ashamed of them. Soon after I began, the Minister rebuked me because my command held the record for incidents of this kind. I told him it was because we were trying to get and send honest reports. And now I really think we have completely stopped torture. The other problem is more difficult: summary executions of prisoners in the field, especially on night patrols. I can't say we have stopped that completely, but I think we have gone most of the way.'

[2] At a particularly delicate moment in Franco-Tunisian relations a member of the Prime Minister's office announced quite falsely that two Moslems, about whose arrest the government was negotiating with the Tunisians, had been handed over to the F.L.N. and shot. The same man falsely told the press that de Gaulle had pardoned thirty Algerians at one stroke. He was not moved (*Le Monde*, 27 February 1959, and 23 July 1959).

dare not mention integration openly because the mainland had still to be educated into accepting it. Less exalted figures let it be known that if de Gaulle proved soft he would be 'dealt with'. Within the army, attacks on the War Minister, Guillaumat, were obviously aimed at the President himself. The Left was increasingly anxious, fearing that de Gaulle had lost his freedom to act, and that the degradation of the Algerian war was taking root more deeply than ever.

Throughout the spring the angry pressure of the activists mounted. There had been no new measures which might be interpreted as integration in deed without the word, while in March de Gaulle returned again to the suspect 'Algerian personality' and announced that Algeria's 'political destiny will appear in the spirit and the votes of her children'.[1] The steady drafting of unreliable officers to safer posts was increasingly evident. Algiers felt itself being insidiously cut off from its indispensable ally. Each announcement of reprieves for terrorists brought fresh outbursts. Martel stormed, 'Every time the army gets the upper hand the government commits an act of weakness, as if it wanted to feed the rebellion'. Even a hothead like Lagaillarde, now a deputy, was accused of having sold out, while the President of the Republic was freely treated as a traitor.

The patriotic organizations decided to boycott the official celebrations of 'the days of May'. As a gesture of appeasement the government—irritating the Left yet again—agreed to celebrate the 13th rather than the 'miracle' of the 16th. But it refused to give the reassuring declaration on integration that the activists were demanding. Instead, de Gaulle explained 'What have I been doing since I came to power. . . . Is that not integration?' and 'What is the political significance of (*Algérie française*)? That Algeria is French. Is it useful to say so, since it is so?' Such ingenuous evasions were scarcely satisfying, when combined with a reminder that 'those who shout the loudest for integration today are those who were formerly against it. What they want is to be given *Algérie de papa*, but *Algérie de papa* is stone dead, and if they do not understand that they will die with it.'[2] These

[1] *Le Monde*, 27 March 1959.
[2] *Le Monde*, 2 May 1959.

declarations provoked a tactical debate among the activists which sent the C.S.P. into its death throes. The ultras maintained their boycott and celebrated 12 May to cries of 'de Gaulle to the gallows' and '*Vive Pétain!*' At the official celebrations there were few Europeans, but many Moslems. Even Massu had stood firm against the bluster from the Right.

Now the moderates took courage. Liberal organizations came into the open. Even in the C.S.P.s Moslems drew away from the defiant intransigence of the Europeans. Here and there opinions were voiced which a year earlier would (at best) have brought imprisonment. Motions of confidence began to mingle with the customary outraged communiqués which had formerly passed for the opinion of Algiers. The municipal and senatorial elections in April and May revealed the same trend. In Médéa the contestants debated that classic parish pump issue, water supplies, more than either integration or *Algérie française*. The activists suffered the consequences of their open disarray, while many familiar political figures made their return. At Algiers a *gros colon*, Senator Schiaffino, was re-elected against a liberal list (Baujard and Ali Khodja), with Sérigny a bad third; Baujard was endorsed by Chalandon and Sérigny by Soustelle, and U.N.R. members were on both their lists. More moderates stood as Gaullist supporters of the Constantine Plan; here and there a liberal mayor or senator was elected. Among them was Benhabylès, a friend and former neighbour of Ferhat Abbas who was clearly destined to be one of de Gaulle's new elite. On reaching Paris he appealed for a federal solution for Algeria.

Even among the *mal élus* of November opinion was shifting. Tension mounted steadily between the diehard integrationists and those who, trusting de Gaulle, preferred to press for social and economic progress. Despite the deliberate omission of 'integration' from its manifesto, the 'Unity of the Republic' group of Algerian deputies lost several Moslem members to the less illiberal U.N.R. When Lagaillarde told the Assembly that it was not a question of 'integrating one million Europeans with nine million Moslems, but of integrating ten million Frenchmen of Algeria with the forty-five millions of the mainland', a Moslem member at once retorted that Lagaillarde spoke only for himself.[1] Mme Khebtani, a veiled woman only a year before, denounced '*Algérie de papa* with its train of corruptions', and argued that true integration would be possible only with the spread of education, irrigation, 'a decent standard of life, and the right to work'.[1] The restive Right had to endure Moslems repudiating the work of the *colons*, rebuking Debré for making concessions to the Europeans, demanding further clemency, and protesting against arbitrary internments. One Moslem deputy took 'the disastrous situation of the Algerians' as ground for setting up a commission of peace and reconciliation.[1] At the other extreme men like Ahmed Djebbour still called for 'a sacred union around *Algérie française*' and insisted that the referendum had fixed for ever the destiny of Algeria.[1] The original united front had cracked; whatever their views, many Moslem deputies were manifestly daring to think for themselves.

The growing independence of the Moslems contributed to the frustration of the Right. At the close of the first parliamentary session its members found themselves no closer to integration, outmanœuvred by Debré, unable to reach the real enemy in the Elysée, and suspect in the eyes of many who had elected them. Increasingly they feared that Debré was the screen behind which de Gaulle was plotting scuttle. While more hopeful of the President's intentions, the Left was alarmed at Debré's apparent tendency to close doors that the President had carefully left open.[2] The central government still had incomplete control over the army and administration.[3] At every turn the General's intentions seemed to be thwarted by passive resistance.

De Gaulle was waiting. Many abuses remained untouched, part of the price he was ready to pay for the confidence of

---

[1] *J.O.*, 10 June 1959, pp. 810–20.

[2] For example: de Gaulle: 'I do not have to recognize this Organization, the F.L.N. It represents, of course, an important force, but in my eyes it does not represent Algeria' (2 May 1959). And Debré: 'The rebellion has no representative value' (5 June 1959). 'The members [of the "G.P.R.A."] represent nothing' (27 June 1959).

[3] The army's determination to play politics was amply demonstrated by a communiqué following a fight near Bône (*Le Monde*, 26 June 1959) which opened, 'With the aim of supporting the campaign for

the army and for preparing the next move. Some of his opponents were silently eliminated. In Kabylia, 'Operation Binoculars' was launched to a great fanfare of pronouncements that a military solution was possible. But General Faure admitted that 'what we are doing out in Kabylia is a labour of Penelope. Every day the work we have undertaken must be begun again. . . . If we do not succeed in having the population with us the war will have no end.' A Moslem deputy said that 'the people here are tired of this war', and envisaged discussions with the F.L.N. after a cease-fire. The cost of the war, particularly to the Moslems, was brought home by the disastrous plight of prisoners and *regroupés*, and the assassination of Senator Benhabylès by the F.L.N. Within France there were signs of growing support for a new attempt to bring peace. Moreover, Debré's irascible insistence on complete support from France's allies, underlined with threats to break up N.A.T.O. and the Common Market underlined the growing isolation of France in the international community.

At last de Gaulle was ready. He had been preparing opinion during his presidential tours by referring to hopes of an early peace. The army and administration were more nearly under control. He chose a moment when, with the United Nations session at hand, he could argue that an initiative was essential to avoid the condemnation of the world. It would also permit parliamentary opinion to mature before the new session. De Gaulle summoned the cabinet to outline on paper their views on Algeria. Then he retired to the Elysée to 'arbitrate'. Next a return to Algeria—his first as President. The army was reassured that there was no question of negotiating with the F.L.N., and that it could 'carry on with the job' until pacification (of which its conception was not exactly his) was complete. But unfailingly every speech to the Moslems, however brief, found place for 'peace'.

Revealing his solution in September, de Gaulle insisted again that he would never negotiate Algeria's future with the

negotiation at present launched in metropolitan France by the F.L.N.'s traditional backers, and to develop terrorist action, a combat group was sent . . .' As the army later discovered, the combat group had no political—or even military—objective; it was simply lost. But F.L.N. propagandists gleefully spread the story which the army spokesman had invented to embarrass the Left.

F.L.N.[1] 'The fate of the Algerians belongs to the Algerians, not by imposing it with knife and sub-machine gun, but according to the desire they will express legitimately by universal suffrage.' But first there must be peace—whether a cease-fire or the success of pacification (defined as the stage when not more than 200 were killed in a year). This must be followed by a transitional period of up to four years 'to allow normal life to begin again, to empty the camps and prisons, to let the exiles return, to re-establish the exercise of individual and public liberties and to allow the population to become fully aware of what is at stake'. Then the Algerians could choose by referendum between secession, 'francisation' and association.[2]

De Gaulle did not hide his belief that 'secession, in which some believe they will find independence' was the worst. 'Improbable and disastrous', it would result in overwhelming poverty, political chaos, widespread butchery, and Communist dictatorship. (This outcome was scarcely rendered less likely by his warning that an independent Algeria would not get the slightest help from France.) 'But the demon must be exorcised, and by the Algerians themselves.' Should they choose independence he promised to 'regroup and establish' those who wished to remain French, while the 'exploitation, transport and shipping of Sahara oil . . . will be assured whatever happens'.

Francisation complète was a degaullism for all-out integration, granting both communities total equality. If de Gaulle did not show any explicit preference, his tone in referring to association was noticeably warmer. This involved 'government of the Algerians by the Algerians', with federal institutions in Algiers (to safeguard minority rights), and with foreign affairs, defence, education, and the economy linked with those of France. Meanwhile, until hostilities ended, pacification was to continue and, the 'democratic way' was to be followed with the election of departmental councils in

[1] *Le Monde*, 18 September 1959.

[2] Two questions were to be submitted to referendum: 'Do you want Algeria to fulfil her destiny with France or without France' and, 'Since you have chosen to be with France, do you want to be administered like metropolitan departments or [under the special regime outlined by the government]?'

1960. From these, administrative, economic, and social councils were to be formed in Algiers—just such specifically Algerian institutions as the Europeans had so bitterly fought at the time of the *loi-cadre*.

Almost every element in the initiative had been underlined repeatedly in various forms in his earlier speeches (even self-determination).[1] But now he said clearly that this could go even as far as 'secession', and that the decision must be totally free. This was a challenge to the F.L.N. It could still claim that without the rebellion none of the measures de Gaulle had introduced, or was promising, would have been granted. In this the rebellion had justified itself. But now de Gaulle was offering self-determination, for which they had been fighting for years, insisting all the while that 90 per cent of Moslems would choose independence in a free vote. What more could they hope to win? As de Gaulle demanded, 'What can be the sense of insurrection?'

But the decision was not so simple. The F.L.N. was being asked to disappear, trusting that its members would be allowed to return to normal life. It must have confidence not only in de Gaulle's continued health and total good faith, but in his ability to force the army to accept independence if need be. Some sections of the declaration remained vague, notably the conditions for the referendum. Remembering earlier elections and the 1958 referendum, the F.L.N. passionately mistrusted any vote organized by a French administration with the army remaining in occupation—no matter how many neutral observers there might be. Yet it was being asked to accept the whole package, ambiguities and all.

This time it dared not risk a brusque rejection, for internal reasons as well as for fear of discrediting itself internationally. After twelve days of deliberations in Tunis it acknowledged the progress which had been made (attributing it to the rebellion), declared it was ready to submit to a genuine popular verdict, attacked the partition of the country (which seemed implied in the offer of secession) and condemned the

[1] He is reported to have told Maurice Clavel in 1957 that if he returned to power 'France is going to give to the maximum; she dislikes half-measures which turn against her. She likes great concessions which bring all back to her.... The more the Algerians are free the more they will be united to the French' (*Le Monde*, 8–9 September 1957).

subordination of the result of the referendum to ratification in France. Yet, while insisting that it was 'the trustee and guarantor of the interests of the Algerian people until it has made known its decision', and reiterating that five years of war had justified its claim to be representative, the 'G.P.R.A.' declared itself prepared to forgo its status as a provisional government (self-proclaimed, but recognized by sixteen other countries). This renunciation of its claim to exclusive representation of Algeria was the F.L.N.'s counter-concession to 'secession'. Moreover, it was prepared to negotiate the political and military conditions of a cease-fire, and the terms of self-determination.

The harsh tone of the F.L.N. reply raised sighs of relief on the Right; pacification could continue. 'This "yes" means "no"', cried L'Aurore, joining in the attempt to prove that no common ground could exist. Yet the F.L.N. was bound to reassure its militants (as de Gaulle had reassured his in making his offer) by cloaking appreciable concessions in unacceptable language. In fact, the F.L.N. communiqué showed that there was still hope, even if de Gaulle's terms were not wholly acceptable. No doors had been closed, but the assurances and clarifications could be given only if the two sides could be brought together.

Predictably, the extreme Right stigmatized de Gaulle's offer as unconstitutional and treasonable. 'Even by referendum, not even the nation has the right to give its consent (least of all hypothetically) to the amputation of territory', asserted Bidault.[1] 'Surrender is on the march'; 'little by little the scuttlers are triumphing'; 'self-determination is the surrender of Algeria': such were the diehards' reactions. Again the Algerians were divided. While Unity of the Republic boycotted the Algeria debate in the Assembly in protest, one Moslem deputy declared that 'self-determination, including that of those who are fighting and of those who are interned, is the only way that permits account to be

[1] Le Monde, 20–21 September 1959. But the President simply made a declaration which was approved (subsequently) by both the cabinet and Parliament. There was therefore no question of the declaration itself infringing any article of the constitution, although constitutional revision might be needed to put the plan into effect. See also below, p. 258, and Article 53 (para. 3) of the constitution.

taken of the human realities without which nothing durable can be done'. All but three of the twenty-four Moslem senators approved de Gaulle's policy and called for the use of 'all the necessary ways and means, *excluding none*, to achieve a speedy end to the fighting'. The Left and the Centre gave their approval gladly, while even the Communists (who at first denounced self-determination as a mere manœuvre) were to come grudgingly into line after Khrushchev's speech encouraging de Gaulle.

But many on the orthodox Right, and a large section of the army, were distressed. How could the three-part offer be explained to ill-educated peasants? De Gaulle had outlined procedures without telling the officers in the countryside what their goal was to be. The army was to oppose secession, but was forbidden to show a preference between the two 'French solutions'. It had been zealously rallying the villagers by promising that it would never leave them, but would remain to carry through the transformation de Gaulle had promised. Only by giving Moslems the certainty that their trust would not be betrayed could it win their allegiance. For the Right feared that the Moslems were overwhelmingly *attentiste* (whereas de Gaulle seemed to picture them as frustrated Frenchmen). The Right therefore believed that by admitting the possibility of secession he was undermining the army in the psychological battle. By 'institutionalizing doubt' he had tipped the scales to the F.L.N., for who would risk offending them if they were soon to be ruling Algeria? Accordingly, when the Assembly voted overwhelmingly its support for the President's policy, many in the C.N.I. and U.N.R. bowed only to loyalty to the General, or to the manifest popularity of the offer among their constituents. Many, unreconciled, set out at once to organize the campaign for *francisation*, with conceptions of a free consultation far from de Gaulle's.

Algiers founded Committees of Resistance Against Surrender, but for the moment its fury was impotent. In a joint letter to Algerian deputies the activists' organizations bitterly declared, 'We see the man we carried to power renounce the work of the army and use the arms that we forged for him to destroy us'. For Senator Paulian of Algiers the lesson was obvious: 'de Gaulle cannot be intimidated. He spoke to

France and to the world. He cannot repudiate himself . . .
while it is constitutionally impossible to overturn him. . . .
De Gaulle is not MacMahon; he has an enormous popular
appeal. . . . The 13 May succeeded because of a miracle, a
conjuncture which brought Algiers, the army and the mainland together with the same aims at the same time. This
conjuncture will not be repeated. A new 13 May will find no
echo on the mainland.'[1] Such indeed might be the immediate
situation, but if Challe declared that the army was one behind
its chief, Juin, Weygand and Zeller all showed their hostility
to the President's policy, and Massu tried to explain it away.
De Gaulle found it necessary to remind the army (in much
milder terms) of words he had used in August. 'You are the
army of France. You only exist by her, because of her, and
for her. You are at her service, and that is your *raison d'être*.'[2]
If a cease-fire were accepted, could de Gaulle keep the loyalty
of this restive army and thwart the plotters who were already
working for a new insurrection? On the answer hung the fate
of the regime.

[1] *Le Monde*, 4–5 October 1959.
[2] *Le Monde*, 1 September 1959.

P

Conclusion

The Gaullist Transition: Pre-Fascism or New Deal?

Un régime, c'est d'abord un style; rarely has this been more
evident than under the Fifth Republic. Few systems of
government have been so conscious of their style. The Fifth
Republic was born of a revolution which rejected the style of
the old regime as fiercely as its policies. Its creators sought to
replace the System not simply with fresh institutions, leaders
and policies, but with a whole new approach to government.
Their new regime was to be stable, cohesive, bristling with
efficiency and, above all, independent and authoritative. By
asking what is the Fifth Republic's style we therefore ask
not only how it governs, but what success it has had in
making reality match this vision.

Inevitably the performance has fallen short of the promise.
Like so many revolutionaries, the founders of the Fifth Republic overestimated the freedom of action power would
bring. Many of them apparently believed that if they found
the right institutions and a fresh set of rulers, their 'certain
image' of France would be revealed in its pristine splendour.
In the best revolutionary tradition, they reckoned without
original sin. For the old System was in many ways an expression of French society. That society was being steadily
changed by the spread of an international culture, the pressure of industrialization and urbanization, and the stirrings
of competition in sectors once dominated by the cult of the
small man. Such changes will continue independently of
anything the Fifth Republic may contribute. But the complete elimination of the System would demand a root and
branch attack on French society itself.

The new leadership applies a mildly reforming and mana-
gerial conservatism to a social structure which the peaceful
revolution of 1958 left practically unscathed. Since the society
from which the Fifth Republic springs is changing so gradually,

210

it is not surprising that—except at its most exalted pinnacle—the new regime bears many similarities to its predecessor. Perhaps these are relics which time will liquidate, perhaps the System has left ineradicable roots; provisional judgments may prove cruelly unjust or mercifully forbearing. The Gaullist proconsulship is clearly transitional—but to what, no man can tell.

The regime falls short of the dynamic decisiveness it promised. This is most evident in de Gaulle's handling of the Algerian war. Before revealing his proposals to the cabinet and the nation in September 1959, he travelled to Algeria to reassure himself about military opinion. The army, and not the people or even de Gaulle—despite his claim to have 'arbitrated'—determined the limits within which France could meet Moslem aspirations. If progress has been painfully slow since June 1958, this is mainly because a military veto would be fatal.

De Gaulle's success has been a product more of his genius for manœuvre and his personal prestige than of the new institutions. The State still dare not assert its authority. De Gaulle's conception of the President as arbiter means little when an army which has tasted the blood of one Republic confronts a political void. His achievements in Algeria have been bought by unsentimental sacrifices elsewhere. He has not squandered his 'capital' by challenging openly the insubordinate soldiers who twist and frustrate his policies, or publicly punishing military practices he must abhor (although offenders are often dealt with behind the scenes). His refusal to recognize such problems publicly still inhibits the revival of independent political forces to fill the vacuum in France itself.

While de Gaulle was not responsible for the disintegration of the central power which now limits his freedom of action, many of his supporters were loud in encouraging the army to think politically. Once the genie of the pronunciamento is summoned from the bottle it is not easily put back. Many of the Fifth Republic's leaders were so closely associated (even compromised) with the military in 1958 that they still only half-heartedly support the President's attempt to restore discipline. Not until peace comes can de Gaulle seriously hope to re-educate the army into obedience to the civil power. Meanwhile the regime lives dangerously.

The Algerian problem breeds indecision or partial ineffectiveness in quite different fields. Today, resources absorbed by the war cannot be used for housing, education and social welfare on the scale the country needs. But the problem goes far deeper, for unless she secedes, Algeria will remain a crushing burden long after a cease-fire. Because of the weakness of the State, other policies are subordinated to the overriding necessity not to prejudice an Algerian solution. Unpleasant decisions must be shelved or avoided in order not to alienate groups whose allegiance is essential, or disturb the prevailing political apathy. By seeking to be all things to all men the government sometimes seems to institutionalize indecision.

The founders of the Fifth Republic clearly expected the government's greater unity and sense of purpose to produce greater decisiveness. Liberated from the tyranny of 'politics', they could treat policy as a series of technical problems. Not even the greater (and welcome) discretion about cabinet deliberations can conceal the failure of this hope. There have been persistent disagreements over certain policies, while ministers have sometimes implemented agreed decisions in quite contradictory ways.[1] The deplorable slowness with which such dissensions are resolved derives partly from a chronic failure of co-ordination, and partly from the oppressive role of the Elysée.

For the moment de Gaulle *is* the Fifth Republic, responsible for both its virtues and its vices. Subject to the problem of controlling the military, when de Gaulle wishes to decide, he decides (despite the declaration in the constitution that 'the government guides and directs the policy of the nation'). His message to the army about his Algerian policy states explicitly: 'On my own responsibility, and in full knowledge of the facts, I have decided what our action in Algeria must be.'[2] His cabinet and the U.N.R. leaders recognize as his exclusive domains Algeria, the Community, defence and diplomacy

---

[1] See above, pp. 161–2.
[2] *Le Monde*, 30 October 1959.

(all confided to technician-ministers). Other ministries, notably Housing and Finance, have never been more independent. But no one is wholly exempt from the President's intervention. When de Gaulle's attention was caught by the rapid rise in prices, he brusquely summoned the economic ministers to the Elysée for an unsolicited 'arbitration' of their differences. Conversely, the Arbiter often declines to rule on problems he considers beneath his attention. A disagreement over competence in Community affairs between Pinay, Janot and Lecourt dragged on for months, with de Gaulle simply counselling moderation. Debré has never completely established himself as a subsidiary arbiter. Whether and when the President will intervene is unpredictable. Even in his own domain he does not attempt to lay down every detail of policy. The effective limits to his power are blurred and shifting.

When de Gaulle lays down a verdict it must still be interpreted by his ministers and executed by an administration which he does not personally control. Even given complete harmony, the oracular character of the General's utterances can cause uncertainty, and policies are inevitably subtly reinforced or diluted as they pass downwards. The correction of errors and misunderstandings is complicated and laborious. A senior civil servant summed up: 'For forty years we have had governments with no power; now we have a power but no government.'[1]

The Fifth Republic has indeed had moments as humdrum, as indecisive—and as squalid—as the Fourth. Even 'strong' government does not confer the ability to do everything at once. But de Gaulle's priorities were plain. From the beginning he insisted that the constitution, Algeria and the colonies came first. There could be no final solution of secondary problems until the prime objectives were attained. Within this system of priorities the record is encouraging. The government has contributed to economic recovery and has pursued a foreign policy which is at least vigorous. The constitution has been changed, the colonial question all but settled, and the Algerian problem attacked, perhaps decisively. By any normal standard these are substantial achievements. Few

[1] *Le Monde*, 16 April 1959.

other French leaders would have tackled these problems, and none could have travelled even half as far on the road to success.

Style

The Fifth Republic is a benevolent despotism partially tempered by republican democracy. Behind the screen of secrecy around the making of decisions, courtiers are intriguing for the ear of a sovereign whose attentions are unevenly divided. Those who have his blessing prosper; some lesser figures work in fruitful independence; others languish from inability to capture his interest. But because the regime has dispensed with much of the public confusion and controversy which are inherent in democracy, it can maintain the impression of that tranquil efficiency vaunted by every 'strong' government.

This authoritarian tinge, and the character of some supporters of the regime, have inevitably brought charges of monarchism, bonapartism, boulangism, or fascism. Traces of all these can be found. The Fifth Republic is based on an alliance between the *homme providentiel* and the people. It is indifferent or hostile to politicians, representative institutions and the normal processes of democratic discussion. Government is a matter for the rulers; the citizen should merely accept decisions, and from time to time ratify them. Indifference to public affairs and the abdication of independent criticism are treated as civic virtues. The new philosophy exalts the Nation—not the nation as it exists, but the General's romanticized vision of the quintessence of France. She is to fulfil her destiny by a 'policy of national ambition' based on a belief in 'the higher interest of France, which is something quite different from the immediate advantage of Frenchmen'.[1]

Yet the Gaullist regime clearly distinguishes itself from totalitarian systems in refusing to impose itself by force. Although the state of public liberties in France still leaves much to be desired, no one can reasonably brand this as a regime which persecutes its critics. Every point of view can be read and heard; infringements of freedom of speech are

[1] General de Gaulle, *Mémoires de Guerre*, Vol. III, p. 28.

few, despite the attention they rightly receive. Where abuses remain—torture, arbitrary internment, interference with the press and the right of association—the Fifth Republic has a markedly more liberal record than the last governments of the Fourth. De Gaulle has set his face against even moral coercion, such as verbal excommunication of his opponents from the national community. Where totalitarians (including some of his own supporters) have normally aroused hatred, de Gaulle has preached brotherhood and reconciliation. The contrast was caught in his call to the Algerians at Constantine:

> Why kill? It is living that matters. Why destroy? Our duty is to build. Why hate? We must co-operate. . . . Before the human race today there are two roads—war or fraternity—in Algeria and everywhere else. France for her part has chosen fraternity.[1]

Apart from the referendum, the State has used the means of persuasion at its disposal no more extensively than earlier governments. De Gaulle has never encouraged a personality cult, or even sought to perpetuate his system.

Here, in the succession, is the heart of the dilemma—as in fully authoritarian regimes. Not merely the person of the next President, but the whole form of government after de Gaulle is in question. Personal presidential rule will no doubt die with him. But there is no certainty that Debré's *régime parlementaire* will step smartly into the breach. It is not only the democrats who wait for the General's passing. For, although the resort to de Gaulle will surely have justified itself if he can resolve the Algerian problem, and despite the great services he can render to France in other fields, the very methods he is—perhaps necessarily—employing are paralysing the forces making for a healthily democratic succession.

To de Gaulle the political institutions and movements which comprise his Republic are apparently a necessary evil. They must be reckoned with, and used as counters for manœuvre, but he scarcely seems to conceive that they might play a truly constructive part. He apparently regards them as Sieyès viewed second chambers: if they agree they are

---

[1] Quotations from de Gaulle in this chapter are taken from *L'Année Politique* 1958, pp. 561, 567, 545, 540, 567.

superfluous; if they disagree, obnoxious. An angry Algerian deputy commented, 'Never has a regime paid so much attention to elections and so little to the elected.' While de Gaulle so completely dominates the political scene, there seems little hope either of the cabinet establishing its independence and authority, or of Parliament attaining the stature Debré expected.

The problem is aggravated by the General's insistence on national unity. The search for consensus is admirable in a country whose political wounds are so deep, and where partisanship is so often excessive or irresponsible. But de Gaulle and Debré have felt it necessary to seek unity by avoiding debate, by concealing their intentions, and by trying to remove major issues from politics altogether. When Mollet resigned over the economic measures of December 1958, de Gaulle replied, 'The budget is an affair of the moment. I admit that you might not approve of it; I admit that you might not sign it. But this disagreement over one point does not in the least justify your departure.' Yet if the cost of living or Algeria are not political issues, what are?

Gaullist government has thus further debilitated political life. Even the Communists have lacked bite. Their ageing and unimaginative Stalinist leadership has failed to exploit economic difficulties, while the General's master-stroke in coaxing a favourable word for his Algerian policy from Khrushchev forced them into yet another dismal somersault and weakened their attack still further. The myth of its invincibility shattered, reduced to a handful in Parliament, the party is for the moment impoverished and impotent. Nevertheless, scattered election results suggest that it is recovering most of its lost voters.

The state of the democratic Left is equally parlous. Its parliamentary position is weak, and its lack of popular strength, revealed so nakedly in May 1958, still persists. Although hostile to the government's economic policy, it cannot press its opposition effectively. For even the most rabid anti-gaullists have now realized that if it comes to the test with the fascists or the military, they must stand shoulder to shoulder with de Gaulle. The attempt to fashion the left-wing groups into an effective alternative to the S.F.I.O. has made some progress; and the P.S.A. won a notable convert to Socialism in Mendès-France. But it may be years before this reformed Left can test its strength at the polls. Meanwhile it has no parliamentary representation and makes hardly any impact on the public.

More important for the immediate future is the dilemma of the U.N.R. It exists purely to support de Gaulle. Yet he has always declined to be identified with it (since he belongs to the entire nation), and he regards it with manifest suspicion. Its function is to be the finest mass of brute votes in Europe. On 'presidential' questions it must have no mind of its own and, since the General's thoughts turn to almost anything, it should not commit itself too forcefully on other matters. The party has been deterred from launching a widespread recruiting campaign, or from implanting the local organizations which have enabled M.R.P. (also a mushroom party) to establish itself over the years. Its march along the path to political suicide is magnificent in its way—but it is not politics.

In these conditions the U.N.R. can scarcely hope to develop into a coherent political party. But its very survival is an achievement. It has shown surprising resistance to the efforts of its rivals to hasten its disintegration. Hardly any of its rank and file followed the leaders of the right wing out of the movement in October 1959. And the Left Gaullists' successive attempts at founding a party have failed. De Gaulle, aloof above the battle, has given them no leadership and little encouragement. Not surprisingly, their militants are few and their spokesmen divided.

'The leaders of the Fourth Republic', de Gaulle has said, 'were men of worth, honesty and patriotism. But, never representing anything other than fractions, these rulers did not identify themselves with the general interest.' Neither de Gaulle nor Debré conceives of the general interest emerging from the clash of political forces. Neither has much sympathy for—or even understanding of—the motives of party men. Few politicians have more zealously guarded their doctrinal purity than Debré; few have shown more scorn for the mindless compromising of the parties of the System. And yet both men expect the parties to accept without question the General's policies, whatever their own doctrine may be.

No party escapes the malaise which the present system induces. The pattern of political life has become more unreal and confused than ever. Critics have been hoping for years for the disintegration of the old barriers of partisanship and bigotry. But such political atrophy is dangerous and sterile unless political forces regroup and reform in a more coherent and rational way. The policy of mystification and anaesthesia frustrates this development. Unless political life can be given more meaning, the Fifth Republic will find its parties as ambivalent and undisciplined as the old Radical-Socialists. This is the breeding ground for a renaissance of the System.

The System and the *régime parlementaire* are not the only contenders in the struggle for the Gaullist succession. In a country with so revolutionary a political tradition, the extremes can never be forgotten. Both de Gaulle and Debré have warned that if the Fifth Republic failed the outcome might be Communist or fascist totalitarianism. Numerically the fascists are utterly insignificant. But men like Dr. Lefèvre are ready:

> I shall wait for events to prove me right. I shall wait for the discrediting of the Fifth Republic. I hope to help make the *régime parlementaire* disappear. I do not know how long that will take, but I am sure that parliamentarianism is doomed.[1]

Such forces are nurtured in a climate where the play of normal political life seems futile, where decisions are left to a leader, and where public interest in political life is undermined. The Algerian war is sowing seeds of hatred, violence and conspiracy—usually sinister and occasionally serious. And, while the Communists are sluggish today, a fascist take-over bid might well revive—by reaction—their own enthusiasm and their power of attraction. The discrediting of parliamentary democracy could only play into the hands of one or the other extreme.

On the day when de Gaulle told the Assembly of his proposals to meet the crisis he added, 'But all this would bring only temporary relief to a disastrous state of affairs unless we decide to put an end to the profound cause of our trials'. Seeing this cause in the political system, he seems to believe

---

[1] *Les Paroles Restent . . .* (Pretoria recording, 25 TNV 3).

the problem solved with the voting of the constitution. In December 1958 he wrote to Mollet: 'One question dominates everything: to restore the Republic to its place. This will be done on 8 January.' But the battle for French democracy is far from won. The convalescence cannot be completed without deep-seated social change. Meanwhile the regime faces two dangers: the totalitarian threat, and relapse into the old ways. Democracy cannot flourish in a climate which makes it seem irrelevant. The last two Republics died for lack of the affection and respect of the people.

De Gaulle believes that France is made for triumph or catastrophe—not for mediocrity. He despises political leaders who set their sights lower. Yet politics and statesmanship are not opposed but complementary. De Gaulle, who has urged France to 'marry her epoch', is well aware that a twentieth-century country cannot be ruled by eighteenth-century methods, and accepts the necessity of democracy. But today public assent to a regime cannot be mobilized without parties which actively concern themselves with 'the immediate advantage of Frenchmen' as well as 'the higher interest of France'. Such independent forces can be revived only from below: not from above. Regrettably, de Gaulle, amid all his immense services to his country, is smothering instead of fostering their growth. But a more vital political life is urgently needed to enable the renovated Republic to defy the extremist challenge, and to survive the departure of its founder. Without this, French democracy will be in danger, and catastrophe more probable than triumph.

EPILOGUE

The second year of the Fifth Republic opened with a double crisis: in Paris, the defection of Pinay and his followers of the parliamentary Right; in Algiers, an armed rising by the *colons* which strained the precarious loyalty of the army and threatened the very existence of the regime.

The tension between government and Parliament, President and politicians recalled the friction which, just fourteen years before, had led de Gaulle to retire from public life. In Paris, authoritarian 'new men', impatient with defeatism at home and 'scuttle' in the Community, formed strange links with Fourth Republican survivors, wedded to parliamentary traditions and concerned for European and Atlantic solidarity; their aims were opposed, but each hoped to gain from a crisis. In the countryside, discontent evoked memories of the Third Republic as well as the Fourth. Behind such noisy skirmishers as the *bouilleurs* and the ex-servicemen were more formidable forces. Debré's 'final solution' of the schools question enraged the Left, whose leaders, after labouring to recruit platoons for the battles of the last eighteen months, suddenly found a volunteer host enthusiastically re-fighting the anti-clerical campaigns of the last century. The peasantry was even more exasperated than usual at the government's neglect, particularly its abandonment of the sliding scale for agricultural prices. Pinay, the farmers' main target, was himself at odds with almost all his colleagues (especially Jeanneney, the 'technocratic' Minister for Industry); hostile to the cabinet's foreign policy, its insufficiently clerical schools bill, and its new 'social' measures[1]; in dispute with the Premier over the powers of his own office, and utterly at odds with de Gaulle, who accused him of living in the wrong Republic.[2] Refusing to resign, he was dismissed on 13 January 1960, and retired

[1] A more generous wages policy, Jeanneney's state-capitalist projects for marketing Saharan oil and developing distressed areas, and Michelet's bill for workers' representation on boards of directors (which Pinay called 'sovietization of business').

[2] *Le Monde*, 17 December 1959.

to his personal Colombey at St. Chamond, 'holding himself at the country's disposal'.[1]

His successor, Wilfrid Baumgartner, Governor of the Bank of France since 1949, shared his financial views. Yet the change marked a turning-point. Pinay was the last non-Gaullist parliamentarian in a key post, the only minister except Soustelle with any personal standing with the French public, and the only one with the weight or self-confidence to oppose de Gaulle. Without him the government would look (and be) more technocratic, more presidential than ever. This would not help its relations with Parliament, where its base was now dangerously narrow. For the Socialists and Radicals, who on Algerian and Community policy might have been tempted to enter an alternative majority, had just been utterly alienated by the church schools bill. And the old majority was falling away. The strong opposition within the C.N.I. launched a violent all-round attack in the official party paper, accusing de Gaulle of wrecking friendships, dislocating alliances and sabotaging European union. 'Has he not so undertaken his task that he can neither interrupt it, nor conceive of anyone succeeding him . . . without catastrophe threatening or breaking out . . . his glory, his mission, his task ending in failure and more than failure, in defeat and disaster?'[2]

The government's credit was already wearing away even before Pinay went. Though the C.N.I. were to claim all the credit for his policies, three-quarters of them had in December voted against his budget (like the Radicals and Algerians) or abstained (like M.R.P.). The majority fell below fifty (220–172), and included only 42 non-U.N.R. members. Even in the U.N.R. group itself, nearly thirty defected (8 actually voting against); and strong pressure for Delbecque's return promised trouble for the new secretary-general, Richard (who was making even less effort than Chalandon to build a party

[1] Pinay was the first victim of the new rule to prevent a parliamentarian who took office retrieving his seat on resigning it. But his electoral colleague and parliamentary successor (see p. 252) at once offered to resign the seat so that Pinay could return at the ensuing by-election. So, in February, did Soustelle's substitute. If this (predictable) practice grows, it will eliminate the benefits sought by excluding ministers from Parliament.

[2] *France Indépendante*, 11 January 1960; it followed *L'Humanité* in calling de Gaulle 'the General-President'.

machine). When Pinay made his grievances public at the New Year, he opened a grave *crise sèche*; once the cabinet would have fallen, but now it merely broke in pieces behind half-closed doors.[1] 'Back to the days of great manœuvres', commented Jacques Fauvet, claiming that the Right was using Pinay as a stalking-horse to get rid of de Gaulle himself.[2] If the President retaliated by dissolving the Assembly, the C.N.I. fully expected to profit from the destruction of the U.N.R.

Parliament again seemed the domain of the System. New members no less than old evaded the rules against absenteeism, read their speeches, concentrated on parochial grievances, introduced trivial and demagogic bills. The *bouilleurs'* debate was as squalid as under the System; indeed their chief lobbyist handed down his orders from the strangers' gallery just as Poujade had once done. Standing orders were ingeniously perverted. Though special committees had been invented to weaken pressure groups, these found them easy to pack; the *bouilleurs'* spokesmen even protested when the bill was sent to an ordinary committee.[3] When electronic voting switches came in, members received individual keys to them, symbols of their independence—which they promptly (and quite improperly) handed over to their party leaders or *boîtiers*, whose status—like that of savage chiefs—came to depend on the weight of metal ornaments they carried.[4] Though deputies complained constantly of their impotence, they could still wrest concessions from a divided or indecisive government. Pressure exerted through them forced it to bring in a schools bill; their amendments destroyed the fragile compromise which had just preserved its unity. In rapid succession they drastically altered the fiscal reform bill, drove Debré to promise to restore some ex-servicemen's bonuses in

[1] Less severe previous ones were Berthoin's and Houdet's resignation (p. 153n.), the revolt against self-determination (pp. 117–8), and Boulloche's resignation over the schools bill a week before.

[2] *Le Monde*, 9 January 1960.

[3] *J.O.*, 3 December 1959, p. 3152. By convention, the ordinary committees concerned came to choose the special committee members; naturally they picked those most interested—in both senses—in the subject. A special committee was set up on the energy tax to escape the Finance Committee's hostility: *J.O.*, 3 November 1959, pp. 2145–7.

[4] According to P. Viansson-Ponté in *Le Monde*, 7 January 1960.

the next budget, and mangled to death the bill on the *bouilleurs*.[1]

But members' discontent was understandable. In December the Constitutional Council ruled out any attempt to introduce bills which modified decrees.[2] In a major foreign affairs debate the Socialist spokesman (Conte) protested at having to discuss the foreign policy of an irresponsible President, while Bidault even refused to take part in a 'so-called debate' of 'a Parliament reduced to uselessness'.[3] The rigidity of the constitution could harm the government. Since Article 34 allowed Parliament to deal only with the 'fundamental principles' of education, ministers were obliged to retain complete control over the administration of the new aid to church schools—the central point in the dispute—and found it hard to appease their critics by concessions; while the clerical party, distrusting Debré's zeal in their cause, tried to make him give specific pledges on how he would use these 'purely executive' powers.

Many difficulties of the new regime were brought out by the treatment of the budget. A special session had to be called to solve the time-limit problem (see p. 155, note 2). The joint committee procedure was applied to a conflict nominally between the two houses, but really between both and the government; intended to protect ministers against one hostile house, it in fact enabled them—amid extreme confusion—to thwart both.[4] Using the 'package' vote procedure

[1] Yet the last may have been a Pyrrhic victory, for the government could still allow Mendès-France's decree, so often postponed, to go into force. Unless it does so it can hardly repeat its proud boast, '*Le pouvoir ne recule pas*'.

[2] Two M.R.P. senators had brought in a bill to abrogate a decree for increasing farm leases. Debré (using Art. 41) claimed it was out of order as outside the domain of the law; the Council upheld him.

[3] *J.O.*, 28 December 1959, p. 3672; *Le Monde*, 30 December 1959.

[4] The Assembly passed the budget on 28 November, only 109 votes being cast for a censure motion (see p. 144n). The Senate amended and accepted it (174–80, 13 December). A conference committee then agreed a text which, with government amendments, passed the Assembly (220–172, 19th) but was lost in the Senate (128–73, 21st). The Assembly now had to revert to the *original* text as first amended by the Senate, into which it then reintroduced those conference committee amendments which the government had accepted (moved by the Finance Committee) and the government's own amendments (moved by the Minister). Deputies themselves were understandably confused; the first amendment

ruthlessly,[1] Debré still prided himself not only on passing the budget by Christmas (for the first time since 1927) but also on his liberalism—the House of Commons, he claimed, passes the budget in a single vote after less than a day's debate![2] But Reynaud, chairman of the Finance Committee, protested at 'conditions hardly compatible with the proper work or even the dignity of the Assembly', hoping they would never be repeated; and even Chaban-Delmas warned the government that the separation of powers should not prevent their co-operation.[3]

There were also difficulties within the executive branch. Once ministers ceased to agree, the new secrecy and solidarity of their deliberations proved fragile growths. Edifying details spread abroad, from the argument over the cabinet minutes on the schools bill which ended with Boulloche resigning, to the effort to dissuade him by issuing with the bill a commentary 'qualifying it to the point of contradiction'.[4] The R.T.F. strikers (p. 163) could claim they were not forcing the hand of the government, but strengthening that of the minister responsible for the service (Frey) whose plans to fulfil overdue government promises were being blocked by Finance Ministry obstruction. (The technician-ministers, who had mostly established surprisingly cordial relations with Parliament, now showed themselves as vigorous controversialists as their 'political' colleagues.)

Policies laid down by the monarch still suffered sabotage by the 'lesser barons'. And, wrote a shrewd observer of the court, 'Those who approach the summit . . . dare not say

proposed by a member—an old hand first elected in 1946—was 'pointless', said the *rapporteur général*. 'Its aim is to restore the Senate's text. But we are debating the Senate's text.' (*J.O.*, 22 December 1959, p. 3555.) As amended, the bill passed the Assembly (248–133, 22nd) and the Senate (116–100, with 82 abstaining or not voting, 23rd). Had the Senate rejected it, the Assembly would then have had the last word.

[1] He demanded one vote on the whole bill *and* the most controversial clauses, which were thus never voted on—sometimes not even debated—separately. The Assembly changed its standing orders to get a Constitutional Council ruling on this stifling form of guillotine; the Council disallowed the amendment.

[2] *J.O.* (*Sénat*), 21 December 1959, p. 1923.

[3] *J.O.*, 30 December 1959, p. 3751.

[4] 'This isn't a government, it's an open forum' was the *Canard Enchaîné*'s comment.

anything disagreeable to hear, or hint there has been disobedience. Would they `even get a hearing? From time to
time, a number of warning signals do get through all the
barriers and filters, right to the head of state's desk. But then,
isolated from their context, they are in danger of appearing
. . . tiresome but happily isolated and exceptional cases.'[1]
Administrative muddle and obstruction, warned two ex-
Ministers of Overseas France, were endangering all de Gaulle's
designs for the Community.[2]

Inert or deliberate sabotage could undo much but by no
means all that he was trying to do. At Dakar in December he
announced a sweeping change in the conception of the Community, accepting Mali's demand for independence ('which
I prefer to call international sovereignty') and promising a
rapid adaptation of the Community's institutions.[3] Other
member states, led by Madagascar, at once sought the same
status. Senghor welcomed the new 'contractual Community',[4]
and pithily summarized the complicated present and doubtful
future. 'At Paris', he said, 'Gaullism may mean ambiguity,
and at Algiers danger—but at Dakar it means progress and
emancipation.'[5]

In Algiers the danger was growing acute. There above all
de Gaulle's clear intentions became distorted in application.
Torture persisted despite official instructions: when four
Catholic officers denounced the courses in it given at one army
training centre, Guillaumat protested that these practices
were punished and the centre had been closed—but did not
deny the facts.[6] Le Monde published a Red Cross report on

[1] Le Monde, 8 January 1960 (P. Viansson-Ponté).
[2] Gaston Defferre in L'Express, 23 December 1959, and Le Monde,
15 December 1959; P.-H. Teitgen in Le Monde, 29 December 1959.
Lecourt, Minister for the Community, admitted: 'The slightest operation
proposed by one of the States of the Community involves the opening
of files, the meeting of numerous committees, interminable comings and
goings. At present we are considering almost a thousand files . . .',
Le Monde, 31 December 1959. (However, at the end of 1959 the Pacific
islands of Wallis and Futuna voted to become an Overseas Territory.)
[3] Le Monde, 15 December 1959. Art. 86 could hardly remain intact.
[4] ibid.
[5] L'Express, 17 December 1959.
[6] Le Monde, 24 December 1959. Similarly, over La Gangrène, the
examining magistrate rejected the government's grounds for seizing the
book. It was then republished.

internment camps, which welcomed improvements over the last year and commended conditions in most camps under Gambiez (Oran) or Olié (Constantine)—but severely condemned over a third of those in the Algiers command.[1] The familiar gap between policy and execution, so often exposed by the critics and covered up by official spokesmen, was now to widen until it threatened the Fifth Republic's very existence.

Tension mounted rapidly among the Europeans of Algeria. They had felt momentary relief in November when the F.L.N. named Ben Bella and his fellow-prisoners as negotiators (see p. 196), and de Gaulle flatly refused to deal with 'those who are *hors de combat*', or to discuss political conditions. (If the F.L.N. hoped to impress the United Nations they failed; France again narrowly escaped condemnation by a two-thirds majority.) But the *colons'* satisfaction was short-lived. First, terrorism—in decline everywhere else—had a sudden and murderous revival in Algiers and the surrounding plain. Next the F.L.N. held a long conference at Tripoli (far from both Nasser and Bourguiba) and reorganized the 'G.P.R.A.' to confront de Gaulle, as he had demanded, with military men who enjoyed the prestige to risk unpopular concessions and the authority to enforce them.[2] Then de Gaulle called a high-level Algerian conference at the Elysée. Was a new political move impending? The warnings and danger-signals multiplied; Georges Bidault was banned from Algeria.

The army apparently decided to sound the alarm. Massu (whose departure from Algiers was already expected) was the Lacoste of the January 1960 rising. In an interview with a leading German journalist (introduced by General Challe himself), the violence of his reported criticisms of de Gaulle's policy forced the issue into the open. Despite protests from the Minister of Armed Forces, de Gaulle insisted on Massu's recall. For the apprehensive Europeans of Algiers this was the last straw.

[1] *Le Monde*, 5 January 1960. Only one other Paris paper reported this matter objectively; most concealed it completely from their readers. The Red Cross also protested against the F.L.N.'s continued refusal to allow it access to prisoners or even a list of names (*Le Monde*, 23 January 1960).

[2] Among the seven ministers dropped were all the four who had visited Communist China, and two friends of Nasser. The moderate politicians and the soldiers stayed; effective power passed to three of the latter.

Sunday, 24 January, was tense. After day-long demonstrations in defiance of the authorities, the gendarmerie were suddenly fired on by ultras of the French National Front (an offshoot of Martel's organization). As in 1958, paratroops replaced them. The F.N.F. leader, Joseph Ortiz (a counter-terrorist and bazooka plot suspect), barricaded the city's main square; Martel set up headquarters nearby, and Lagaillarde in the University. The Algiers Europeans gave the 'insurgents' full moral support (though few took any active part), and among the many political leaders who gave their approval were Paulian and a 'liberal' senator, as well as the inevitable Alain de Sérigny. A general strike was called, and spread rapidly throughout Algeria. But though Oran was tense for a time, no other city followed the capital's lead as they had twenty months before. And the Moslems stayed completely aloof. From the Casbah, which had mustered scores of thousands to cheer for de Gaulle, Lagaillarde's fellow-deputy Kaouah could raise barely a hundred to demonstrate against him. At Mostaganem territorials fired on a Moslem crowd shouting *'Vive de Gaulle!'* Never had the communities been further apart.

Once again the army had the crucial role. Some officers had encouraged the insurgents to act; others had allowed arms and reinforcements to reach them; none wanted to fire on fellow-countrymen demanding the right to remain French. Yet few were ready for open disobedience. Their problem would be solved if only de Gaulle would make policy concessions to satisfy the *colons*—and the army itself.[1] Ministers and senior officers pleaded with him to do so, or at least opposed the use of force against the insurgents. But de Gaulle would not budge. On Friday, 29 January, he broadcast to the nation, and to the army above all. He pledged that it would supervise the freedom of the referendum on Algeria's future, and denounced the 'liars and plotters' who suggested that he would greet with anything

---

[1] Many assumed he would; the Algerian deputies compared him unfavourably with Mollet, who had refused to fire on Frenchmen.

'I hate the idea of military rule or a fascist regime', said Challe to a journalist. 'But . . . if a defeated French army were to return home accompanied by half a million furiously angry Algerians, France would be under dictatorship before three months were up.' *Paris-Match*, 6 February 1960.

but joy a Moslem choice of 'the most French solution'.[1] But he was insistent that that choice must be wholly free, contemptuous of an army which, by placing conditions on its loyalty, became 'an anarchical and derisory collection of military clans', and implacable with the 'guilty men who dream of usurping power'. The army had tried to confront him with the cruel choice: concessions or bloodshed? Skilfully he threw back the dilemma, allowing them to choose their own means to restore order—within forty-eight hours. The F.L.N. could draw their conclusions from his stubborn insistence on keeping his word to the Moslems, even to the point of risking civil war among Frenchmen.

His appeal succeeded. Hitherto the city had been controlled by Massu's paras, the troops most sympathetic to the *colons*, long stationed in Algiers and largely drawn from the town. They had done little to stop the assembly of Sunday's rioters, the erection of barricades, or the rallying of Europeans in defiance of curfew and state of siege. Now the general who had relied on them was removed, and the Foreign Legion and paratroops from another division (Ducournau's) were brought in. The insurgents were cut off from the army and from the civilian sympathizers on whom they relied.

Impressed by de Gaulle's firm speech, the army was further shaken by the unanimity of French opinion. No one now talked of invading the mainland, where approval of the government and condemnation of Algiers were far more widespread, sharp and vocal than in May 1958. A token strike, called jointly by all unions in support of de Gaulle, was highly successful. Socialists and U.N.R. came together to defend the Republic. Only two U.N.R. deputies came out for the insurgents. But the C.N.I. Executive hastened to put out a statement of complete solidarity with the Algiers members who were championing Lagaillarde. Then, as the week passed and the army and opinion rallied to de Gaulle, Duchet denounced the 'untruth' that identified his 'concern for peace' with support for insurrection, and the 'imbecile calumny' that the C.N.I. wanted to overthrow the regime.

[1] By approving Soustelle's phrase for integration (but only on condition the Moslems chose it), de Gaulle allowed some of his opponents to save face—and others to distort his position.

Others remembered that, unprovoked, the insurgents had killed fourteen and wounded 120 of their fellow-countrymen. De Gaulle would not hear of immunity for their leaders; Lagaillarde, Kaouah, Biaggi, Lefèvre and Sérigny were arrested, and Le Pen prosecuted. But the repression was not fully effective. Some of the more sinister conspirators in the shadows remained at liberty. The Paris police carried out orders with little zeal, many of those arrested were soon released, and from the Algiers 'redoubts' surrounded by troops, Ortiz and Martel escaped as easily as Kovacs before them.[1]

A purge was clearly needed. Though Gambiez in Oran and Olié in Constantine had stayed loyal, all de Gaulle's cautious military politics had failed to secure obedience in the city where it was crucial. The familiar plotters of 6 February 1956 and 13 May 1958 had yet again been allowed to build up their private army, and had almost succeeding in forcing Paris to capitulate once more. Yet could a purge of disloyal individuals meet the case? The first victim was Colonel Godard, director of security and the last surviving military architect of 13 May. But what had been gained by removing all his colleagues—or indeed the 4,000 other officers posted by de Gaulle—when their successors were tempted on to the same path by the circumstances of the war itself? Like 'liberal' Governors-General, 'reliable' officers soon succumbed to the atmosphere of Algiers and the 'logic' of the war.

The purge was extended to the cabinet. Soustelle and Cornut-Gentille were dismissed for opposing action against the insurgents; Terrenoire took over Information, and Guillaumat, accused of 'softness', relinquished the Ministry of Armed Forces to a liberal Gaullist, Messmer (a high colonial official, then serving as a reserve officer in Algeria). More than ever the *Canard Enchaîné* seemed justified in saying 'We have a shadow cabinet, just like the British—only ours is in office'.

Throughout the crisis Parliament had remained in recess, and no emergency powers had been invoked—for the constitutional armoury, so carefully stocked against foreign invasion or

[1] One of the first acts of the insurgents had been to liberate Kovacs' accomplices in the bazooka plot, whose state of health had—by a strange coincidence—brought all of them to a comfortable incarceration in an Algiers hospital. They too disappeared from the 'redoubt' before the capitulation.

parliamentary obstruction, could provide no solution to the problem of military disobedience (see p. 127). Only when the insurgents disbanded and the crisis ended was Parliament summoned—for a mere twenty-four hours—to confer special powers (not under Article 16, which was scarcely applicable and highly unpopular, but under Article 38) to maintain order, defend the State and constitution, pacify and administer Algeria. These were vague terms, and as the government insisted that the powers must last a year Parliament could not debate their use until April 1961. The need to strike hard at the plotters hardly seemed to justify a Parliament (which had shown no disloyalty) abdicating so much power for so long to ministers many of whom—from the Premier downwards—had themselves faltered in face of the insurrection. But, to proclaim their confidence in de Gaulle, members voted the bill by huge majorities: 441–75 in the Assembly, 225–39 in the Senate. And less than a tenth of the 72 Moslem '*mal élus*' joined with the *colons* and Communists who opposed the President.[1]

In Algeria the government made prompt use of its powers. The insurgent leaders were moved to prisons in France, and their cases transferred to the capital. Policemen from Paris took over control of security; a new public prosecutor was appointed; and the prefects recovered their normal powers from the army. The psychological warfare branch, the chief stronghold of the military extremists, and the territorial units which had been their instrument, were both dissolved. Twenty senior officers were removed from Algeria, and three generals (including Faure and Gribius) retired from the army.

The soldiers were given some compensation. Procedure for trying terrorists was speeded up, and an ugly precedent was set when well-known defence counsel for the F.L.N. were prosecuted for sedition. Seizures of newspapers became rather more frequent and arbitrary. Yet on balance Moslem opinion welcomed the government's measures as the first serious check ever inflicted on the Europeans. More confident in de Gaulle

---

[1] For the bill were 32 Moslem deputies (out of 48), 20 senators (out of 24), 8 Algerian European deputies and one senator; against it, 7 Moslem deputies and no senator, 14 European deputies and two senators. The opposition also included a quarter of the Conservative deputies, rather fewer senators, and one or two left-wingers like Mitterrand.

than ever before, Moslems might lose patience with a completely intransigent F.L.N. To exploit this mood, the government brought forward the departmental council elections; boundaries were to be re-drawn on ethnic lines, so that the new departments could form the bases for a federal structure, if the referendum went in favour of association, or for partition if the vote were for independence. The early elections thus afforded both a means of pressure on the F.L.N. to make a new offer (for fear of partition), and also a foundation for an alternative policy if it refused. In Algeria, therefore, the stage was set for a new act.

In France the crisis marked a long step away from a parliamentary regime. For if few democratic leaders have enjoyed the popular support that de Gaulle commands, few have paid it less attention. Though not despising this support, he takes it for granted, as being in the nature of things. In his broadcast he called for obedience in the name, not only of the people's vote, but of the respect due to the State and to 'the national legitimacy which I have incarnated for twenty years'.

The crisis, which forced the President to take personal responsibility for his policy, might also seem to have exposed and obliterated his unreal conception of *arbitrage*. This is not de Gaulle's view. It would not be in character for him to turn openly to the Left as the Right and the army draw away from him. He still hopes to pursue his course successfully without taking sides between Frenchmen, or rupturing—for the second time in his career—the unity of the nation and of its army, on which he sets so high a value. So he is driven to rely more and more exclusively on his own prestige, rather than on any independent force. Cabinet and Parliament are yet further debased; the regime becomes still more presidential. While the problem of the succession looms, further than ever from a solution, de Gaulle's own eminence has become even lonelier than before.

APPENDIX I

CONSTITUTION OF THE FIFTH REPUBLIC[1]

PREAMBLE

The French people solemnly proclaims its attachment to the Rights of Man and to the principles of national sovereignty as defined by the Declaration of 1789, confirmed and completed by the preamble to the Constitution of 1946.

In accordance with these principles and that of the free determination of peoples, the Republic offers to those Overseas Territories which manifest their will to adhere to them new institutions founded on the common ideal of liberty, equality and fraternity and conceived with a view to their democratic evolution.

ART. 1   The Republic and the peoples of the Overseas Territories who by a freely determined decision adopt the present Constitution, establish a Community.

The Community is based on the equality and solidarity of the peoples composing it.

TITLE I

SOVEREIGNTY

ART. 2   France is a Republic, indivisible, lay (*laïque*), democratic, and social. She assures equality before the law to all citizens without distinction of origin, race or religion. She respects all beliefs.

The national emblem is the tricolour flag, blue, white and red.

The national anthem is the 'Marseillaise'.

The motto of the Republic is 'Liberty, Equality, Fraternity'.

Its principle is: government of the people, by the people and for the people.

ART. 3   National sovereignty belongs to the people, who exercise it through their representatives and by way of referendum.

Neither any section of the people nor any individual can claim exercise to it.

Suffrage may be direct or indirect under conditions provided for by the Constitution. It is always universal, equal and secret.

All French citizens of both sexes who have attained their majority and who possess their civil and political rights are electors under conditions determined by law.

[1] The translators did not conceive it their task to correct defective syntax, re-cast unwieldy sentences or elucidate ambiguities. While not claiming infallibility, they have tried to render 'the worst-drafted of all French constitutions' as faithfully as possible. (P.M.W. and M.H.)

ART. 4 Political parties and groups assist in the expression of the franchise. They are formed and conduct their activities freely. They must respect the principles of national sovereignty and of democracy.

TITLE II

The President of the Republic

ART. 5 The President of the Republic sees to it that the Constitution is respected. By his arbitration he ensures the regular functioning of the public authorities, as well as the continuity of the State.

He is the guarantor of the nation's independence, of its territorial integrity, of respect for Community Agreements and treaties.

ART. 6 The President of the Republic is elected for seven years by an electoral college comprising the members of Parliament, of departmental councils (*conseils généraux*) and of Assemblies of the Overseas Territories as well as the representatives elected by the municipal councils.

These representatives are: the mayor, in communes of less than 1,000 inhabitants; the mayor and first assistant mayor, in communes from 1,000 to 2,000 inhabitants; the mayor, first assistant mayor and a municipal councillor chosen according to the order in which he appears on the council list[1] in communes from 2,001 to 2,500 inhabitants; the mayor and two first assistant mayors, in communes from 2,501 to 3,000 inhabitants; the mayor, two first assistant mayors and three municipal councillors chosen according to the order in which they appear on the council list, in communes from 3,001 to 6,000 inhabitants; the mayor, two first assistant mayors and six municipal councillors chosen according to the order in which they appear on the council list, in communes from 6,001 to 9,000 inhabitants; all municipal councillors, in communes of more than 9,000 inhabitants; in addition, in communes of more than 30,000 inhabitants, delegates nominated by the municipal council at the rate of one delegate for every 1,000 inhabitants above 30,000.

In the Overseas Territories of the Republic the representatives elected by the councils of administrative units are also included in the electoral college under conditions determined by an organic law.

The participation of the Member States of the Community in the electoral college of the President of the Republic is settled by agreement between the Republic and the Member States of the Community.

The detailed application of the present Article is settled by an organic law.

ART. 7 The election of the President of the Republic requires an absolute majority on the first ballot. If this is not obtained, the President of the Republic is elected on the second ballot by a relative majority.

[1] i.e. taken in the order of seniority in office.

Voting is opened at a time fixed by the Government.

The election of the new President takes place not less than twenty and not more than fifty days before the powers of the President in office expire.

If the Presidency of the Republic should fall vacant for any reason, or if the Constitutional Council referred to by the Government certifies by a decision of an absolute majority of its members the incapacity of the President to act, the functions of the President of the Republic, with the exception of those provided for by Articles 11 and 12 below, are provisionally exercised by the President of the Senate. If the Presidency falls vacant, or when the incapacity is certified permanent by the Constitutional Council, voting for the election of the new President takes place, except in the event of *force majeure* certified by the Constitutional Council, not less than twenty and not more than fifty days after the opening of the vacancy or the declaration of the permanent character of the incapacity.

ART. 8   The President of the Republic appoints the Prime Minister. He puts an end to his tenure of office when the latter presents the resignation of the Government.

On the proposal of the Prime Minister, he appoints the other members of the Government and terminates their tenure of office.

ART. 9   The President of the Republic presides over the Council of Ministers.

ART. 10   The President of the Republic promulgates laws within two weeks (*quinze jours*) following the transmission to the Government of the law as finally adopted.

He may, before this period expires, ask Parliament for a new discussion of the law or certain of its articles. This new discussion cannot be refused.

ART. 11   The President of the Republic may, on the proposal of the Government during parliamentary sessions or on the joint proposal of the two assemblies, published in the *Journal Officiel*, submit to a referendum any government bill dealing with the organization of public authorities, carrying approval of a Community Agreement or proposing to authorize the ratification of a treaty which, without being contrary to the Constitution, would affect the functioning of institutions.

When the bill has been adopted by referendum, the President of the Republic promulgates it within the time laid down in the preceding article.

ART. 12   The President of the Republic may, after consulting the Prime Minister and the Presidents of the assemblies, declare the National Assembly dissolved.

A general election takes place not less than twenty and not more than forty days after the dissolution.

The National Assembly meets automatically the second Thursday following its election. If this meeting takes place outside the periods

234

laid down for ordinary sessions, a session of two weeks is automatically opened.

A new dissolution cannot be effected within the year following this election.

ART. 13 The President of the Republic signs ordinances and decrees deliberated upon in Council of Ministers.

He appoints to the civil and military posts of the State.

Conseillers d'Etat, the Grand Chancellor of the Legion of Honour, ambassadors and envoys extraordinary, senior councillors of the *Cour des Comptes*, prefects, representatives of the Government in the Overseas Territories, general officers, rectors of academies and directors of central administrations are appointed in Council of Ministers.

An organic law determines the other posts to be filled in Council of Ministers as well as the conditions under which the appointing power of the President of the Republic may be delegated by him to be exercised in his name.

ART. 14 The President of the Republic accredits ambassadors and envoys extraordinary to foreign powers; foreign ambassadors and envoys extraordinary are accredited to him.

ART. 15 The President of the Republic is the chief of the armed forces. He presides over the higher councils and committees of national defence.

ART. 16 When the institutions of the Republic, the independence of the nation, the integrity of its territory or the execution of its international commitments are gravely and immediately threatened and the regular functioning of the constitutional public authorities is interrupted, the President of the Republic takes the measures required by these circumstances after official consultation with the Prime Minister and the Presidents of the assemblies as well as with the Constitutional Council.

He informs the nation of these measures by a message.

These measures must be inspired by the will to assure to the constitutional public authorities, within the shortest possible time, the means of fulfilling their tasks. The Constitutional Council is consulted on these measures.

Parliament meets automatically.

The National Assembly cannot be dissolved during the exercise of the exceptional powers.

ART. 17 The President of the Republic has the right of pardon.[1]

ART. 18 The President of the Republic communicates with the two parliamentary assemblies by messages which are read for him and which cannot be debated.

If Parliament is in recess it is specially recalled for this purpose.

ART. 19 The acts of the President of the Republic other than those

[1] '*Le droit de faire grâce*' covers an unlimited right of reprieve, pardon and commutation of sentence.

provided for in Articles 8 (paragraph 1), 11, 12, 16, 18, 54, 56 and 61 are countersigned by the Prime Minister and, where applicable, by the appropriate ministers.

TITLE III

THE GOVERNMENT

ART. 20   The Government determines and guides the policy of the nation.

The administration and the armed forces are at its disposal.

It is responsible to Parliament under the conditions and according to the procedures provided for in Articles 49 and 50.

ART. 21   The Prime Minister directs (*dirige*) the action of the Government. He is responsible for national defence. He ensures the execution of the laws. Subject to the conditions of Article 13, he exercises rule-making power (*le pouvoir règlementaire*) and makes civil and military appointments.

He may delegate certain of his powers to ministers.

When necessary, he deputises for the President of the Republic as the president of the councils and committees provided for under Article 15.

In exceptional instances, he may preside in his place at a meeting of the Council of Ministers by virtue of an express delegation and for a specific agenda.

ART. 22   The acts of the Prime Minister are countersigned, where applicable, by the ministers responsible for their execution.

ART. 23   The office of member of the Government is incompatible with the exercise of any parliamentary mandate, with national office in any 'professional'[1] organization, with any public employment, or with any professional activity.

An organic law determines the conditions in which provision is made for replacing the holders of such mandates, offices, or employments.

The replacement of members of Parliament takes place in conformity with the provisions of Article 25.

TITLE IV

THE PARLIAMENT

ART. 24   Parliament comprises the National Assembly and the Senate.

Deputies to the National Assembly are elected by direct universal suffrage.

The Senate is elected by indirect suffrage. It ensures the representation of the territorial units of the Republic. Frenchmen resident outside France are represented in the Senate.

[1] The French text is '*toute fonction de représentation professionnelle à caractère national*' (see p. 251).

Art. 25 An organic law determines the duration of the powers of each assembly, the number of its members, their remuneration, the system of ineligibilities and incompatibilities.

It also determines the conditions under which are elected the persons called to replace deputies or senators whose seats fall vacant, until the complete or partial renewal of the assembly to which they belong.

Art. 26 No member of Parliament may be prosecuted, sought out, arrested, detained or tried because of the opinions or votes expressed by him in the exercise of his duties.

During parliamentary sessions, no member of Parliament may be prosecuted or arrested for any crime or misdemeanour without the authorization of the assembly of which he is a member, except *in flagrante delicto*.

When Parliament is not in session, no member of Parliament may be arrested without the authorization of the *bureau* of the assembly of which he is a member, except for cases of *flagrante delicto*, previously authorized prosecutions or confirmation of sentence.

The detention or prosecution of a member of Parliament is suspended if the assembly to which he belongs demands it.

Art. 27 All imperative mandates are null and void.[1]

The voting rights of members of Parliament are personal.

The organic law may authorize proxy voting in exceptional circumstances. In this case, no person may receive more than one proxy.

Art. 28 Parliament meets automatically in two ordinary sessions a year.

The first session begins on the first Tuesday in October and ends on the third Friday in December.

The second session opens on the last Tuesday in April; its length may not exceed three months.

Art. 29 Parliament meets in special session at the request of the Prime Minister or of the majority of the members forming the National Assembly, on a specific agenda.

When the special session is held at the request of the members of the National Assembly, the decree of closure takes effect as soon as Parliament has exhausted the agenda for which it was called and at the latest twelve days from the date of its meeting.

Only the Prime Minister may ask for a new session before the end of the month which follows the decree of closure.

Art. 30 Apart from cases in which Parliament meets automatically, special sessions are opened and closed by decree of the President of the Republic.

Art. 31 Members of the Government have access to the two assemblies. They are heard at their own request.

[1] The prohibition of *mandats impératifs* is apparently intended to prevent the practice employed by some Communist and right-wing parties of forcing members of Parliament to deposit undated resignations.

They may be assisted by commissioners of the Government.

ART. 32 The President of the National Assembly is elected for the duration of the legislature. The President of the Senate is elected after each partial renewal.

ART. 33 The sittings of the two assemblies are public. The verbatim report of the debates is published in the *Journal Officiel*.

Each assembly may meet in secret session at the request of the Prime Minister or of one-tenth of its members.

TITLE V

RELATIONS BETWEEN PARLIAMENT AND THE GOVERNMENT

ART. 34 Laws are voted by Parliament.

Laws determine the rules concerning:

—civil rights and fundamental guarantees accorded to the citizens for the exercise of public liberties; the national defence obligations imposed upon the persons and property of citizens;

—the nationality, status and legal capacity of persons, the law of matrimony, inheritance and gifts;

—the determination of crimes and offences as well as the punishments applicable to them; criminal procedure; amnesty; the creation of new orders of jurisdiction and the rights and duties of the judiciary (*statut des magistrats*);

—the basis, rate and methods of collection of taxation of all types; the system of issuing money.

The law also determines the rules concerning:

—the electoral system for the parliamentary assemblies and local assemblies;

—the creation of categories of public corporations (*établissements*);

—the fundamental guarantees accorded to civil and military employees of the State;

—the nationalization of undertakings (*entreprises*) and the transfer of the property of undertakings from the public to the private sector.

Laws lay down the fundamental principles:

—of the general organization of national defence;

—of the free administration of local government units, of their powers and their resources;

—of education;

—of the status of property, real estate laws and civil and commercial obligations;

—of the law pertaining to employment, unions and social security.

The budget determines the revenues and obligations of the State under the conditions and with the exceptions provided for by an organic law.

Programme-laws determine the objectives of the State's economic and social activities.

The provisions of the present article may be detailed and completed by an organic law.

ART. 35 The declaration of war is authorized by Parliament.

ART. 36 The state of siege is decreed in Council of Ministers. Its extension beyond twelve days can be authorized only by Parliament.

ART. 37 Matters other than those which are in the domain of the law fall within the rule-making sphere.

Texts in legislative form intruding in these matters may be modified by decrees taken after an opinion has been given by the *Conseil d'Etat*. Such texts arising after the entry into force of the present Constitution may not be modified by decree unless the Constitutional Council has stated that they fall within the rule-making sphere under the preceding paragraph.

ART. 38 For the execution of its programme, the Government may ask Parliament to authorize it to pass by ordinances, during a limited period, measures which are normally in the domain of the law.

Ordinances (*Les ordonnances*) are passed by the Council of Ministers after an opinion has been given by the *Conseil d'Etat*. They come into force upon their publication, but become null and void if the ratification bill is not submitted to Parliament before the date fixed by the enabling act.

At the end of the period mentioned in the first paragraph of the present article, the ordinances may be modified, in those matters which are in the legislative domain, only by a law.

ART. 39 The right to introduce bills belongs concurrently to the Prime Minister and to members of Parliament.

Government bills are discussed in Council of Ministers after the opinion of the *Conseil d'Etat* has been taken, and are handed to the *bureau* of one of the two assemblies. Budget bills are submitted to the National Assembly first.

ART. 40 Proposals (*propositions*)[1] and amendments drafted by members of Parliament are out of order when their adoption would have as a consequence either a diminution of public revenue or the creation or the increase of public expenditure.

ART. 41 If it becomes apparent in the course of the legislative process that a proposal (*proposition*)[1] or amendment is not in the domain of the law or is contrary to a delegation accorded by virtue of Article 38, the Government can ask for it to be ruled out of order.

[1] '*Propositions*' may be '*de loi*' (private members' bills) or '*de résolution*' (private members' motions). The latter were declared unconstitutional by the Constitutional Council, see above p. 140n.

289

In the event of a disagreement between the Government and the President of the assembly concerned, at the request of either, the Constitutional Council gives a ruling within a period of a week (*huit jours*).

ART. 42   In the first assembly to which they have been submitted the discussion of government bills proceeds upon the text presented by the Government.

An assembly receiving a text voted by the other assembly deliberates on the text which is transmitted to it.

ART. 43   At the request of the Government or of the assembly to which they have been submitted, bills[1] are sent for study to committees specially designated for this purpose.

Bills[1] for which no such request has been made are sent to one of the permanent committees, the number of which is limited to six in each assembly.

ART. 44   Members of Parliament and the Government have the right of amendment.

After the opening of the debate, the Government may oppose the consideration of any amendment which has not been submitted previously to the committee.

If the Government so request, the assembly considering it decides by a single vote on all or part of the text under discussion, in which only the amendments proposed or accepted by the Government are retained.

ART. 45   Every bill[1] is examined successively in the two assemblies of Parliament with a view to the adoption of an identical text.

When, as a result of a disagreement between the two assemblies, it has not been possible to pass a bill[1] after two readings by each assembly or, if the Government has declared it urgent, after a single reading by each of them, the Prime Minister is entitled to call for a meeting of a joint committee, drawn equally from both assemblies, with the task of proposing a draft on the provisions still under discussion.

The text drawn up by the joint committee may be submitted by the Government for the approval of the two assemblies. No amendment is in order except with the Government's agreement.

If the joint committee does not succeed in adopting a common text or if this text is not adopted under the conditions set forth in the preceding paragraph, the Government may, after a new reading by the National Assembly and by the Senate, ask the National Assembly to make the final decision. In this case, the National Assembly may take up either the text drawn up by the joint committee, or the last text voted by itself, modified if need be by one or more of the amendments adopted by the Senate.

ART. 46   The laws on which the Constitution confers the character of organic laws are passed and amended according to the following rules.

[1] *Projets et propositions de loi*, i.e. both government and private members' bills.

The bill[1] is not submitted for deliberation and vote in the first assembly to which it is referred, until a fortnight has expired since its introduction.

The procedure laid down in Article 45 applies. However, failing an agreement between the two assemblies, the text can be adopted by the National Assembly at the final reading only by an absolute majority of its members.

Organic laws relative to the Senate must be voted in identical terms by the two assemblies.

Organic laws may not be promulgated until the Constitutional Council has declared them in conformity with the Constitution.

ART. 47   Parliament votes budget bills under conditions laid down by an organic law.

If the National Assembly has not concluded its first deliberation with a decision (*ne s'est pas prononcée en première lecture*) within a period of forty days after the introduction of a bill, the Government refers it to the Senate, which must come to a decision within a fortnight. The procedure then follows in accordance with the provisions set forth in Article 45.

If Parliament has not decided within a period of seventy days, the provisions of the bill may be put into operation by ordinance.

If the budget bill fixing revenue and expenditure for a fiscal year has not been introduced in time to be promulgated before the beginning of that fiscal year, the Government asks authority from Parliament, as a matter of urgency, to collect taxes, and allocates by decree the credits relating to the estimates [already] approved.

The time-limits set forth in the present article are suspended when Parliament is not in session.

The *Cour des Comptes* assists Parliament and the Government in the supervision of the execution of the budget.

ART. 48   The agenda of the assemblies includes, by priority, and in the order determined by the Government, the discussion of bills introduced by the Government and of private members' bills accepted by it.

At one sitting a week priority is given to the questions of members of Parliament and replies by the Government.

ART. 49   After deliberation by the Council of Ministers, the Prime Minister stakes the existence of the Government before the National Assembly on its programme or, possibly, on a declaration of its general policy.

The National Assembly calls into question the existence of the Government by the vote of a motion of censure. Such a motion is in order only if it is signed by at least one-tenth of the members of the National Assembly. The vote cannot take place until forty-eight hours after its introduction. The only votes of which a count is taken are those favourable to the motion of censure, which can be adopted only by a majority

---

[1] See footnote, p. 240.

of the members forming the Assembly. If the motion of censure is rejected, its signatories cannot propose a new one in the course of the same session, except in cases provided for in the following paragraph.

After deliberation by the Council of Ministers the Prime Minister can stake the existence of the Government before the National Assembly on the vote of a text. In this case, this text is considered as adopted, unless a motion of censure, put down during the following twenty-four hours, is voted in the conditions set forth in the preceding paragraph.

The Prime Minister has the right to seek the Senate's approval of a declaration of general policy.

Art. 50 When the National Assembly adopts a motion of censure or when it disapproves the programme or a declaration of general policy of the Government, the Prime Minister must give the President of the Republic the resignation of the Government.

Art. 51 If necessary the closure of ordinary or special sessions is automatically postponed to allow the application of the provisions of Article 49.

TITLE VI

Treaties and International Agreements

Art. 52 The President of the Republic negotiates and ratifies treaties.

He is informed of all negotiations leading to the conclusion of an international agreement not subject to ratification.

Art. 53 Peace treaties, commercial treaties, treaties or agreements relative to international organization, those which involve the finances of the State, those which modify provisions of a legislative nature, those which are relative to the status of persons, those which require cession, exchange or acquisition of territory, can be ratified or approved only by a law.

They take effect only after having been ratified or approved.

No cession, exchange, or acquisition of territory is valid without the consent of the populations concerned.

Art. 54 If the Constitutional Council, consulted by the President of the Republic, the Prime Minister or the President of either assembly, has declared that an international commitment contains a clause contrary to the Constitution, the authorization to ratify it or to approve it can take place only after the revision of the Constitution.

Art. 55 Treaties or agreements regularly ratified or approved have, upon their publication, an authority superior to that of laws, on condition, for each agreement or treaty, that it is applied by the other party.

TITLE VII

THE CONSTITUTIONAL COUNCIL

ART. 56 The Constitutional Council consists of nine members, whose term lasts nine years and is not renewable. One-third of the Constitutional Council is renewed every three years. Three of the members are appointed by the President of the Republic, three by the President of the National Assembly, three by the President of the Senate.

In addition to the nine members provided for above, former Presidents of the Republic are *ex-officio* life members of the Constitutional Council.

The President is appointed by the President of the Republic. He has a casting vote in case of a tie.

ART. 57 The duties of a member of the Constitutional Council are incompatible with those of a minister or a member of Parliament. Other incompatibilities are determined by an organic law.

ART. 58 The Constitutional Council supervises the regularity of the election of the President of the Republic.

It examines complaints and announces the results of the vote.

ART. 59 The Constitutional Council rules, in case of dispute, on the regularity of the election of deputies and senators.

ART. 60 The Constitutional Council supervises the regularity of the conduct of a referendum and announces the results.

ART. 61 Organic laws, before their promulgation, and standing orders of the parliamentary assemblies, before they come into force, must be submitted to the Constitutional Council, which decides upon their conformity to the Constitution.

To the same ends, laws may be referred to the Constitutional Council, before their promulgation, by the President of the Republic, the Prime Minister or the President of either assembly.

In the cases provided for by the two preceding paragraphs, the Constitutional Council must give its ruling within a period of one month. However, at the request of the Government, if the matter is urgent, this period is reduced to a week.

In these same cases, reference to the Constitutional Council suspends the time-limit for promulgation.

ART. 62 A provision declared unconstitutional may not be promulgated or put into force.

The decisions of the Constitutional Council are subject to no appeal. They are binding on public authorities and all administrative and juridical authorities.

ART. 63 An organic law determines the rules of organization and functioning of the Constitutional Council, the procedure which is followed before it, and particularly the time-limits allowed for referring disputes to it.

TITLE VIII

THE JUDICIAL AUTHORITY

ART. 64   The President of the Republic is the guarantor of the independence of the judicial authority.

He is assisted by the High Council of the Judiciary.

An organic law lays down the rights and duties of the judiciary (*magistrats*).

Judges (*Magistrats du siège*) are appointed for life.

ART. 65   The High Council of the Judiciary is presided over by the President of the Republic. The Minister of Justice is its *ex-officio* Vice-President. He may deputize for the President of the Republic.

In addition the High Council includes nine members designated by the President of the Republic in conditions determined by an organic law.

The High Council of the Judiciary makes recommendations for the appointment of judges of the *Cour de Cassation* and of First Presidents of *Cours d'Appel*. In conditions fixed by the organic law, it gives its opinion on the recommendations of the Minister of Justice in respect of the nominations of other judges. It is consulted about pardons in conditions determined by an organic law.

The High Council of the Judiciary gives rulings as the disciplinary council of the judges. It is then presided over by the First President of the *Cour de Cassation*.

ART. 66   No one may be arbitrarily detained.

The judicial authority, guardian of individual liberty, ensures the respect of this principle under conditions provided for by law.

TITLE IX

THE HIGH COURT OF JUSTICE

ART. 67   A High Court of Justice is established.

It is composed of members elected by the National Assembly and by the Senate, from among their own members and in equal numbers, after each complete or partial renewal of these assemblies. It elects its President from among its members.

An organic law determines the composition of the High Court, its rules of operation and the procedure applicable before it.

ART. 68   The President of the Republic is accountable for the acts performed in the exercise of his duties only in the case of high treason. He can be indicted only by the two assemblies ruling by identical vote in an open ballot and by an absolute majority of their members. He is tried by the High Court of Justice.

Members of the Government can be brought to trial for acts performed in the exercise of their duties and recognized as crimes or offences at the moment they were committed. The procedure defined above applies to them as well as to their accomplices in the case of a plot against the security of the State. In the cases laid down in the present paragraph, the High Court is bound by the definition of crimes and offences and also by the determination of punishments such as follow from the penal laws in force at the moment when the acts were committed.

TITLE X

The Economic and Social Council

ART. 69   The Economic and Social Council, consulted by the Government, gives its opinion on government bills, draft ordinances or decrees, as well as on private members' bills which are submitted to it.

A member of the Economic and Social Council may be designated by it to explain before the parliamentary assemblies the opinion of the Council on the proposals (*projets ou propositions*) which have been submitted to it.

ART. 70   The Economic and Social Council may also be consulted by the Government on any problem of an economic or social character affecting the Republic or the Community. All plans or [governmental] programme-bills[1] of an economic or social character are submitted to it for advice.

ART. 71   The composition of the Economic and Social Council and its rules of operation are determined by an organic law.

TITLE XI

Territorial Units

ART. 72   The territorial units of the Republic are communes, departments, and Overseas Territories. Any other territorial unit is created by law.[2]

These units administer themselves freely through elected councils and under the conditions provided for by law.

In departments and territories, the delegate of the government has charge of national interests, administrative supervision and respect for the laws.

ART. 73   The legislative system and the administrative organization of the Overseas Departments may be the subject of measures of adaptation required by their special situation.[3]

ART. 74   The Overseas Territories of the Republic have a special organization taking account of their particular interests within the interests of the Republic as a whole. This organization is defined and

---

[1] i.e. bills specifying plans for more than one financial year.
[2] See below, p. 258.
[3] See below, p. 258.

modified by law after consultation with the territorial assembly concerned.

ART. 75   Citizens of the Republic who do not have ordinary civil status (*statut civil de droit commun*), the only status referred to in Article 34, retain their *statut personnel* as long as they have not renounced it.[1]

ART. 76   The Overseas Territories may retain their status within the Republic.

If they express the will to do so by deliberation of their territorial assembly within the period fixed in the first paragraph of Article 91, they may become either Overseas Departments of the Republic or, grouped among themselves or not, Member States of the Community.

TITLE XII
THE COMMUNITY

ART. 77   In the Community established by the present Constitution the States enjoy autonomy; they administer themselves and manage their own affairs democratically and freely.

There is only one Community citizenship.

All citizens have equal rights, whatever their origin, their race and their religion. They have the same duties.

ART. 78   The field of competence of the Community includes foreign policy, defence, currency, common economic and financial policy, and also policy on strategic raw materials.

It further includes, except by special Agreement, supervision of justice, higher education, general organization of external and common transport, and telecommunications.

Special Agreements may establish other common fields of competence or regulate any transfer of competence from the Community to one of its Members.

ART. 79   Member States benefit from the provisions of Article 77 as soon as they have exercised the choice provided for in Article 76.

Until the measures required for the application of this title come into force, matters of common competence are settled by the Republic.

ART. 80   The President of the Republic presides over and represents the Community.

The Community has an Executive Council, a Senate and a Court of Arbitration as institutions.

ART. 81   The Member States of the Community participate in the election of the President according to the conditions set forth in Article 6.

The President of the Republic, in his capacity of President of the Community, is represented in each State of the Community.

ART. 82   The President of the Community presides over the Executive Council of the Community. It consists of the Prime Minister of the Republic, the heads of government of each of the Member States of

---

[1] This refers to the legal status of French Moslems.

the Community, and the ministers responsible on behalf of the Community for common affairs.

The Executive Council organizes the co-operation of Members of the Community in the spheres of government and administration.

The organization and functioning of the Executive Council are determined by an organic law.

ART. 83 The Senate of the Community is composed of delegates whom the Parliament of the Republic and the legislative assemblies of the other Members of the Community choose from their own membership. The number of delegates from each State takes into account its population and the responsibilities it assumes in the Community.

It holds two sessions a year, which are opened and closed by the President of the Community and may not exceed one month each.

When referred to by the President of the Community, the Senate deliberates on common economic and financial policy before laws in these fields are voted by the Parliament of the Republic, and, where applicable, by the legislative assemblies of the other Members of the Community.

The Senate of the Community studies the acts and the treaties or international agreements specified in Articles 35 and 53 and which commit the Community.

It takes decisions having the force of law in the fields where it has received a delegation of power from the legislative assemblies of the Members of the Community. These decisions are promulgated in the same form as laws in the territory of each of the States concerned.

An organic law lays down its composition and determines the rules for its functioning.

ART. 84 A Community Court of Arbitration settles disputes occurring between Members of the Community.

Its composition and competence are determined by an organic law.

ART. 85 Notwithstanding the procedure laid down in Article 89, the dispositions of this Title which concern the functioning of the common institutions are amended by laws voted in identical terms by the Parliament of the Republic and by the Senate of the Community.

ART. 86 A change of status of a Member State of the Community may be requested either by the Republic, or by a resolution of the legislative assembly of the State concerned, confirmed by a local referendum for the organization and supervision of which the institutions of the Community are responsible. The detailed arrangements for this change are determined by an Agreement approved by the Parliament of the Republic and the legislative assembly concerned.

Under the same conditions a Member State of the Community may become independent. It thereby ceases to belong to the Community.

ART. 87 The special Agreements concluded for the application of this Title are approved by the Parliament of the Republic and the legislative assembly concerned.

TITLE XIII

AGREEMENTS OF ASSOCIATION

ART. 88 Either the Republic or the Community may conclude Agreements with states which wish to associate themselves with it to develop their civilizations.

TITLE XIV

REVISION

ART. 89 The initiative for amending the Constitution belongs concurrently to the President of the Republic on the proposal of the Prime Minister and to members of Parliament.

The bill for amendment (*le projet ou la proposition de révision*) must be voted by the two Assemblies in identical terms. The amendment becomes effective after approval by referendum.

However, the bill for amendment (*le projet de révision*)[1] is not submitted to a referendum when the President of the Republic decides to submit it to Parliament convoked in Congress; in this case, the bill for amendment is approved only if it obtains a majority of three-fifths of the votes cast. The *bureau* of the Congress is that of the National Assembly.

No amendment process may be initiated or proceeded with when the integrity of the national territory is impaired.

The republican form of government is not subject to revision.

TITLE XV

TEMPORARY DISPOSITIONS

ART. 90 The ordinary session of Parliament is suspended. The mandate of members of the present National Assembly will expire the day the Assembly elected under the present Constitution meets.

Until this meeting, the government alone has the authority to convoke Parliament.

The mandate of members of the Assembly of the French Union will expire at the same time as the mandate of members of the present National Assembly.

ART. 91 The institutions of the Republic prescribed by the present Constitution shall be set up within a period of four months reckoned from its promulgation.

This period is extended to six months for the institutions of the Community.

The powers of the present President of the Republic will expire only when the results of the election provided for in Articles 6 and 7 of the present Constitution are proclaimed.

[1] There is no mention of a *proposition de révision*.

The Member States of the Community will participate in this first election under conditions derived from their status on the date of the promulgation of the Constitution.

The established authorities will continue in the exercise of their functions in these States according to the laws and regulations in force at the moment when the Constitution comes into effect until the establishment of the authorities provided for by their new system of government (*nouveau régime*).

Until it is permanently constituted, the Senate consists of the present members of the Council of the Republic. The organic laws which will determine the permanent constitution of the Senate must be tabled before 31 July 1959.

The powers conferred on the Constitutional Council by Articles 58 and 59 of the Constitution will be exercised, until the establishment of the Council, by a committee composed of the Vice-President of the *Conseil d'État* as President, the First President of the *Cour de Cassation* and the First President of the *Cour des Comptes*.

The peoples of the Member States of the Community continue to be represented in Parliament until the measures necessary for the application of Title XII enter into force.

Art. 92   The legislative measures necessary for the establishment of the institutions and, until that establishment, for the functioning of the public authorities, will be taken in Council of Ministers, after advice from the *Conseil d'État*, by ordinances having the force of law.

During the period prescribed in the first paragraph of Article 91 the Government is authorized to determine, by ordinances having the force of law and adopted in the same form, the electoral system for the assemblies provided for by the Constitution.

During the same period and under the same conditions, the Government may also adopt in all domains the measures which it shall deem necessary to the life of the nation, the protection of the citizens or the safeguard of liberties.

APPENDIX II

BRIEF SUMMARY OF OTHER CONSTITUTIONAL PROVISIONS

The organic laws which supplement and clarify the constitution contain much material beyond what has been directly mentioned in earlier chapters. Most have been collected in *Constitution, Ordonnances portant Lois Organiques et ordonnances relatives aux Pouvoirs publics* (*Imprimerie des Journaux officiels*, 1959), but many—notably the electoral laws—are scattered with their train of corrigenda through the swollen issues of the *Journal Officiel* for the period. In the following pages some of the more important points which have not been made already are briefly summarized.

PRESIDENT OF THE REPUBLIC AND OF THE COMMUNITY

The President serves for seven years and is re-eligible. The constitution lays down no criteria of eligibility.

The composition of the electoral college in 1958 was: metropolitan France, 76,310 electors; Overseas Departments (D.O.M.), 1,266; Overseas Territories (T.O.M.), 3,853; Algeria (which at that time had no elected councils), 83. The representation of the Overseas Territories then included all colonial possessions; the representation of those T.O.M. which became member states of the Community will be negotiated with them before 1965. The constitution lays down no criteria or procedure for this.

In metropolitan France Article 6 of the constitution indicates automatically the electors in communes of under 30,000 inhabitants. In the larger communes, where additional electors must be chosen, these are elected by a list system of proportional representation at meetings held at least twenty days before the presidential ballot. Substitutes are chosen in case any elector is unable to vote. Voting is compulsory on pain of a fine of 30 new francs.

Nominations for the Presidency, signed by at least fifty members of the electoral college, are examined for regularity by the Constitutional Council at least twelve days before the first ballot. The Constitutional Council checks that the candidate accepts nomination, and that it is in order, and the government publishes the final list of candidates at least ten days before the first ballot.

The electoral college meets in the chief town of the department (or constituency overseas) under the president of the *tribunal civil*. Electors may not deliberate before voting. Election requires an absolute majority of votes cast on the first ballot, a relative majority on the second—held the following Sunday. A new candidate cannot come forward on the second ballot unless two candidates at the first ballot

250

stand down for him. The count is made immediately the poll closes in the presence of the electors. The Constitutional Council is responsible for the general count and announcing of results.

MINISTERIAL INCOMPATIBILITIES

Ministerial office is incompatible with membership of any parliamentary assembly (including the Economic and Social Council). A member of Parliament who becomes a minister must choose within one month between leaving the government and losing his place in Parliament. During this period—which permits a safe retreat if the ministry is still-born—he may not vote in the assembly to which he belongs.

If he remains a minister his place in Parliament is filled for the remainder of its normal term by a substitute, whose name figured with his on the ballot paper at the election. (Exceptionally, in the departments electing senators by proportional representation, the vacancy is filled by the highest unsuccessful candidate on the list on which the minister was elected.) A substitute who replaces a member of Parliament cannot (with the same exception) stand against him in the same constituency at the next election.

Civil servants who become ministers are suspended (*mis hors cadre*) while they are in the government, returning to their former rank on leaving it. Ministers may not continue in any remunerated professional activity. This is apparently intended to suppress the dubious practice of lawyer-ministers accepting briefs. Membership of the government is also incompatible with 'any office of professional representation of a national character'. While the organic laws lay down no list of such positions, this probably applies to any leader of a major economic or professional group accepting office.

Ministers leaving the government receive their salaries for six months unless they resume paid employment (except when they had previously been in 'private employment'). During this period they may receive no appointment incompatible with membership of Parliament (see below), except to return to a position previously held. Thereafter they could be consoled with an embassy, a special mission, or a seat on the board of a nationalized industry.

PARLIAMENTARY INCOMPATIBILITIES

Ineligibilities: The minimum age for election to the Assembly is 23, to the Senate 35. Candidates must have completed their military service and be French citizens of at least ten years' standing. Convicts, and persons legally declared incapable of handling their own finances or deprived of civil rights, are not eligible.

Some public servants may not stand in constituencies where they have recently exercised jurisdiction. In general terms these are:

—regional prefects, prefects, and colonial chiefs of territory, disqualified for three years;

—Parisian mayors and their *adjoints*, sub-prefects and secretaries-general of prefectures, for one year;

—most officials holding general inspectorates or posts of either regional or departmental coverage in the administration, armed forces, or the judiciary, for six months.

Membership of Parliament is also incompatible with holding certain positions, notably: the exercise of any paid functions on behalf of a Member State of the Community, a foreign power or an international organization, or the effective continuance in any non-elective position under the State. This includes members of the boards of nationalized industries (except those representing Parliament); directors of companies which either receive discretionary state aid or contract extensively for the government; directors of concerns having 'exclusively a financial object and appealing publicly for saving and credit'. Lawyers who are members of Parliament may not act for any of the above categories of business, unless they were accustomed to do so before election; nor may they act in any criminal case involving the press, offences against the State, or 'injury to credit and saving'.

No ineligible person may become a candidate, but if one should be elected, or if a member of Parliament accepts any of these posts, he automatically loses his seat on discovery.

ELECTIONS TO THE NATIONAL ASSEMBLY

(a) Metropolitan France and the D.O.M. Single-member constituencies, with an average of 93,000 inhabitants. Election at the first ballot requires the votes of more than half those voting (and of at least a quarter of the registered voters). If no candidate has an absolute majority, a second ballot is held the following Sunday at which the candidate with the most votes is elected.

(b) Algeria and the Sahara. The number of members varies between constituencies. At a single ballot the list with the most votes is elected *en bloc*. In Algeria, valid lists must contain Moslem and European candidates in proportions fixed according to the constituencies, but which attain a ratio of 2 Moslems to 1 European over all.

(c) T.O.M. Each territory has only one seat, except Comoro Is. with two. The candidate (or two-man list in Comoro) with most votes is elected in a single ballot.

Candidates must put down 1,000 new francs deposit. If they win 5 per cent of the vote they receive their deposit back, and the State pays election costs worth about 4,000 new francs. Candidates polling under 5 per cent are eliminated automatically from the second ballot, for which no new candidates may come forward.

ELECTIONS TO THE SENATE

The senatorial electorate is almost identical with the presidential electoral college, and with the electorate of the former Council of the

Republic. The representation of large towns is slightly greater than under the Fourth Republic, but slightly less than in the presidential college.

The constituency is the department, and voting takes place in the chief town. The systems used are:

(a) In T.O.M., D.O.M., Sahara, and 83 Metropolitan departments choosing four senators or fewer, the two-ballot system. Candidates receiving over half the votes cast on the first ballot are elected. At the second ballot, held the same day, the remaining places are filled by those receiving the most votes.

(b) In seven metropolitan departments with five or more senators, the list system of proportional representation with a single ballot.

(c) In Algeria. Two ballots. If a list receives an absolute majority on the first ballot it is elected *en bloc*. If no list has an absolute majority, the list with the most votes is elected *en bloc* on the second ballot. The proportion of Moslem and European candidates comprising a valid list is laid down for each constituency; over the whole country there must be 22 Moslems and 10 Europeans.

(d) Senators representing Frenchmen abroad are elected by the Senate on the nomination of the High Council of Frenchmen Abroad, which in turn chooses its nominees from its various geographical sections.

PARLIAMENT

Composition: The National Assembly has 552 members: 465 from metropolitan France, 71 from Algeria and the Sahara, 10 from D.O.M. and 6 from T.O.M.

The Senate has 307 members: 255 for metropolitan France, 34 for Algeria and the Sahara, 7 for D.O.M., 6 for Frenchmen resident abroad, and 5 for T.O.M.

Term: Unless the Assembly is prematurely dissolved, its term expires at the beginning of the April session in the fifth year following general elections. General elections are held within two months of this date.

Senators serve nine years. The Senate is renewed by thirds every three years.

Sessions: The first session begins for both houses on the first Tuesday in October, and ends on the third Friday in December. The second runs for up to three months from the last Tuesday in April. Special sessions are held at the request of the government or of a majority of deputies (but not of senators). Only the business for which the special session is called may be discussed. Special sessions called by the Assembly may not exceed twelve days, and only the Prime Minister can call another within the following month.

Committees: The permanent committees of the Assembly are: Finance, General Economy and the Plan; and Foreign Affairs (60 members); National Defence and Armed Forces; and Constitutional Laws,

Legislation and General Administration of the Republic (90 members); Cultural, Family and Social Affairs; and Production and Exchange (120 members). In the Senate two committees which shoulder the great bulk of business (Finance, Budgetary Control and Economic Accounts of the Nation; and Constitutional Laws, Universal Suffrage, Standing Orders and General Administration) have 35 members. Three (Cultural Affairs; Foreign Affairs, Defence and Armed Forces; and Social Affairs) have 54, and one (Economic Affairs and the Plan) has 80. Members of the Assembly's permanent committees are chosen by proportional representation of groups with 30 or more members. These choose their own nominees, the committees can then elect additional members from smaller groups. The Senate uses P.R. for all seats. Permanent committees are elected each October. *Ad hoc* committees are chosen by proportional representation in the Assembly and by consultation between the Presidents of permanent committees in the Senate.

Each house can set up temporary committees of enquiry or scrutiny whose life is limited to four months, and which may not then be reconstituted for a further twelve. Such committees may not be set up, or continue hearings, if a question becomes *sub judice*. Committees may enquire into the administrative, financial or technical management of the public services and the nationalized industries. Although reports may be published, the proceedings are secret and breaches may be punished. Members are chosen by majority vote—which permits the elimination of minorities. Requests for the raising of a member of Parliament's immunity from arrest are referred to *ad hoc* committees of 15 members in the Assembly and 30 in the Senate, chosen by proportional representation.

Voting: Members of Parliament are allowed to delegate their vote only if they are absent on a temporary governmental mission or on military service, or are participating in the work of an international assembly on the nomination of either house, or are prevented from attending by illness, accident or grave family event, or if they are absent from metropolitan France during a special session. Notice of delegation, stating the length of time it is to be in force, the reason, and the name of the proxy must be given to the President of the assembly concerned. No one may hold more than one proxy. The Assembly can now vote electronically, but the Senate divides, as in Britain.

ECONOMIC AND SOCIAL COUNCIL

For a moment during constitution-making the old Economic Council seemed likely to be merged in an expanded Senate. Its survival (still under the presidency of a Fourth Republic figure, Emile Roche) is one of the constitution's minor surprises. The founders of the Economic Council intended it as an advisory chamber which, representing the main economic, social and cultural groups, could attract specialist advice from men who would hesitate to enter politics, and encourage groups to see the difficulties of reconciling their demands with the national nterest. But while it made useful contributions to the debate on important issues as diverse as distributive costs, the national Plan, the Schuman Plan, and alcoholism, the Council's virtues were never recognized. Unknown to the public, suspect to the assemblies who rarely heeded its opinions, its disappearance would have been little noticed or mourned.

Yet the new Economic and Social Council has a role and status greater than its predecessor. It is now intended to advise on both domestic problems and the development of Algeria and the Community. Its 229 seats are allocated as follows:

Employees	45	Producers' co-operatives, tourism, export trades, regional development bodies	7
Industry and Commerce	41		
Agriculture	40		
'Persons qualified in the economic, social, scientific or cultural fields'	15	'Middle classes'	2
		Specialists in overseas development and franc zone	10
'Social activities' (such as family associations, housing and savings organizations, public health bodies and consumers' co-operatives)	15	Algeria and Sahara	20
		Overseas departments and territories	10
		Community (two from each state)	24

Members serve for five years. Most are chosen by 'the most representative organizations in each field', but the government appoints 65 (compared with only 14 to the old Economic Council). It may also appoint 'persons with special competence' to any of the Council's working sections at any time.

Governments *may* consult the Council on any economic or social question; they *must* consult it on 'all plans or government programme-bills of an economic character', with the traditional exception of the budget. The Council gives its views on any bill which is sent to it, with the new right to send a spokesman to either assembly to explain its views. The government may consult it before publishing decrees, or seek its help in preparing economic or social legislation. The Council cannot initiate legislation, but it may 'call the government's attention' to measures it thinks would 'encourage the adaptation of economic or social institutions to new techniques'. It may press for reforms to encourage the 'collaboration of occupational groups among themselves and their participation in the government's economic and social policy'. At any time it may give the government its views on the execution of economic or social plans.

The Council remains the one institution in which the static and conservative elements in the economy (notably distribution and the small craftsman) are not over-represented. It is clearly intended to be a force for economic expansion and modernization. Accordingly the government tried to assure the Council a parliamentary audience, and agreed that the Prime Minister should make an annual report to it on the action the government has taken on its recommendations. The Council will probably continue to exercise a quiet yet significant influence on its own members and the other organs of government.

HIGH COUNCIL OF THE JUDICIARY

Its new powers and composition show that the battle to free the judiciary from political interference is not over. The Council was set up in 1946 to help the President exercise his right of pardon, and to deal with judicial promotions and discipline. The Ministry of Justice, which never reconciled itself to the loss of its former influence, seems to have won some of it back. Under the Fourth Republic the Council's fourteen members were the President of the Republic and the Minister of Justice *ex-officio*, six judges (two chosen by the President and four selected by the judges themselves); and six chosen by the Assembly outside its own ranks—who were in practice jurists rather than politicians. It had considerable success.

Under the Fifth Republic the President is guarantor of the independence of the judiciary. The two *ex-officio* members remain: the President selects the nine appointed members: two directly, seven taken from three lists, containing twenty-one names, drawn up by the *Cour de Cassation* and the *Conseil d'Etat*. Formerly the High Council effectively appointed and promoted all members of the judiciary except members of the *parquet*. Now it 'makes proposals for nomination' to higher judicial posts, which are filled by the President. And it merely 'gives its opinion' on the Minister of Justice's proposals for other judicial posts. While several provisions in the Statute of the Judiciary limit the room for political appointments, it is far from certain that the danger is entirely eliminated.

EXECUTIVE COUNCIL OF THE COMMUNITY

The Council meets approximately every four months in Paris or one of the overseas Republics. Its members sit *ex-officio*, but other ministers may substitute for heads of government with the President's permission. The President may summon ministers of any member state to assist in debates on specific subjects. In addition to its consideration of common policy the Council decides how the cost of matters of common competence and of running the Community's institutions shall be shared by the members.

The Council's agenda and proceedings are secret, but a communiqué is published at the close of each meeting. There are five special committees of representatives of each state, sitting at the Secretariat-General for the Community, which prepare for Council meetings by studying economic and social affairs, transport and telecommunications, justice and higher education, relations between the Community and international organizations, and the demarcation between common affairs and the domain of the member states. Working parties on other questions are set up as needed. Administration is in the hands of the Secretary-General (Janot), who is appointed by the President 'in Executive Council'. All officials of the Community are appointed by and responsible to the President. Outside sessions of the Executive Council the states have access to the President through the High Commissioner and the Secretary-General—although the formal procedures are often by-passed.

THE SENATE OF THE COMMUNITY

Normally the Senate meets for two sessions of one month each year, sitting in the Palais du Luxembourg. Sessions are convoked and closed by the President of the Community, who may summon special sessions of up to ten days. It may be addressed by members of the Executive Council of the Community (including ministers responsible for common affairs), when they are delegated by the Executive Council.

The Senate elected in 1959 has 284 members—one for every 300,000 of population in each state, with a minimum of three. Its composition is:

French Republic	186	Etat du Sénégal	8
(including D.O.M., T.O.M., Algeria)			
République malgache	17	République du Dahomey	6
,, soudanaise	13	,, Centrafricaine	4
,, voltaïque	12	,, du Congo	3
,, de Côte d'Ivoire	11	,, gabonaise	3
,, du Tchad	9	,, islamique	
,, du Niger	9	mauritanienne	3

Senators are chosen by the legislative assemblies of the states from among their members. Delegates from the French Republic are chosen half by the Senate, half by the Assembly by majority vote. Members serve for as long as they hold their seats in their domestic legislature, up to a maximum of five years, and are re-eligible.

COMMUNITY ARBITRATION COURT

The Court decides all litigation between member states arising from the interpretation of the law governing their relationships, notably the constitution and organic laws, Community Agreements or conventions concluded between member states, or decisions of either the President or Senate of the Community. The President of the Community may take its opinion on such questions of interpretation. Its jurisdiction may be extended by agreement between member states.

Cases may be brought before the Court only when the normal course of justice in the member state has been exhausted. The Court has full jurisdiction over questions within its competence—it may interpret the law, annul decisions contrary to it, and award damages when the law has been violated or falsely interpreted. Its decisions are subject to no appeal, and are binding on all members of the Community.

Disputes over the regularity of the appointment of delegates from the legislative assemblies of the member states to the Senate of the Community are referred to the Court by the President. In other matters cases are brought before the Court by governments, or in the name of the Community—presumably by the President.

The Court comprises seven judges appointed for six years by the President of the Community. They are irremovable and re-eligible. Four of de Gaulle's first appointees came from France, three from overseas. Members of the Court must have been either Professors of Law, or judges in the regular or administrative courts for ten years; or have 'acquired juridical qualifications' by holding other positions for at least twenty years. This last category would include men like M. Pignon, a former colonial governor-general, who was among the first appointees.

The Court's procedure is similar to that of the *Conseil d'Etat* which is the administrative appeal court of the Community. Other cases may be appealed to a special section of the *Cour de Cassation*. The President has the right of pardon throughout the Community.

ALGERIA AND THE CONSTITUTION

Whether Algeria can be granted independence or 'association' within the present constitution is doubtful. The drafters of the controversial Articles 72 and 73 clearly intended to leave scope for a liberal solution. Algeria might become either a new entity under Article 72 or remain (as the *Conseil d'Etat* has held) a group of Overseas Departments benefiting from the 'measures of adaptation' allowed by Article 73. However (as the *Conseil d'Etat* has also held) these Articles do not permit profound changes in the political relationship between France and Algeria; they must be read in conjunction with Article 2 proclaiming the Republic indivisible. The roundabout course of making Algeria an Overseas Territory and then permitting it to opt for membership of the Community (Article 76) seems barred because this possibility is categorically limited to the constitution's transitional period. M. Debré's conclusion that within the present constitution Algeria cannot become a T.O.M., a member of the Community, or a wholly independent state (*J.O.*, 28 April 1959, p. 351), seems juridically preferable to Professor Duverger's contention that the constitution is supple enough to permit the most liberal solution (*Le Monde*, 18 August 1959). But Article 53 (para. 3) does envisage the cession of territory provided the inhabitants consent. Once the political obstacles to Algerian independence or 'association' were removed, a revision could rapidly solve the constitutional problem.

REIGNING FAMILIES

Members of families which have reigned over France were, in the Third and Fourth Republics, ineligible for the Presidency (in the former, also for Parliament). The new constitution omits this provision, allegedly by de Gaulle's wish.

INDEX

Important references are set in **bold** type

271